THOMAS J. BANDIERA

The
Revised & Expanded
Canadian
Tax & Investment
Guide

The Revised & Expanded Canadian Tax & Investment Guide

Henry B. Zimmer

Hurtig Publishers
Edmonton

Hurtig Publishers Ltd.
10560 – 105 Street
Edmonton, Alberta
Canada   T5H 2W7

Canadian Cataloguing in Publication Data

Zimmer, Henry B., 1943–
    The revised & expanded Canadian tax &
investment guide

    Previous ed. published under title: Zimmer's
1983 Canadian tax & investment guide

    ISBN 0-88830-273-8

    1. Tax planning – Canada – Popular works.
2. Income tax – Canada – Popular works.   3.
Investments – Canada.   I. Title.   II. Title:
Zimmer's 1983 Canadian tax & investment guide.
KE5682.Z82Z54 1984   343.7105′2   C84-091289-7

Printed and bound in Canada
by D.W. Friesen & Sons Ltd.

Contents

Acknowledgements

This book is dedicated to the many executives, professionals, and business owners who have attended my seminars and have encouraged me to put it all in writing.

I wish to thank my good friend Dr. Norman Schachar, who was kind enough to read the text for the first edition of *The New Canadian Tax & Investment Guide* and whose valuable criticism helped me to keep sophisticated and technical material simple.

I also would like to acknowledge the efforts of Frank Solomon, formerly of Revenue Canada, who helped me put together the chapter on dealing with the tax collector.

A special thank you is reserved for my editor, Elizabeth Munroe, and my wife, Shana, who provided hours of painstaking work and technical assistance.

H.B.Z.

Introduction

The Government of Canada has brought down three budgets since the predecessor to this book, *Zimmer's 1983 Canadian Tax & Investment Guide*, disappeared from the shelves of your local bookstore in the spring of 1983. Though these budgets contained fewer technical income-tax amendments than those of prior years, there are, nevertheless, many major changes that will affect your pocketbook.

For example, in May 1985 Finance Minister Michael Wilson proposed a broad-based capital-gains exemption to be phased in between now and 1990. This is seen as a major initiative for business owners and entrepreneurs to encourage risk-taking and investment in both small and large businesses. On the other hand, the income-attribution rules have been tightened, making it far more difficult for married individuals to split income by making interest-free loans to each other.

The government also proposed a major overhaul for the entire pension system, including changes in deductible limits, as well as sweeping reforms such as pension portability (if an individual changes jobs) and a splitting of benefits in the event of marriage breakdown. A major simplification of the small-business tax system, which has tremendous implications for owner-managed businesses, has recently been implemented.

There are some important changes for home owners, too, such as the new Mortgage Rate Protection Plan and amendments to the Interest Act governing mortgage prepayments, although the Registered Home Ownership Savings Plan has been repealed.

At the time this is being written, some of these proposals are merely in the discussion stage. However, it is important to note from the outset that *none of the government's suggestions are offensive to anyone. There is every likelihood that all of these*

15

provisions will be introduced. Thus, you must understand these provisions *now* and plan for these proposed developments.

There have also been many other important changes in the last three years, which are already law. For example, amendments to the tax rules for company cars necessitate a complete rethinking of whether or not an automobile furnished by an employer is still a valid fringe benefit. A decline in prevailing interest rates also sets the stage for some aggressive tax planning for those of us who have loans from employers for the purchase of our homes.

The last couple of years have also seen a certain type of life insurance policy emerge as a new tax shelter. This is at a time when other shelters such as movie films or multiple unit residential buildings have lost their glamour or have been "outlawed."

In addition to the new rules for simplification of small-business taxes which I mentioned briefly before, there are other important changes in planning for the owner-managed business. As you will see, it is no longer as easy as it once was to split income among members of a family by arranging for each person to own a separate class of shares. On the other hand, it now appears that there *is* an opportunity to remunerate family members through loan-guarantee fees, even in cases where these people are not active in a family business.

Beyond discussing all these changes in detail, this *Revised & Expanded Canadian Tax & Investment Guide* contains five brand-new chapters covering material that I have never dealt with before in previous editions. The topics are: tax planning for the commissioned salesperson, tax planning for separation and divorce, planning for the retirement years, planning for new business ventures, and how to deal with Revenue Canada.

In the last year or so, Canada began to take some major steps down the road towards economic recovery. The recession that began in the fall of 1981 was a long one but for most of us, the worst is now over. Nevertheless, it may be a long time before the business and investment climate recaptures the euphoria that marked the general boom of the late 1970s.

Because the overall economic climate indicates that we are in for a turbulent decade, the key to your own financial survival is flexibility, especially in the area of tax planning. Many of the larger economic struggles will be fought in the taxation arena, for taxation is like a chess game. The government makes a move

16

and then it falls upon taxpayers and their advisers to make countermoves. Remember, each individual is entitled to order his or her affairs within the framework of the law to pay the least amount of tax possible. While many of the discussions in the book will be familiar to you if you read any of the previous editions, the new approaches and new material will be just as useful. *If you can pick up one new idea each year, your savings can be many thousands of dollars.*

CHAPTER ONE

Your Silent Partner

What This Book Will Do for You

This is not a book to assist you in preparing your tax return. Nor will it save you money if you read it just before you file in March or April next year. By then, it will be too late. Tax planning is a twelve-month-a-year exercise, one that should take place every time you are up for a pay increase, or manage to put away $1,000 for investments, or think about starting (or buying) a business.

If you have bought this book, you probably already realize that you are paying too much tax. Any Canadian whose taxable income reaches $35,000 will begin to pay between 45% and 50% out of each additional dollar of earnings to a silent partner—Revenue Canada.

If you are earning $200,000 or $300,000 a year, things tend to fall into place by themselves. You can afford the best professional advice and you may be able to use certain tax write-offs. Corporations as a vehicle for sheltering income are also more readily available. However, for the vast majority of people, who earn less than a six-figure income, many of these opportunities are not as accessible. Any legitimate advantage in dealing with the silent partner should therefore be pursued. To some extent, this is difficult since the government is the one that makes up the rules of the game. However, if you learn the rules, playing the game can be fun as well as profitable.

Certainly, the situation today is not as bleak as it was last year and the year before. Several harsh changes proposed in November 1981 concerning employee benefits have been modified or rejected. Contrary to the amendments proposed, the government will *not* be taxing employer contributions to private health-care programs, or discounted travel passes for most employees of transportation companies. The value of subsidized board and lodging at remote worksites remains a tax-free benefit, as well. Lower interest rates are certainly another good sign and, as in the past, Canadians may continue to rely heavily on the use of leverage to accumulate capital, by borrowing against their earning power on a tax-deductible basis in order to make investments. Although the November 1981 Budget proposed severe restrictions on the deductibility of interest write-offs, the government then had a change of heart. Each and every one of us must use the new system to our best advantage. This book will help you in this complex and difficult endeavour.

Actually, taxation concepts are not especially difficult to understand. Over the past few years, I have presented some four hundred and fifty seminars to perhaps thirteen thousand business owners, executives, and professionals across Canada. These people have shown that the average Canadian not only wants to understand how the system works, but with just a little effort, also can make the system work for *him* or *her*. All anyone needs is a translation of the tax rules into plain English.

As you read through this book, you will find that learning the tax rules is easy. Also, formulating an effective investment policy for yourself does not necessarily require a crystal ball. You do not need an accounting or legal background. You need only assimilate some facts, and use some common sense and a bit of imagination. If you are capable of reaching a 45% tax bracket, you should be able to appreciate the logic of the tax and investment suggestions that this book contains. Of course, you may choose to disregard some or all of my suggestions and think independently. However, unless you are an extremely sophisticated person and have done extremely well in the past on your own, there is no reason why you shouldn't seek independent advice from your own advisers.

When to Use the Experts

An important point must be put into proper perspective. While the cost of an hour's time with a tax accountant or lawyer can exceed $150, rarely will the development of a tax and investment planning outline take more than three or four hours in total. The actual implementation of the ideas can then be accomplished with the assistance of non-specialist advisers whose rates are considerably cheaper. I have been consulting on these matters almost exclusively to small businesses and executives for the past eight years. In very few cases has my charge exceeded $500. This is not because I undercut the competition, but because I leave the implementation of my proposals to my clients' regular advisers.

What if you don't think that you have a problem? You will still find that a tax and investment check-up is important. In the same way that it is worthwhile for you go to your physician for a physical check-up at least once a year, a periodic tax and investment check-up can save you money by detecting problems and outlining planning opportunities that you may not even know exist. While $150 an hour sounds expensive, a fee of a few hundred dollars is not costly if you can save considerably more.

The key to proper planning, however, is to ask the right questions. Since the price for legal and accounting services is high, many business owners, executives, and professionals have expressed to me a desire to educate themselves to discuss tax and investment matters intelligently—especially since accountants and lawyers often have difficulty coming down to a layperson's level. As one of my clients said to me two or three years ago, "I've got to learn what this is all about. After all, it's *my* money."

How to Use This Book

This book is a collection of the topics with which I have dealt in seminars on tax and investment all over Canada. I have found speaking to the public extremely gratifying. A year or two ago, an Edmonton businessman said that he had learned more in one day from me than he had from his accountants in eleven years, and a Vancouver doctor told me, during the first coffee break in the morning, that he had already absorbed enough to cover the cost of my seminar and the loss of a day's earnings. Invariably, I have been asked by participants to produce a book in order to cover the material that I teach. I therefore wrote *The New Canadian Tax & Investment Guide*, which was published in the fall of 1980.

As you have already seen, however, the rules of the game have changed completely. As I write this, I am dismayed by the suggestion that I made on page 5 of the first edition. I said, "a tax plan, once initiated, should be effective for many future years." Fortunately, I also suggested that the ongoing benefits of any program are dependent on the general structure of the tax laws remaining the same. I, for one, never dreamed that the rules could change so greatly in such a short span of time.

So here is the 1985 update. There is still room for planning that uses fringe-benefit programs, such as group health and life insurance packages, employee loans, and business-pleasure trips, where the value of these benefits is often much more than a (fully taxable) raise in pay. Although some of the tax advantages have been lessened, a good fringe-benefit program is still important. While recent legislation plugs certain loopholes with respect to retiring allowances and termination arrangements, the material in this book will show you that these concepts can still be of great value. A high-salary income can be converted to a post-retirement allowance to provide a cash flow for retired executives and business owners. In Chapter Eleven, you will also be brought up to date on the tax-deferral advantages of personal-service companies, especially for doctors, dentists, and commissioned salespeople. The 1981/82 tax changes plugged certain loopholes previously used by various executives and athletes, although a consultant capable of earning revenues from different sources can still avail himself or herself of the benefits of incorporation.

Chapter Six explains the rule changes which have taken place in the real estate area. In addition, the topic of life insurance shelters will be covered. As in the past, I must emphasize the importance of first finding a good *investment* before concentrating on tax-shelter aspects. Then, you can use the information in this chapter to take advantage of any shelter an investment may provide. Certainly, recent changes have eliminated some of the shelter features of real estate investments. As I predicted three years ago, in the short run (without these tax incentives) real estate values did, in fact, fall substantially. Today, however, with lower interest rates, we have a new situation. If you understand the scenario that is now unfolding in this country, you will find that large profits are still obtainable. An understanding of the tax rules will then enable you to retain as much of these profits as is possible.

Another chapter explores ideas for maximizing investment yields by splitting income with family members, both by way of direct transactions and through the use of investment corporations. Important changes to these guidelines have been made necessary by the most recent federal budget. You will also be alerted to some of the misconceptions pertaining to investment yields, which can result from erroneously trying to apply U.S. guidelines to Canada. For example, U.S. rules do not differentiate between the earning of interest and dividend income. However, for most Canadians in 45% or 50% tax brackets, a Canadian dividend is worth at least one and a half times as much as an equivalent yield of Canadian interest on an *after-tax* basis. Thus, if a stock pays a 6% dividend, this is equivalent to pre-tax interest of 9%.

I will show you that for many individuals, the difference between buying a blue-chip Canadian stock and investing in a term deposit or Canada Savings Bond is only a 3%–4% net annual cash difference in favour of the interest-bearing security. However, when you take capital appreciation potential and inflation into account, the balance will often swing in favour of share investments.

I am not, however, suggesting that this is necessarily the time to invest in the stock market. As I predicted in the 1982 edition of this book, the stock market did decline severely in the first half of that year. Recently, there have been some substantial gains on certain days and losses on others. I personally don't think that a clear trend will become evident until the government gives us some assurance on what the medium-term outlook for interest rates will be. In spite of Finance Minister Michael Wilson's comments that he thinks interest rates will remain low, remember that the huge deficit and government borrowing requirements will create some upward pressures. However, also remember that stock-market patterns are cyclical. The trick is to know when to buy and when to sell. Very few people can make substantial profits going against market trends. Looking for "special opportunities" in a bad market may be akin to trying to find the proverbial needle in a haystack.

I am not suggesting that you desert your stockbroker and leave him to starve during periods when the market is falling. With proper planning, you can make as much money in a "down" market as you can when the economy is in an upswing. Explore the various methods of "selling short" with your broker. *This is where an investor sells a stock which he does not own.* The idea is to buy it back later and cover the short position when the price has dropped. The difference becomes profit.

Selling short has its risks—but the reward may easily warrant them and they can be minimized.

We will also examine the major tax-planning concepts for owner-managers of private companies. Legislation passed in 1983 and 1984 creates brand-new guidelines and *renders all previous tax plans obsolete*. Business owners must learn to cope with the new 12.5% corporate-distributions tax (see Chapter Thirteen), which reduces a company's ability to pay dividends to its shareholders. Fortunately, the new guidelines are readily understandable and they can be applied to salary and dividend policies so as to optimize after-tax retentions in any active business situation.

For anyone planning to buy a business, I will explain how there is a "right way" and a "wrong way." Without proper planning, anyone who buys the shares of a Canadian private company could be *overpaying income taxes by as much as $33,000 for every $100,000 of the purchase price*. With proper planning, this needless tax can be legitimately avoided. Other material introduces estate-planning concepts, such as the points that a will should contain, and suggests some guidelines for a common-sense approach towards allocating assets to family members.

Before we go any further, however, a word of caution is in order. My intention is not to replace your accountants and lawyers. Nor am I trying to make you into a "tax expert." My purpose is to show you what is available so that when you sit down with your own advisers, at least you have a common starting point. After having read this book, you should be able to discuss specific matters with the professionals who are there to assist you in implementing the proposals that I suggest. In many cases, your own advisers will be able to make important modifications suitable to your own specific circumstances.

Another word of caution is also warranted. The contents of this book are based on the tax law in force at the end of 1984 with provision for budget amendments to May 23, 1985. Although some of the most recent changes are slated to become effective in 1985, they are not yet law and may be revised yet again before becoming part of the Income Tax Act. In other words, there may be important modifications that are brought in before the legislation is implemented. Keeping up with the tax rules is an ongoing process. *This book is your starting point*. Beyond checking out

24

specific tax-planning concepts with your own advisers, I strongly recommend that you keep up to date by reading digests of budget proposals, which appear in publications such as the *Financial Post* or the *Financial Times*. If there are important modifications before any laws are passed, your own accountant should be able to explain the relevant changes a few days after these are implemented.

It is also important to understand how to properly evaluate tax changes. Before becoming excited about a legislative amendment or an opportunity for planning, always compare the tax theory to the actual dollars of tax cost or saving, as the case may be.

In addition to saving taxes, I hope that you will learn *tax awareness* from this book. One thing I have learned in the last few years is that there is no such thing as permanent or long-term investment policies. You must be aware of how the economy fluctuates at all times and cultivate political awareness as well. Perhaps, most important of all, you must learn to think in terms of after-tax dollars and discount additional income that you receive by the tax burden of earning it.

To take a common example, most of us who earn employment income from one source or another receive cost-of-living increases. If the cost of living goes up by 6% in one year, then a 6% raise is often received exclusive of merit increases. However, for most of us a raise in pay will now translate on an after-tax basis to only about fifty cents on the dollar. Thus, our 6% cost-of-living increase becomes only 3% in our pockets. It is true that to the extent that certain of our costs are fixed, we may be unaffected by increases in the cost of living. How many of us envy our neighbours who have owned their homes for the last ten or fifteen years and were thus "immune" to the jump in house prices in the late 1970s? Nevertheless, 6% still equals 3%—maybe not in mathematics but in "real life" arithmetic.

As you increase your understanding of the Canadian tax structure, you will also become aware that while certain loopholes have, in fact, been blocked, other valid opportunities for planning will always present themselves. Parliament giveth, Parliament taketh away....

CHAPTER TWO

Minimize Your Salary and Maximize Your Benefits

Whether you own your own business or work for someone else, you probably derive at least a portion of your income from salary. In general, you should only draw as much salary as you need to meet your particular living requirements after income taxes. Once you earn sufficient salary to pay living expenses, the next step is to look for fringe benefits. These benefits can actually be worth more than a salary increase, since your employer can provide goods and services that you want without the full impact of taxes otherwise payable on an equivalent amount of salary.

This chapter will deal with some of the more common and readily available fringe-benefit programs you can obtain by virtue of employment. Naturally, if you are self-employed, you are more likely to be able to take advantage of these opportunities than if you have to ask someone else for them. However, as you will see, it is often advantageous for the employer as well to provide some of these benefits, because the cost may be less than salary or about the same.

However, you must be careful. While most fringe benefits are, in fact, benefits, remember their status is always subject to change. Thus, even if you have an established fringe-benefit package, you should review it annually to ensure that it is the right one under the circumstances. For example, the company car that was such a bonus in previous years may no longer be a viable "perk" for many individuals. Because of the major tax changes in this area, I will deal with company cars first.

Company Cars

For many years the best benefit you could have obtained from employment was a company car—an automobile owned or rented by your employer, who covered all operating expenses as well. In order to enjoy this benefit, however, it was always important that each employee have at least some business requirement for the vehicle that would justify the cost to the company providing it.

Technically, Revenue Canada has always insisted that employees report a taxable benefit for personal use of a company car. In theory, a reasonable calculation of such a benefit would reflect any operating expenses paid for by the employer that were, in fact, attributable to personal use. In 1972, however, in order to eliminate the complex bookkeeping required to segregate costs on a car-by-car basis, the Income Tax Act adopted the concept of a minimum stand-by charge, that is, a benefit based on *availability* for personal use. Actually, two formulas were incorporated into the Income Tax Act. If an automobile was owned by the employer, the benefit was computed at 1% per month multiplied by the original cost of the car multiplied by the number of months of availability. If the car was leased, the computation took into account one-third of the monthly car rental (exclusive of insurance and maintenance) multiplied by the number of months of availability. These formulas were certainly straightforward and allowed Revenue authorities to easily verify the taxable benefits. The formulas took into account availability of the car for personal use, not actual use.

To understand why a company car was considered the best available fringe benefit during this ten-year period, let's take some simple numbers and apply them to the minimum stand-by charge formula in use until 1982. For example, assume that a $15,000 car was owned by a company and was available to a particular employee. Under the formula, the taxable benefit was $1,800 ($15,000 × 1% × 12 months). If the individual was in the 50% tax bracket and had $1,800 added to his income, his only cost was a maximum of $900. For an out-of-pocket cost of only $75 a month, the employee had a $15,000 car available throughout the year for which his employer paid all the expenses. What better benefit could one ask for? Most executives were certainly willing to forgo increases in pay (which would be fully taxed) in favour of a $15,000 car at a cost of only $900 a year.

Unfortunately, the government saw fit, starting in 1982, to *double* the taxable benefit under the minimum stand-by charge formulas. Where an automobile is owned by an employer, the benefit is now 2% of the capital cost of the car per month. If the automobile is leased, the benefit is two-thirds of the lease cost. There is one minor concession that applies if an employee uses the company car less than 1,000 kilometres a month for personal purposes. In such case, the formulas permit the employee to reduce the benefit for tax calculations. You should note, however, that such low personal use appears to be quite unusual in practice. The workings of the new stand-by charge formula are illustrated in Figure 2-1. The example assumes that a $10,000 car is owned by an employer and is provided to an employee throughout the year.

Figure 2-1   **If Automobile Is Owned by Employer**

	Case One	*Case Two*
Capital cost	$10,000	$10,000
Number of months available for employee's use	12	12
Total kilometres driven	10,000	24,000
Personal use in kilometres	5,000	12,000
Taxable benefit calculation	$2,400 × 5,000	$2,400 × 12,000
	12,000	12,000
Taxable benefit	$ 1,000	$ 2,400

Formula:

$$2\% \times \text{capital cost} \times \text{no. of months available} \times \frac{\text{no. of personal km.}}{1,000 \times \text{no. of mos.}}$$

You can see that in Case One, even though the car is used half the time for personal purposes, the benefit is only five-twelfths of the total maximum benefit of $2,400. In the second example, on the other hand, the full $2,400 must be reported as income even though the automobile is again only used half the time for personal purposes. This is because in Case Two the individual does in fact get a full 1,000 kilometres a month personal use.

If the government had simply decided to double the taxable benefit under the formulas, most individuals would still probably consider a company car as the best available fringe benefit. However, the government has also decided that a stand-by charge or availability benefit is *not enough*. In addition to the formula computations, the actual use must now also be considered where an employer pays an employee's operating expenses for personal use. In other words, the total taxable benefit is now the sum of *two* calculations—the stand-by charge *plus* an operating benefit. The operating benefit takes into account the actual operating expenses in relation to personal kilometres driven. Its workings are illustrated in the example in Figure 2-2.

Figure 2-2   **Effect of Second Tax on Company Cars**

Capital cost of automobile	$10,000
Total operating costs	$ 2,100
Number of days automobile available to employee/shareholder	360 days
Total kilometres driven for the period	24,000 km
Personal kilometres driven for the period	15,000 km

Operating benefit:
$$\frac{15,000 \text{ km}}{24,000 \text{ km}} \times \$2,100 = \qquad \$1,312.50$$

Stand-by charge:
$$\$10,000 \times 2\% \times \frac{360 \text{ days}}{30 \text{ days}} \times \frac{12,000 \text{ km*}}{1,000 \text{ km} \times 12 \text{ mos}} = \qquad \underline{\$2,400.00}$$

Total benefit $3,712.50

Comparable benefit in 1981:
$$\$10,000 \times 1\% \times \frac{360 \text{ days}}{30 \text{ days}} = \qquad \underline{\$1,200.00}$$

*Since the 15,000 personal kilometres exceed the formula minimum of 12,000, the lesser distance must be taken for the calculation of the stand-by charge.

As you can see from this simple case study, the total benefit is $3,712.50—over three times as much as the equivalent benefit for 1981, when administrative practice was to refer to the stand-by charge alone (at that time 1% per month). This is clearly a case of overkill.

Recent Changes

When the concept of an operating automobile benefit was introduced into the Income Tax Act, the government began to bear the brunt of much criticism. Not only is the total cost of a company car onerous but, as well, to comply with these rules, careful cost and distance records have to be kept. This presents a serious problem, not only for the individual employee but also for the employer, especially in a case where several individuals use the same credit card numbers for gasoline purchases and other operating costs.

In his Spring 1984 Budget, former Finance Minister Lalonde therefore took steps to make the record keeping simpler. He proposed an optional alternative for calculating the taxable benefit pertaining to operating costs for a car provided by an employer to an employee or shareholder. Instead of calculating the actual benefit with reference to specific costs incurred and the actual personal distance driven, the operating benefit may now be computed at the rate of 50% of the stand-by charge pertaining to that automobile. In other words, if the employer decides to ignore actual operating costs, the stand-by charge becomes 3% per month of the cost of the car (if the car is owned by the employer) multiplied by the number of months the car is available for personal use by the individual employee. For a leased car, the total taxable benefit becomes an amount *equal* to the rent paid by the employer, instead of two-thirds of this amount.

With this new alternative, the total taxable benefit calculated in Figure 2-2 would become $3,600 ($2,000 × 3% × 12) instead of $3,712.50, a difference of only $112.50.

While simplifying the calculations, the government has, unfortunately, done nothing in response to the many complaints that the tax on this benefit is excessive and unfair.

Thus, employers who still provide company cars must carefully rethink the value of this benefit. In cases where employees do a lot of business-related driving, it might be better to have the individual purchase or lease a vehicle and charge the employer a fee for each kilometre driven. Before deciding on a course of action, you should determine the actual out-of-pocket costs under both alternatives.

A Company Car for Owner-Managers

Certainly, there are some instances where a company car is still worth considering. For example, a Canadian small business will often pay, at most, a tax of only 25% on its profits. Thus, as shown in Figure 2-3, a company can afford to pay for a $15,000 car using only $20,000 of "earning power." The individual owner would, on the other hand, need at least $30,000 of additional gross salary (assuming he or she is already in a 50% tax bracket) to net the same $15,000. So there is a tremendous saving in earning power if you own a business and the corporation purchases a car.

Figure 2-3 **Pre-Tax Dollars Required to Purchase $15,000 Car**

	Gross Earnings	Taxes Payable		Net Cash Flow for Car
Ownership by corporation in most provinces	20,000	5,000	(25%)	15,000
Ownership by individual	30,000	15,000	(50%)	15,000

For larger companies, it would generally be more expedient to lease automobiles for key executives. The employees could sign agreements stating that in the event of resignation or dismissal, they would assume the balance of the leases. (If an employee is not financially stable, the company would presumably withhold this benefit.) Since turnover is greater among new staff, company cars could be reserved for employees who have attained high income levels and a certain length of service.

Tax Planning for Company Cars

Depending on how much business driving you do relative to your personal use, your employer may still want to provide you with a company car. If so, there are several other planning points that you should consider. First, if your lifestyle is such that you take an annual one-month vacation outside Canada and you leave your company car at home, I suggest that you park it in the employer's parking lot instead. Under these circumstances, the car cannot be said to be available for personal use during the time you are outside the country. It appears to me that you are entitled to approach your employer and have your taxable benefit recalculated accordingly. Similarly, if your job requires you to travel extensively, and you leave your car for several days at a time at an airport parking lot, you are also entitled to have your benefit reduced since, on those days, the vehicle cannot be said to be available for personal use.

Consider, as well, your position if you are driving a company-owned car that is several years old. Remember that the benefit for tax purposes is based on original cost. It might pay to have the employer sell the car to a leasing company at book value (cost minus depreciation) and lease it back for a further two or three years at a relatively cheap rate. Your taxable benefit will then be based on the leasing cost instead of the original cost.

Another interesting opportunity for effective tax planning is to buy a company car at the cheapest price possible and to settle for a reduced trade-in value. For example, what if your employer is buying you a $20,000 car and is entitled to a $7,000 trade-in on your old company vehicle? In these circumstances, the car dealer must receive a cheque for $13,000 to complete the purchase. Why not structure the deal so that the new car costs only $16,000 and a mere $3,000 trade-in allowance is provided for the old one? If this is done, the dealer would still receive $13,000 in cash but your taxable benefit would now be based on a car that has a smaller cost. Of course, you must use some discretion. I would not recommend that the dealer actually sell the new vehicle to the company for less than cost.

Loans to Individuals to Buy Their Own Cars

In many cases, it might be a good idea for a corporation to lend money to an individual towards the purchase of his or her own car, especially where that individual is an employee-shareholder. Where the car is to be used by the individual in the performance of duties as an employee of the corporation, Canadian tax law allows a car loan to be repaid over a reasonable period of time. This would probably be somewhere between three and five years.

A loan to buy a car would provide today's dollars to the individual employee, which need only be repaid with dollars that will presumably be worth less because of inflation. Then, instead of repaying the loan in cash only, the employee could charge the company as much as twenty-five or thirty cents a kilometre for business use. In this way, over a three or four-year period, he or she could conceivably "work off" the bulk of the debt.

Loans to Employees and Shareholders

If a business makes a loan to an employee, there are no requirements in the Income Tax Act governing the repayment of that loan within any specific time—as long as the employee is not a shareholder of the corporation. Thus, a loan from an employer to an employee can be made for an indefinite period and can remain outstanding as long as both parties agree. If the loan is ever forgiven, the forgiveness of debt would, at that time, create income from employment. This rule is to prevent tax-exempt and other non-profit organizations from making advances to their employees (instead of paying salaries) and then, later on, forgiving these loans. A non-profit organization would not need a tax deduction, and in the absence of the above rule, an employee could escape taxation.

Where an employee is also a shareholder, there are, however, some very strict repayment rules that apply when a loan is made. The reason for these rules is that the government does not want shareholders borrowing money initially taxed at comparatively low corporate rates without the imposition of personal taxes. In the absence of any special rules, a corporation with profits of $10,000 would have an average of $7,500 of funds available for shareholders' loans after paying Revenue Canada taxes of about 25% of its profits.

The general rule on shareholder loans is that if a loan is outstanding on two successive year-end balance sheets of a company, it is *retroactively* included in the shareholder's income. Thus, the maximum length of time that a loan can remain unpaid is two years less one day. (The "two years less one day" would only apply if the loan is taken out on the first day of a company's fiscal year.)

You cannot subvert the system by simply repaying a loan just before the deadline and borrowing back the funds. Other provisions within the Tax Act provide that a "series of loans and repayments" is equivalent to not having repaid the loan at all. In addition, you cannot have a series of family members take loans to extend the length of the borrowing. A loan to a member of a shareholder's family becomes the equivalent of a loan to the shareholder.

There are four specific exceptions to the above rules, which provide an individual with an opportunity to borrow money for an extended period of time. These exceptions are:

- A loan made in the ordinary course of business by a company whose ordinary business consists of making loans.
- A loan made to a shareholder who is also an employee to acquire shares of the company out of treasury under a stock-option or stock-purchase plan.
- A loan to acquire an automobile to be used by a shareholder-employee in the performance of his or her duties.
- A loan to a shareholder-employee to acquire or construct a house to live in.

In all cases, the Income Tax Act requires that a reasonable repayment schedule be decided upon at the time the loan is made and that it be subsequently followed.

The first exception is of limited significance. It is in the Act in order to prevent unfair tax treatment of an individual who borrows money from a chartered bank in which he or she has a few shares. Thus, if I deal with the Royal Bank of Canada and borrow $40,000 for business purposes, it would be somewhat ridiculous for me to have to consider that amount as income if, by coincidence, I have one hundred shares of Royal Bank in my investment portfolio.

The second exception, however, is very important when it comes to "buying into" a business—whether that business is privately owned or whether the stock-option or purchase plan involves a public company. It appears that the government wants to encourage employees to become shareholders of (or extend their shareholdings in) corporations that employ them. Thus, where a corporation makes a loan for this purpose, a reasonable period may be used in order to effect repayment. It must be stressed, however, that the exception applies only to *shares issued out of treasury* and not to shares acquired by an individual from another shareholder.

Until recently, the third exception has been of minor significance because the greatest benefit from employment was always a company car. Thus, a loan to an individual to buy his or her *own* car was of limited use. However, as explained previously, a company car will now result in a double taxable benefit, one based on availability and the second based on use. For many of us, the balance now swings over in favour of personal ownership. In these circumstances, the employer could lend the individual money to buy a car—even if he or she is a shareholder—and the employee could then charge the company for actual business use.

While the value of loans for cars must be assessed on a case-by-case basis, it is clear that the best tax deal emanates from the fourth exception, which is a housing loan. The first advantage of such a loan arises because corporate tax rates tend to be significantly less than personal rates. Where the employer is a privately owned company, often around seventy-five cents out of each dollar of profits is left over after tax. These funds can be used as an advance to the owner for purposes of buying or building a home. This is much cheaper than using only fifty cents out of each dollar of after-tax *personal* earnings.

Figure 2-4 **House-Purchase Alternatives**

Personal after-tax funds:

Salary to shareholder-employee	$100,000
Less: Personal taxes of 50%	50,000
After-tax funds available to purchase a home	$ 50,000

Corporate after-tax funds:

Earnings taxed in corporation	$100,000
Corporate taxes (25%)	25,000
After-tax funds available to shareholder as a loan for a home	$ 75,000

The second advantage is that the employee-shareholder gets the use of corporate dollars *today*, which he or she must only repay over a period of time, presumably with "cheaper" dollars because of inflation. A reasonable repayment program for the principal itself might be ten or fifteen years.

If you own a controlling interest in an incorporated business, I suggest that you speak to your advisers with regard to such a loan *before* you purchase or build any residence. The residence need not be a city home. A country house (or second home) will also qualify, as long as it will be owned primarily for personal use and could not be construed as a rental property.

Note that the very generous provision in the Income Tax Act permitting such a loan applies only in situations where a house is being built or bought. It does not apply to the refinancing of your present home. However, if your intention is to make a major extension to an existing residence, it may be possible to get an advance ruling from Revenue Canada allowing a company loan for that purpose under the same favourable tax conditions.

"Imputed" Interest on Loans

Before 1979, I would have classified a non-interest-bearing or low-interest loan as the best of the employment benefits. This is because there was no requirement that interest be charged on loans to either employees or to shareholders—or that interest be calculated as a taxable benefit. All this changed on January 1, 1979, and further modifications were made in 1982.

According to the new rules, if interest is not charged by an employer, it must be calculated at a set rate and added on to the T-4 slip as a taxable benefit. During most of the last few years, the prescribed rate of interest was around 10%. (Prior to 1982, the calculated rates were set annually. A Budget amendment on November 12, 1981, changed this practice to a quarterly calculation based on treasury-bill rates.)

Before 1982 the tax rules provided three exceptions to the requirement for calculating interest. These have now been either withdrawn or modified. The first was where the interest on a loan was less than five hundred dollars. The second was in cases where the loan was used for the purpose of acquiring shares in the employer's company under a stock-option or stock-purchase plan. The government encouraged employees to buy into their employers' companies and a loan for that purpose was afforded very favourable tax conditions. Amendments to this second exception in particular appear to represent a rather surprising reversal of policy. Fortunately, interest calculated as a taxable benefit on share-purchase loans also qualifies as a tax-deductible carrying charge against the investment itself. It therefore seems that there will be no net tax cost as a result of such a loan.

A further exception to the imputed interest rules allowed a corporation to make interest-free relocation loans of up to $50,000 (per family unit of husband and wife) where an employee was moved from one place in Canada to another pursuant to a change of job location. The purpose of this provision was to encourage employee mobility. A relocation loan was also availa-

36

ble to induce an individual to accept a new job that involved a move. Unfortunately, the $50,000 exemption was removed for loans made in 1982 and subsequent taxation years. In the last federal budget, however, Finance Minister Michael Wilson proposed to exempt from tax certain benefits received by an employee as a result of an interest-free or low-interest housing loan received from an employer where the employee relocates in order to maintain employment or to begin a new job. The new alleviating measure applies for 1985 and subsequent years, provided employment at the new location in Canada begins after May 23, 1985.

Under the proposal, the maximum annual tax-free benefit is limited to the benefit resulting from an interest-free housing loan of $25,000 and will be available for the first five years of the loan. The exemption applies in the same circumstances as the tax rules governing the deduction of moving expenses. These require the new residence to be at least 40 km closer to the new job than the old residence.

Where housing loans are made in circumstances other than employee relocation, there is now a taxable benefit. This is explained further on. However, if a loan actually bears interest at prevailing market levels, a taxable benefit will not apply.

Let's now look at housing loans other than those specifically for relocation.

New Planning for Housing Loans

Remember that at the time the government introduced the tax changes on housing loans, interest rates were moving up. As a result, the legislation brought in some rather important provisions. The new rules provide that there is no taxable benefit if the rate of interest payable on a housing loan is equal to or greater than the rate of interest in effect *at the time the loan was made*. This would protect the individual from increases in interest rates after the loan is received. However, if the term of a loan is greater than five years, the tax-exempt status of the loan with respect to interest is reassessed at the end of each five-year period.

These new provisions set the stage for some interesting tax planning. As we move towards the end of 1985, general interest rates have now declined to the point that the taxable-benefit calculation rate is only 10%. The chances of a substantial decline in interest rates below this level appear quite remote; it is more likely that over the next few years interest rates will escalate as the government is forced to borrow more and more money to meet its rising deficits.

In the past, most individuals have chosen to live with the taxable benefit without paying any interest to their employers. At the time when the rate of calculated interest was 16%, the common thinking was that paying 8% out-of-pocket in taxes was preferable to actually paying non-deductible interest to an employer. In fact, this was the planning which I recommended in previous editions of this book. Now, however, it appears to me that this thinking is obsolete.

By definition, a home-purchase loan includes not only a loan made to an employee or shareholder to acquire a home, but also a loan made to repay a loan or debt to acquire a home in the first place. In other words, a loan made to *replace* a home-purchase loan is itself now treated as a home-purchase loan.

Suppose you are an individual in the 50% tax bracket and you have a $50,000 non-interest-bearing loan towards the purchase of your home. If the interest rate stabilizes at 10%, your annual taxable benefit is $5,000 and your out-of-pocket tax cost is $2,500. Let's say you now renegotiate your home-purchase loan for a five-year period and actually agree to pay to your employer $5,000 a year—the going rate of interest at the time the loan is renegotiated. At the same time, your employer gives you a $5,000 raise in pay.

From your employer's perspective, the $5,000 interest income and $5,000 additional salary expense offset one another. However, from your point of view, the $5,000 increased salary represents a net take-home pay of $2,500, although you would then be laying out $5,000 of after-tax money to pay the interest on your loan. When the smoke clears you are still out-of-pocket $2,500. This is the same exact amount that you would be paying if you continued to submit to a $5,000 annual taxable benefit on which your tax liability is 50%.

In other words, matching a loan payment to your employer with an equivalent raise in pay produces no adverse tax consequences to the employer and the net after-tax cost to you, the employee, is the same. What, then, is the advantage? It will simply *stabilize the actual tax cost of the loan to acquire your* house for the next five years. Thus, for example, if interest rates move back up to 16%, you would not have to worry about an $8,000 taxable benefit (16% × $50,000) and a $4,000 tax bite.

Of course, no one knows for certain in which direction interest rates are going to move. If the calculated or imputed rate drops as low as 8%, you might be a bit unhappy because you would now be overpaying. On the other hand, there does not appear to be any restriction against a further renegotiation for a five-year period beginning at that time. And yet, as I mentioned previously, what if rates go back up to 16%, 18%, or even 20%? The opportunity to stabilize your out-of-pocket cost should be well worth your while. This is illustrated in Figure 2-5.

Figure 2-5 **Home-Purchase-Loan Alternatives**

Alternative 1

Loan of	$50,000
Taxable benefit (10%)	$ 5,000
Out-of-pocket cost	$ 2,500

Alternative 2

Loan of	$50,000
Interest charged by employer (non-deductible)	$ 5,000
Net proceeds from $5,000 raise	(2,500)
Out-of-pocket cost	$ 2,500
Employer's position:	
Interest received	$ 5,000
Raise in pay to employee	(5,000)
Net effect	Nil

Private Health-Care Programs

One of the most common and yet valuable fringe-benefit programs is an employer-sponsored private health-care (including dental services) package. Under such a program, the employer pays for insurance, which reimburses the employee if he or his family incurs medical or dental expenses not covered under provincial medicare. Such costs would include prescription drugs, eye glasses, and dental care. In the November 1981

Budget, the government proposed that employer contributions to such programs would become taxable starting in 1982. Because of public outcry, however, these proposals have been retracted.

A private health-care program thus continues to be a valuable benefit for two reasons. First, the cost of group coverage for insurance is much cheaper than personal coverage. Second, where an individual pays the costs of medical or dental services (not covered by medicare) the payments are only tax-deductible to the extent that they exceed 3% of annual net income. Thus, most Canadians would not obtain worthwhile tax relief from medical expenses if these were paid for personally. In addition, remember one of the cardinal rules of tax planning—*a reimbursed expense is worth a hundred cents on the dollar while a tax-deductible expenditure only results in a recovery of half the outlay.*

Holiday Trips, Including Travel Expenses for an Employee's Spouse

Revenue officials take the position that the value of a holiday trip, prize, or incentive award must be included in an employee's income as a fringe benefit—even if the person paying the costs is a customer or supplier of the employer. Travel benefits include the expenses of an employee's spouse as well. However, within this rather general framework there are a number of exceptions. The most important would be the case where a holiday trip can be combined with a valid business purpose. Where a business purpose exists, the taxable benefit can be reduced or even eliminated in some cases.

A friend of mine who is a chartered accountant was asked by a Canadian client of his to prepare a report on the tax consequences of investing in U.S. real estate. My friend informed his client that although a significant amount of research could be done from Canada, it would still be advantageous for him to meet with a tax accountant or lawyer based in the United States to discuss some of the finer points involved. The client readily agreed. It so happened that my friend was invited to a family wedding in Los Angeles that was scheduled to take place within the following month. It doesn't take much imagination to guess where my friend made arrangements to meet with a qualified U.S. tax practitioner.

40

Another case involves a privately owned real-estate-brokerage house, which has offices in major cities in both Canada and the United States. This firm services many clients from both Europe and the Orient who want to invest in North American real estate. For several years, this particular company has had a policy of providing a rather interesting fringe benefit to employees. Each year commissioned salespeople who reach their quotas are rewarded with free trips. In year one, the employees based in western Canada go east while the eastern employees go west. In year two, the Canadian employees go south to the United States while the U.S. employees come north to Canada. In year three, the trip is to Europe, in year four to the Orient, and in year five to Hawaii.

In each case, the employee is required to file a detailed report on his or her return. The report must compare real estate prices in the places that he or she has been to those at home, and the employee must, as well, list contacts that he or she has made in the other city or cities. These reports are kept on file by the company. Not long ago, Revenue officials did an audit at the company's head office. They proposed to allow the first four trips as being for business only, without any taxable-benefit implications, while they decided that the fifth year's trip to Hawaii should be treated as a fully taxable benefit.

The company objected on behalf of its employees, stating that many investors are buying real estate in Hawaii and that there is as much business justification for that trip as there is to anywhere else. At one point, the company's controller asked my advice. I suggested that the company back off and allow its employees to be taxed on the value of the Hawaiian trip. My reasoning was simply that even if they could convince Revenue to allow, say, 30% as being for business purposes, the authorities could just as easily change their minds and contend that 40% or 50% of the other four trips was for pleasure. Sometimes, a compromise with Revenue officials will save more in the long run—especially when one takes into account the professional fees incurred in handling a dispute. I don't know if the controller took my advice, but in any event, my message should be clear. Wherever possible, combine business and pleasure. As a general rule, I suggest that you avoid business meetings in both Florida and Hawaii since Revenue Canada appears to take a very negative attitude to expenditures incurred in these two locations.

If you take your spouse on a business trip, Revenue's general outlook is that the costs of taking the spouse are a taxable benefit. The exception is where your spouse accompanies you at the specific request of your employer and for purposes of enhancing the employer's business efforts. In this case you should obtain written instructions from your employer requiring you to bring your spouse along on a trip. The letter should indicate that it is anticipated that there will be meetings in the evenings involving customers, clients, or suppliers and their spouses, and that your spouse is expected to contribute to these meetings by promoting the employer's activities. This letter could be extremely useful during a subsequent Revenue audit— but it will only work where there is an arm's-length relationship between you and the employer. This means you cannot be related by blood, marriage, or adoption. If an employee also happens to own the business, there is no great advantage in getting the individual in his capacity as president of the company to sit down and write himself a letter requiring that he take his own spouse away on business.

When it comes to the employer paying the cost of bringing spouses along to conventions, Revenue's attitude appears to be somewhat mixed. In many cases, the authorities will add on taxable benefits when participants take their spouses along, although, in recent years, many organizations seem to have been making efforts to eliminate or reduce the tax exposure. Most convention agendas now make bona fide attempts to include the spouses of participants in business-related sessions. At one convention where I was a speaker, there was a specific program for wives on how to help their husbands cope with stress. At another convention, a former colleague of mine from the University of Calgary spoke to the association members' spouses on how to interpret financial statements of small businesses. Many of my own programs on personal financial planning are suitable for both spouses.

Discounts on Merchandise Ordinarily Sold by an Employer

If you obtain a discount on merchandise ordinarily sold by your employer, Revenue Canada does not require you to include the value of that discount in your income. Presumably, keeping track of such discounts would involve an effort more costly than the dollars lost to the government coffers. While in late November 1981 it appeared this policy would change, the Minister of National Revenue was subsequently persuaded to back down. Thus, if you are in a position to take advantage of such discounts because, for example, you work for a retail company, feel free to do so.

Note, however, that special rules have always applied to the construction industry. Where an executive is able to acquire a home built by his or her employer, and the cost is less than its fair market value, most of the District Taxation Offices try to label a portion of the difference as a taxable benefit. The amount of the benefit is, of course, subject to negotiation. If you work in the construction industry and are able to benefit from the purchase of a company-built home, avoid any disputes by purchasing at a price that would give your employer at least a small profit margin.

While on the subject of construction companies, I strongly suggest that you stay away from the practice of letting a company pay for improvements to your own residence while charging off the cost of these expenditures against job-construction projects. Anybody who does something of this nature is committing fraud, which is punishable by severe penalties.

Recreational Facilities and Club-Membership Dues

In an attempt to cut back on expense-account living, Parliament passed a law as part of its 1972 Tax Reform prohibiting the deduction as a business expense of membership fees in any club providing dining, recreational, and sporting facilities. Thus, if a company pays these membership fees, they are non-deductible even if the facilities are used for proper business entertainment and promotion. Although the membership fees are automatically disallowed, house accounts (for green fees or the actual cost of meals and beverages) are deductible if it can be shown that these specific accounts arose in the course of business entertainment.

When the above rules were brought in, Revenue Canada was faced with an administrative dilemma. If the department were to adopt the policy of taxing these memberships as a benefit to individual employees, then a double-tax situation would arise. (This results any time an expense is disallowed to a company, while the outlay is also taxed as a benefit to an individual.) In order to circumvent double taxation, Revenue issued an Interpretation Bulletin exempting employees from having to include these benefits in income. Officially, the exemption only applies where an employee uses the facilities *primarily* to further the employer's business objectives. Administratively, however, it appears that the department has taken a rather lax approach in enforcement. Therefore, club memberships paid for by a company can be an excellent benefit for senior executives. This is especially true where the individual is in a substantially higher tax bracket than the corporation that employs him.

The benefit is even greater where the individual happens to be a major shareholder of the company as well. Again, as is the case with company cars, less earning power is needed to pay for a club membership on a after-tax basis where the corporation bears the cost. This is illustrated in Figure 2-6.

Figure 2-6 **Pre-Tax Earnings Needed to Pay Club-Membership Dues of $750**

Personal Earnings

Salary to individual	$1,500
Less: Incremental taxes at assumed 50% marginal bracket	750
After-tax funds for membership dues	$ 750

Corporate Earnings

Profit retained by small-business corporation	$1,000
Less: Taxes at 25%	250
After-tax funds for membership dues	$ 750

Stock-Option and Stock-Purchase Plans

Where an individual is employed by a *public* corporation and the individual obtains the right to acquire shares of his or her employer company out of treasury, the tax rules consider this to be an employment benefit. Until recently, the amount to be added to income was the *full* difference between the price to be paid for the shares and their fair market value at the date the employee exercised his or her option. (The fair market value of the shares on the date the option was granted was not relevant for tax purposes.) This can be illustrated by a simple example:

Fair market value of each share at the time the option is exercised	$20.00
Less: Option price to be paid	14.00
Benefit from employment (per share)	$6.00

For stock-option programs initiated after February 15, 1984, the taxable benefit on the eventual exercise is now limited to *one-half* of the difference between the option price and the fair market value of the shares at the time the option is exercised. This reduces the tax burden of a stock-option program by 50% compared to the burden under rules applicable to previous plans. The new rules only apply, however, if the exercise price for the shares is the same or greater than their fair market value at the time the option was granted. This new incentive should make stock-option programs for employees of public corporations even more attractive than before.

Where the option is for shares in a public corporation, the fact that a taxable benefit arises is not too onerous. These shares generally tend to be marketable and it is usually possible for some of the shares to be sold in order to pay taxes on the benefit. In addition, since these shares are saleable, an employee can often borrow money to pay the taxes by using the shares as collateral.

Stock-option plans are thus quite attractive for employees of public companies who are able to acquire shares at less than the going trading price. Although the individual must contend with a taxable benefit at the time the option is exercised, any future growth beyond that point is treated as a capital gain—only one-half of which is potentially taxable. A capital gain will only arise at the time the shares are sold.

During the early 1970s stock-option programs were rarely, if ever, used with respect to *private* corporations. This was for two major reasons:

- Shares of private companies are not marketable. Thus, an employee cannot sell some of his or her shares to pay taxes.
- Shares of private companies are not readily pledged as collateral for bank financing. Accordingly, an individual faced with a tax liability would be hard-pressed to borrow against his or her shares for the purpose of making payment.

In mid-1977, however, Parliament decided for the first time to differentiate between option plans granted by public corporations and option plans of Canadian-controlled private companies. An employee of a private company is now permitted to buy treasury shares at literally *any price* from one dollar up to fair market value. As long as the employee continues to hold these shares in his or her own name for at least two years after the date of acquisition, no taxable benefit need be calculated. The only tax consequences that will arise occur at the time of sale. One-half of the difference between the actual purchase price and the selling price becomes an employment benefit at that time.

Thus, it is theoretically possible for key employees of Canadian-controlled private corporations to acquire substantial interests in an employer company for as little as one dollar. The only requirement that must be adhered to (in addition to the two-year minimum holding period) is that the employees must deal at arm's length with the controlling shareholder or shareholders. Because of the very generous tax treatment afforded employees of Canadian private companies, a share-interest in the business is definitely one of the key benefits to be negotiated wherever possible.

From the standpoint of the controlling shareholder, admission of key employees as "partners" can be a very viable alternative to an outright sale. Consider, for example, the case where a person has built up a business and now wishes to retire. Unfortunately, no one within the family wishes to assume the responsibilities of administration. The owner could, in such circumstances, issue sufficient shares to one or more key employees so that they wind up with, say, 25% of the equity. These key employees would remain as custodians and would receive salaries for their continued efforts. In addition, if the business does well, 25% of the profits from all future growth will accrue to their benefit, while the rest of the profits would remain within the family of the retired owner.

Other Benefits

Two other fringe benefits that should be considered are travel passes and discount rates for transportation-company employees and subsidized board and lodging in remote work locations. While the November 1981 Budget proposed to tax these benefits, the government has subsequently backtracked, and these perks essentially remain non-taxable. Airline passes available to airline employees are now only taxable if the employee travels on a space-confirmed basis and pays less than 50% of the economy fare available on that carrier for that trip on that day of travel. The value of the benefit will be the difference between 50% of the economy airfare and any amount reimbursed to the carrier for that trip. Employees of bus and rail companies are not, however, taxed on the use of passes. Moreover, retired employees of transportation companies are not taxed on pass benefits under any circumstances. An employee in the travel industry is certainly better off with a "cheap" holiday as a bonus instead of using a fully-taxed raise in pay to subsidize a vacation. Similarly, there is now an excellent incentive for an engineer or other highly skilled employee to accept an assignment in a smaller community where large industrial plants or resource-development facilities are located. Such an individual would be well advised to negotiate a smaller salary in exchange for subsidized board and lodging.

Where an employer owns a vacation property which is used by an employee, it is the opinion of Revenue Canada that the taxable benefit is the amount that the employee would have had to pay a third party for equivalent accommodation less any amount the employee actually pays to the employer. The authorities do recognize that the taxable benefit may be reduced where there is conclusive evidence to substantiate that the employee was involved in direct business activities during the holiday or vacation.

Getting the Competitive Edge

There are many opportunities to capitalize on the differences between the tax rules pertaining to the employee's income and those pertaining to the employer's income. For example, certain expenses are deductible when incurred by a company but are not deductible to employed individuals. Although it is difficult to generalize, a couple of concrete examples should serve to make this point.

Convention Expenses
Under the tax rules, convention expenses are not a proper

deduction in arriving at employment income. Thus, for example, when an individual attends a trade or professional convention and bears the cost personally, the costs would not be deductible unless the individual is self-employed.

Consider an individual who wishes to attend a particular trade or professional conference. He or she asks an employer to subsidize the costs, but the employer refuses on the grounds that it is contrary to company policy. The employer, however, says that the employee may go if he or she is willing to take the time off as part of the annual vacation. If the employee is tax conscious, he or she should then suggest that the employer pay the cost of the convention and reduce his or her salary accordingly.

From an employer's standpoint, it makes no difference whether an amount is paid as a salary or as a convention expense. The full payment in either case can be written off for tax purposes. However, where an employer pays convention costs and reduces an employee's salary, the employee gets a smaller amount reported on his or her T-4 slip. Having less income to report in the first place is equivalent to having a higher income offset by a tax-deductible expense.

This is a prime example of getting the competitive edge— finding a situation where an expense is deductible to an employer that would not be deductible to an individual employee.

Tuition Fees
Here is another fringe-benefit program that you might consider—tuition fees for courses. From an employer's perspective, these are treated as an expense in arriving at business income. On the other side, tuition-fee payments must be included in an employee's income, although the employee also gets a deduction for tuition fees paid on his or her personal tax return. Thus, *the taxable employment benefit and the fee deduction cancel one another.* This is more advantageous than if the employee were to pay these expenses personally. On personally paid tuition fees, you still have to absorb a substantial portion of the fees even if they are deductible. For 1982 and subsequent years, tuition fees for personal-interest (meaning non-job-related) courses may no longer be claimed. Fees relating to university degree programs continue to be tax-deductible.

Tax Avoidance Versus Tax Evasion

The previous examples fall under the definition of effective tax *avoidance*. There is nothing fraudulent about arranging your affairs to produce the smallest tax bite possible in any given circumstances. There is, however, a fine line of distinction between tax avoidance and tax evasion. Evasion is something that you should stay away from since this is an offence punishable under both common and criminal law. To illustrate the difference, here is a short story outlining one of my favourite examples of evasion.

There is a privately owned appliance store that operates in a major Canadian city. Over a period of twenty or twenty-five years the owner of that store got to know his regular customers quite well, and he eventually came up with a very interesting idea for promoting sales. When a customer who owned a business came in to buy, say, a television set for personal use, the store owner would approach him or her with the suggestion that he could invoice the television to the customer's business as an air-conditioning unit. The customer's business could then pay for the set and could also obtain a tax write-off through future depreciation. From the appliance dealer's standpoint it wouldn't make any difference to his cash flow, but from the customer's position, getting a company to pay (on a tax-deductible basis) for a personal expenditure would be an excellent benefit.

Somehow or other, Revenue officials caught on to what was happening. They did an audit of the appliance dealer's operations and compared sales invoices to related shipping documentation. Naturally, the discrepancy became apparent. The invoices described air conditioners sold to companies while the shipping documentation was for television sets delivered to personal residences. Both the appliance dealer and all the customers who had participated in this particular venture lived to regret this little scheme.

Tax fraud is, of course, subject to severe penalties. Granted, it is often difficult for a layperson to differentiate between permissible avoidance and punishable evasion. Usually, if you are in doubt, listen to your stomach. The more queasy you feel about a particular manoeuvre, the more likely it is that you are crossing over into forbidden territory. When in doubt, consult your own advisers. That is one of the reasons you have them. In the meantime, use your imagination. I am sure that most business owners and executives can find ways to *legitimately* get that competitive edge.

CHAPTER THREE

Tax Planning for the Commissioned Salesperson

There are several strategies that commissioned salespeople can use when planning their affairs so that they take maximum advantage of the Canadian tax rules for the recording of income and expenses. In this chapter, strategies are discussed for commissioned salespersons who are employed as well as those who are self-employed. Strategies are also outlined for the self-employed commissioned salesperson who may be able to benefit from incorporating his or her activities. These latter considerations will be discussed briefly towards the end of this chapter and in more detail in Chapter Eleven.

Employment Versus Self-Employment

Tax planning for the individual who receives income from commissions must start with a determination of whether the person is employed or self-employed. It is important that this be decided, because if you are self-employed, you do not necessarily have to report your income on a calendar-year basis. If you are considered to be carrying on your own business, you can initially pick any year end that you want, as long as you are then consistent in following years. This allows regular tax deferrals. Also, if you are self-employed, the Income Tax Act tends to provide much more liberal expense deductions than if you are an employee. So, again, the first and perhaps key distinction is to determine whether you are an employee or an independent contractor.

If you are considered an employee, the company for which you work is required to deduct Canada or Quebec Pension Plan premiums as well as Unemployment Insurance premiums. If there is any problem in determining your status, you are allowed to request a specific ruling, which is valid not only for Canada

Pension and Unemployment Insurance but also for income-tax purposes. To make an application, you must file Form CPT-1 and the related questionnaires which you can obtain from your local District Taxation Office.

Some of the major criteria in distinguishing whether you are an employee or self-employed include the following:

- Are you an officer or director of the company that pays you?
- Are you prohibited from performing your services for other businesses during the same period in the working day?
- Does the company that pays you have a preferred call on your time and efforts?
- Are you required to furnish your own office or does the business which pays you provide you with a place to work?
- How often do you have to report to a representative of the business that pays you?
- Are you required to cover your territory within a specified time or with specified frequency?
- Are you required to meet a quota to retain your position?
- Are you guaranteed a minimum amount of compensation irrespective of your commissions?
- Are your expenses reimbursed by way of an allowance?
- Are you required to perform all services personally?
- Do you have a draw against anticipated earnings?
- Are you covered under various fringe-benefit programs such as a registered pension fund, group insurance, profit sharing, and so on?
- Can your services be terminated at will by the business that pays you?

No one factor or combination of factors is necessarily conclusive except that if the answer to most of the previous questions is "yes," you are probably going to be considered an employee. On the other hand, if you are an independent contractor, you are thus self-employed.

Examine Your Gross Revenues—Timing of Income Recognition

Once you have established your status, the next step is to look at your gross revenues. If you are employed, your gross revenues would presumably include salary or wages as well as commissions. As an employee, your commissions are normally taxable in the calendar year they are received. In other words, employment income is calculated on a cash basis. This is an important consideration because it gives you, perhaps, the first opportunity for planning. Let's assume that you make a very large sale in December 1985. You have already enjoyed a very good year and you recognize that your commission on this sale would be taxed at approximately 50%, the top marginal tax bracket in most provinces of Canada. If you can arrange with your employer to defer the payment of your commission until January 1986, you won't have to account for this income until the subsequent year. If you anticipate a low-income year in 1986, there can be a substantial advantage. From your employer's perspective, delaying the payment of a commission by one month has no effect for tax purposes. This is because the employer calculates income on an accrual basis and can claim a deduction at the point in time that the liability is incurred, even if it is paid later.

On the other hand, you should note that Revenue Canada takes the position that if you receive advances against commissions, they are *also* taxable in the year that they are received, even if they are only earned subsequently. Again, you may have an opportunity for planning. First, if you have a very good year in 1985, you might delay the receipt of an advance to which you are entitled in December 1985 until January 1986. Again, if 1986 is a lower-income year, in the final analysis, you may pay less tax.

Conversely, if 1985 was a relatively bad year for you but you are expecting a significant improvement in 1986, you might ask your employer for an advance in 1985 against 1986's commissions. It's true this will accelerate the payment of your taxes but you may get the advantage of paying in a lower bracket.

If this type of planning appeals to you, I think an hour or so with your own accountant towards the end of the year, but before December 31, would be time and money well spent. My point is that a commissioned salesperson generally has more flexibility than most employees.

If you are self-employed, you must report your income on an accrual basis. This means you are taxable when your income is earned, irrespective of whether it was received before or after the time it was earned. However, as I mentioned earlier, a self-employed person is entitled to adopt an accounting period other than the calendar year. In the first year that you carry on a business, you can pick any year end that you want. After that time, all year ends must remain constant unless you get approval for a change from the Minister of National Revenue. Usually a good valid business reason is required for such an approval to be granted.

What is the advantage of selecting a year end other than the calendar year? The answer is the opportunity to defer taxes for as much as a full year on an ongoing basis. For example, let's assume that you were an employee of a particular company until March 31, 1985. At that point, you decided to go into your own business as an independent commissioned agent. You can pick as your first year end any time from April 1, 1985, to March 31, 1986.

Assume you earn a very large commission in mid-November 1985. You might then pick October 31 as your first year end. Thus, when you file your 1985 return in April 1986 you would only report your employment income for the months of January, February, and March and your profit from your self-employment for the period April through October. In other words, your big commission for the month of November 1985 would only become income in 1986 and you would only have to report this income on filing your 1986 tax return in April 1987. This is a significant tax advantage. However, once you have established an October 31 year end, all year ends thereafter would have to be October 31.

This is only one of many possibilities. As an alternative, you could pick January 31, 1986, as your first year end. Under these circumstances, when you file your 1985 tax return, you would only have to report your employment income for the months of January, February, and March. Your 1985 income from your entire period of self-employment (in other words, April through December) would only be taxable in 1986. Again, your taxes would be paid in April 1987.

If you become self-employed in the middle of a particular year, you don't have to make a decision on when your first year end is going to be until the following March or, if you're prone to waiting until the last minute, even early April. In other words, you've got the benefit of hindsight, although you should make your decision before your next tax return is due the following April 30. In my last example, a decision on what year end to adopt should really be made no later than mid-March or early April 1986. This way, a proper tax return for the 1985 year can be prepared before the April 30, 1986, deadline.

Again, spend some time with your accountant. It would be well worth your while, though, to have available for your accountant's consideration a summary of your income earned on a month-by-month basis and a schedule of related expenses. With this information and some trial-and-error calculations, your accountant can help you make a year-end timing decision that is to your maximum advantage.

So, to summarize everything I have said to this point, your first step is to determine whether you are employed or self-employed. Step two is then to recognize the point in time at which your gross income is subject to taxation, regardless of whether you must report on a cash or on an accrual basis.

Fringe Benefits

If you are an employed commissioned salesperson, it is likely that you are receiving benefits beyond wages, salaries, and commissions. Most fringe benefits are included in income at their value to an individual employee. Some common fringe benefits include holiday trips, prizes, and incentive awards as well as travelling expenses of an employee's spouse, tuition fees for courses, and premiums under provincial hospitalization and medicare programs.

One of the most common fringe benefits allocated to commissioned salespeople is a company car. If you drive a company car, your income for tax purposes will include a two-part benefit, the first calculated on availability of the vehicle and the second based on operating expenses. The double taxable benefit from company cars was discussed in detail in Chapter Two. I suggest that, in at least some cases, it may be more to your advantage for you to provide your own automobile and to charge your employer so many cents per kilometre, or arrange for a reasonable monthly allowance. The allowance should, of course, cover not only the business operating expenses but also that portion of the capital cost of the car applicable to business-related usage.

You should be aware that there are a few employee benefits that are not taxable. For example, if your employer provides you with a distinctive uniform that you are required to wear while carrying out your duties, this does not constitute a taxable benefit. Similarly, if your employer pays for laundry and dry-cleaning of such a uniform, this is also not taxable. A good example of such an arrangement can be found in the case of a number of national real estate companies that provide their salespeople with distinctive blazers.

Perhaps the most important non-taxable benefit for the commissioned salesperson is the use of recreational facilities. If your employer provides you with a paid membership in a club that provides dining, recreational, or sporting facilities, this is not taxable as long as it is to the employer's advantage for you to be a member of the club. In other words, if you use these facilities to entertain customers, clients, or prospective customers or clients, there are no adverse tax consequences for you.

Deductibility of Expenses

Let's now turn to the deductibility of expenses that may be claimed against income from commissions. I will make some general points first which are applicable primarily to employed salespeople and I will then provide some detailed comments on specific expenses, highlighting some of the major differences between being classified as an employee versus a self-employed person.

First of all, an employed commissioned salesperson is allowed to claim "salesmen's" expenses if he or she can answer yes to four specific questions as follows:

1. Are you paid, at least in part, on a commission basis?
2. Are you required to pay your own expenses pursuant to your contract of employment?
3. Are you involved in selling property or negotiating contracts?
4. Are you ordinarily required to carry on your duties of employment away from your employer's place of business?

Those who do qualify for a claim under salesmen's expenses should note that if they receive an allowance for travel expenses, they can record that allowance as income and then claim actual expenses as an offset. The other option is to ignore the allowance and disregard actual travel costs. The option that provides the greater benefit for tax purposes is the one that should be selected.

For many commissioned salespersons, the most contentious item is the question of carrying on duties away from an employer's place of business. For example, if you are involved in selling furniture or appliances, you may not qualify for a claim for salesmen's expenses because you would not ordinarily be required by your employer to involve yourself with customer visits. However, if you are engaged in selling carpeting or draperies and you must make customer calls, then you would likely qualify.

The one area where the Revenue authorities appear to be reasonably lenient is in connection with securities salespeople— in other words, individuals who sell stocks and bonds on a commission basis. The problem here is that a securities salesperson generally operates via the telephone. In other words, he or she may not spend much time away from the employer's place of business during the working day. However, the Revenue authorities seem to allow an expense claim, provided that the employer requires the salesperson to contact clients away from the employer's place of business. Since many securities salespeople feel that face-to-face contact with clients and prospective clients is an important segment of their activities, and since successful securities salespeople tend to spend significant amounts of money on entertainment and promotion of clients outside normal business hours, it appears that this condition can be satisfied.

If an employed salesperson claims salesmen's expenses, there are a couple of points that should be noted. First, the expenses claimed cannot exceed the amount of commissions received in the year with the exception of capital cost allowance (depreciation for income-tax purposes) on an automobile used by the individual in performing his or her duties, along with interest expense on money borrowed to acquire that car. In other words, with the exception of capital cost allowance on a car and interest expense, you are not permitted to claim a commission loss for the year.

The other important point you should note is that if you claim salesmen's expenses you are not eligible for the employment-expense deduction, which is otherwise 20% of your employment income, including commissions, to a maximum of $500. In other words, it is only to your advantage to claim salesmen's expenses (other than travel expenses) if these exceed $500 in total.

If you don't want to make a claim under the category of salesmen's expenses, you may claim your travel expenses only. Travel expenses will include capital cost allowance and finance charges on an automobile used in the performance of your duties. If you deduct travel expenses only, you are also permitted to claim the $500 employment-expense deduction. However, if you claim under the travel-expense rules, you may not include items such as advertising, entertainment, or promotion. A deduction for travel expenses is also prohibited if you receive a reasonable travel allowance from your employer.

Once you determine that you qualify to claim salesmen's expenses, it is necessary to examine what your expenses are and to what extent these may be deducted. If you are an employee, you are limited to those expenses specifically called for under the Income Tax Act. The next part of this chapter will highlight some of the differences between claiming expenses as an employee versus claiming them when you are self-employed. But first, please note that if you are an employee, you may only deduct expenses in the year they are incurred. In other words, you may not carry forward amounts expended in prior years even if your income in those years was too low for you to obtain any substantial benefit.

Car Expenses
For most commissioned salespeople, car expenses are probably the largest single expense deduction. The rules for keeping track of and claiming car expenses appear to be the same whether you are employed or self-employed. Of course, in dealing with car expenses at this time, I make the assumption that you are using your own car, not an automobile provided by someone else.

Legitimate operating expenses that may be claimed for tax purposes include the cost of gas and oil, repairs and maintenance, insurance, parking, licence, car washes, and even short-term rentals while your car is in for servicing. If you lease an automobile, your lease costs will be deductible pursuant to your leasing agreement, provided that they are paid in the year in question. When it comes to repairs and maintenance, you may have to differentiate between expenses and capital costs. For example, if you install a new radio or an air-conditioning system, this should not be claimed as an expense but should be amortized as part of your depreciation allowance. Depreciation allowances (or capital cost allowance, as it is called for tax purposes) are discussed next.

Capital Cost Allowance
Capital cost allowance on an automobile that is owned by a taxpayer and used for business is 15% of the cost of the car in the year of acquisition and 30% on a declining balance thereafter. In other words, if you buy a $10,000 automobile, your first year's depreciation becomes $1,500, 15% of $10,000. In the second year, you may claim 30% of $8,500, or $2,550, and in the third year, your depreciation claim is 30% of $5,950, or $1,785.

If you trade your car in on another one, you simply add the net cost after trade-in allowance to your undepreciated capital-cost-allowance balance at the start of that year. You may claim 30% of the old balance and 15% of your additional net cost for that year.

Unfortunately, the capital-cost-allowance rules are somewhat complex and a detailed analysis is beyond the scope of this book. In the year that you are contemplating the purchase of a car, you might be well advised to spend a few minutes with your own accountant so that he or she can calculate the available depreciation claim based on your anticipated cost.

I also suggest that you consult with your accountant if you plan to sell a car that you use for business purposes and then lease a car from that time on. Depending on the price you get for your old car, you may wind up with a "recaptured depreciation," which you will have to take into income in the year of sale.

If you previously used an automobile for personal purposes and begin to use it to earn income, you are deemed to have acquired it at its fair market value at the time you began to use it for business purposes. That amount becomes the base on which future depreciation is claimed.

If you are an employed commissioned salesperson, you may claim the 15% first year's depreciation on the cost of your car, even if you buy that car on the last day of the calendar year. In fact, it is common practice to acquire depreciable property towards the end of the year to get the maximum tax advantage from a capital-cost-allowance claim. If, however, you are self-employed and your tax year happens to be less than twelve months in length, your depreciation must be prorated based on the number of the days in your business year. As I pointed out earlier, you will generally only have a short year in your first year as a self-employed commissioned salesperson. Again, at the time you get your accounting advice, you might discuss the tax rules pertaining to automobiles with your own adviser.

In most cases, cars are used both for business and personal purposes. Where this is the case, your personal-use portion must be accounted for separately. As distasteful as this might be, you should really keep a log or you run the risk that your expense claim will be disallowed or reduced.

Travel Expenses
For some commissioned salespeople, whether employed or self-employed, a second major expense category is travel expenses other than car expenses. Travel expenses would be incurred while away from home overnight on business and would commonly include hotel accommodations, transportation by way of bus, train, taxi, or airplane, as well as meal costs. When it comes to meal costs, there is an important limitation that applies to employed salespeople. Specifically, a meal is only deductible as a travel expense if you are away from the municipality in which your employer's business establishment is located for more than twelve hours. Thus, to claim travel expenses, you must ordinarily be away from home overnight. Of course, if your meals are taken in the company of clients or customers, even within the municipality in which your employer's business is located, you may be able to claim your expenses as business promotion instead.

Business Promotion
Business promotion involves a wide variety of expenses, including advertising and entertainment. Common advertising costs include give-away items such as calendars, pens, and samples, as well as the cost of business cards, newspaper ads, flyers, and printed pamphlets.

Business entertainment includes the costs of meals and certain expenses incurred in conjunction with the use of recreational facilities. Membership fees in any club that provides dining, recreational, or sporting facilities are not tax-deductible, regardless of whether you are employed or self-employed. However, the actual expenses of *using* recreational facilities, such as green fees, or the costs of food and beverages, are deductible if these costs are incurred as part of legitimate client entertainment.

Promotion expenses will include gift items, such as a bottle of liquor to a customer or client, or (very common in the real estate industry) a house-warming gift to a family that buys a house from a real estate agent. Another tax-deductible promotion expense is tickets to sporting events. I caution you, though, that if you wish to claim gifts and/or the cost of sporting-event tickets, you should keep careful track of who the recipients are. If you can't substantiate that the beneficiaries are clients, customers, or potential clients and customers, Revenue Canada may disallow your claims.

An Office in the Home

From the standpoint of an employed commissioned salesperson, one of the most difficult areas is a claim for expenses incurred in conjunction with an office in the home. Such a claim generally does not trigger the same degree of scrutiny by the authorities if you are self-employed.

There are several conditions that must be met for an employed commissioned salesperson to successfully maintain a deduction for home-office expenses. First and most important, the Income Tax Act specifies that the individual must be *required by his or her contract of employment* to maintain an office at home. If the office is not required, then Revenue Canada is at liberty to disallow all expenses, even if otherwise legitimate.

If you pass the test of having a home office required by your employer, there are several other criteria that will be considered in judging your claim. First, you should set aside a room in your home that is used exclusively as a place to carry on business. You should also be able to establish that a reasonable portion of your activities are carried on from that office.

Generally, Revenue Canada looks with a jaundiced eye on expense claims for a home office when the employer has an office within a reasonable distance from the individual's home. What is reasonable is not defined within the framework of the Income Tax Act itself. Also, if you are reimbursed for the costs of maintaining an office at home, you are not allowed to claim a deduction.

Whether you rent or own your home, legitimate expenses will include utilities, telephone expenses, cleaning materials, and minor repairs. If you are employed, you may not claim mortgage interest or capital cost allowance on the home. Even if you are self-employed, I do not recommend that you claim either mortgage interest or capital cost allowance if you are over the lifetime capital-gains limit, since these claims could jeopardize your exemption from capital-gains tax at the time the house is sold.

Practically speaking, you should keep track of the total costs applicable to your home office and then divide the expenses between business and personal use. The allocation can be based either on the number of rooms used for business as a percentage of the total number of rooms in the home or on the square footage of business space over the total area of the home.

Other Allowable Expenses
If you maintain an office at home, you are likely to incur telephone expenses. Revenue Canada adopts the position that only long-distance phone calls related to business are a proper deduction unless you have a separate business line. If a separate business line is maintained, all telephone costs would then be tax-deductible.

Whether you are employed or self-employed, you are also permitted to claim professional or association membership dues as well as licence fees necessary to maintain a professional status. Association entrance or initiation fees are, however, considered capital outlays and are not tax-deductible.

Salary to an Assistant
One of the trickiest areas is a claim for salary expenses. Again, the problem only arises if you are employed on a commission basis. An employee is only allowed to deduct salary expenses paid to an assistant or substitute if these payments are *required* through the contract of employment, even if the employee can substantiate that payments (not actually required) were bona fide and that services were in fact rendered. This problem does *not* arise if you are self-employed. Your claim for salaries is much less likely to be scrutinized closely.

If you can claim salaries and wages, they may include amounts paid to your spouse or to other family members. However, if you are making payments to a member of your family, you must be very careful to ensure that you can show that these payments are in fact reasonable. Reasonable is considered to be the amount that you would otherwise have to pay an outside party to perform the same services. You should also note, whether you are employed or self-employed, that salaries paid to others are subject to tax deductions at source, including Canada or Quebec Pension Plan and Unemployment Insurance premiums.

The Cost of Supplies
Another area where the Income Tax Act closely regulates expense deductions by an employee is the subject of supplies. Again, a deduction for supplies consumed may only be claimed if the purchase of these supplies was required pursuant to a contract of employment. If you are self-employed, this restriction does not apply. Supplies include such items as pens and pencils, appointment calendars, diaries, stamps, paper clips, and stationery.

Conventions
Another major difference between employed and self-employed commissioned salespersons pertains to convention expenses. Convention expenses are never deductible against employment income; they are only a proper deduction against income from a business. If you are employed and you are required to attend a convention or sales conference, you do not have to add reimbursement costs into your income. However, if you receive a non-accountable allowance to cover your expenses, your allowance would have to be reported as a taxable benefit and your expenses would not be deductible.

If you would like to attend a convention, essentially at your own expense, you might want to ask your employer to pay the expenses directly on your behalf and to reduce correspondingly the rate paid to you as gross commissions. Your employer could claim these convention expenses as a deduction as part of *his* or *her* business activities, and if you show a smaller gross income from commissions, this would be the equivalent of a higher income coupled with a deductible expense. This is certainly one of the many grey areas in the Income Tax Act and I caution you to get professional advice before implementing any planning steps. If you are involved as a commissioned salesperson in either the life insurance or real estate industries and you are employed by a company, I suggest that you speak to representatives of that company so that a suitable policy regarding conventions can be set up on a company-wide basis.

If you are self-employed, you are permitted to deduct the costs of up to two conventions a year, provided that these conventions are sponsored by a business or professional organization and were attended by yourself in connection with a business that you carry on. You need not be a member of the organization sponsoring the convention, but to qualify for a deduction, your attendance must be related to your business.

The Income Tax Act specifies that you may only claim convention expenses at locations consistent with the territorial scope of the organization holding them. Generally, this means that a Canadian business would be bound to hold its convention activities somewhere in Canada if the business is national in scope, while if the organization is provincial, the convention should be held in that particular province. However, since many organizations are multinational, there is no rule that would deny a convention-expense deduction for reasonable costs incurred outside the country.

As a general rule of thumb, I recommend that if you wish to claim the costs of two conventions, one of them should be located in Canada and one may take place outside the country. Revenue Canada does, however, take a rather dim view of conventions held in exotic locations such as the Bahamas or Hawaii, but then again, as long as there is a good business reason, there is no real cause for a disallowance.

If you combine attendance at a convention with a vacation trip, you should prorate your expenses on a reasonable basis. Also, if you are accompanied by your spouse or children, the costs you incur for these people are generally not deductible.

Accounting Fees
Finally, a few words on accounting fees, including the cost of preparing an income-tax return. Revenue Canada has issued an Interpretation Bulletin that indicates that fees incurred for advice and assistance in preparing and filing tax returns are deductible

in computing income from a business, if the business is of sufficient scope to warrant legal or accounting expenses. Accounting fees incurred by an employed commissioned salesperson are also considered to be tax-deductible, if they are reasonable in the circumstances and the individual is making a claim of salesmen's expenses.

Rules for Making Income-Tax Remittances

As I mentioned at the beginning of this chapter, if you are employed, it is encumbent on your employer to deduct income taxes at source from commissions paid. If you are self-employed, you must make quarterly instalments on the last day of March, June, September, and December. Only the difference between the instalments which you have paid and your actual tax liability is due the following April 30 when your tax return is filed. Instalments are required if you had taxable income in the previous year and tax was not deducted at source from at least three-quarters of your net income. You are exempt from instalments, however, if your federal income tax for either the current year or the previous year has not exceeded $1,000. Generally, in your first year as a self-employed salesperson, you will not be required to make any tax instalments. These matters should be reviewed annually with your own advisers because insufficient instalments are subject to non-deductible interest charges.

Incorporation

Incorporation of a commissioned sales agency is only feasible if you are, beyond the slightest shadow of a doubt, self-employed and you receive your gross commission revenues from more than one source. When I refer to more than one source, I mean that you are paid by at least two, if not more, independent entities. It is not sufficient that you yourself service many customers or clients. Instead, the products that you sell must be provided by at least two independent businesses.

Incorporation provides several important tax advantages. First, there is the ability to split income between members of your family. Even if your family members are not active in your business, you can make them shareholders in the corporation and split income by way of dividends. This is explained in

Chapters Nine and Thirteen. Alternatively, any profit not required by your family to meet living expenses can be retained by the corporation. Corporate tax rates for small businesses range around 25% on active business income, which is substantially less than the rate of tax applicable to individuals at middle and upper-income levels. Then, as the retained earnings of a corporation accumulate, the funds represented by these earnings can be invested on your behalf. You are far better off investing about seventy-five cents on the dollar than reinvesting only fifty or sixty cents on the dollar after personal taxes. You should note, however, that there are restrictions governing the use of small-business tax rates. These are covered in Chapter Eleven, which highlights the important changes implemented following the federal Budget of February 15, 1984.

In most cases, the question of whether or not to incorporate cannot be resolved without the assistance of professional advisers. You will, no doubt, pick up some good ideas from Chapter Twelve, "Tax Planning for New Business Ventures." However, you should still make use of the services of your own accountant and lawyer. They should be able to explain your tax position to you and also quantify the benefits that you may hope to derive from incorporation. Since every individual's income, expenses, family situation, and living requirements are different, you cannot simply rely on generalities or on what your friends are doing when it comes to making your own business decisions.

CHAPTER FOUR

Postponing Your Income

Planning for Retirement, Loss of Job, and Transfers Outside Canada

If you are a business owner or executive aged fifty-five or older, you should be giving some thought to planning for retirement. In this chapter, I will show you that a knowledge of the tax rules can certainly be helpful. Even if you are under the age of fifty-five, this material describes opportunities for tax savings that you might have if you ever become a non-resident as a result of a job transfer outside Canada, or if you become unemployed after several years of service to a company.

The basic theme of this chapter is the conversion of income from salary into a "retiring allowance." We have already seen that a raise in pay is simply taxed in your top marginal bracket. With respect to retiring allowances, there are other options—and even a relatively young person may become eligible to receive such payments.

In passing, you should note that Chapter Ten contains a general discussion of *all* aspects of planning for the retirement years. This chapter concentrates on earned income only.

Non-Statutory Deferred-Compensation Programs

There are two kinds of deferred compensation. The first is referred to as "statutory" deferred compensation. This means that specific rules governing these concepts are set out within the Income Tax Act. Statutory deferred compensation programs include retirement savings plans and company pension plans which will be dealt with in Chapter Five. The second type of deferred compensation is "non-statutory." Non-statutory means that these plans are not covered specifically within the framework of the Income Tax Act. Actually, non-statutory deferred compensation is based on a *voluntary negotiated agreement* between an employee and an employer.

Let us begin with an example relevant to an employee of a large corporation, perhaps a public company, which has been in existence for many years. (Later on, you will see that retiring allowances can be extremely useful as a tax-planning vehicle for owner-managed businesses as well.) The following is a typical scenario involving a large company.

The chairman of the board calls a senior vice-president into his office. The vice-president is earning a salary of $70,000 a year—enough to put him into the top marginal tax bracket. The vice-president is fifty-five years old, has been with the company for twenty years, and is ten years away from retirement. Assume that the company does not have a corporate pension plan or registered deferred profit-sharing program. The chairman of the board suggests that the last thing that the vice-president really needs is additional salary. After a raise, about fifty cents on the dollar would only disappear as additional taxes.

The chairman then advances a proposal that would allow the executive to defer all or part of the *additional* compensation he would receive by way of annual raises over the next ten years. If the vice-president accepts this offer, his salary will become relatively frozen at its current level. Of course, if the executive does require additional funds from time to time, these arrangements can be altered.

Some of the additional salary that the vice-president would otherwise receive on an ongoing basis from year to year is then "put away" by the company, and at the time of retirement, *a lump sum is paid out as a retiring allowance.* The lump sum would reflect the forgone salary plus (presumably) an interest factor that had previously been negotiated between the parties.

What is the advantage of such an arrangement? There are actually two opportunities to save taxes when retiring allowances are received instead of ordinary salary.

First, by simply retiring *early* in a given taxation year, the vice-president can take a substantial portion of the allowance into his income and gain a significant tax advantage.

It is important for you to understand the difference between *marginal tax brackets* and *effective taxes*—the marginal rate is considerably higher. On the first $100,000 of a retiring allowance, for example, the tax bite would only be about $40,000 if this is the executive's *only income* in the year of retirement. The *effective* tax rate becomes 40% rather than the 50% *marginal* rate that would have applied all along had this retiring allowance been received on a year-by-year basis as (additional) salary. There is an absolute tax saving of 10%. If the executive can organize his affairs to keep his other income in that year small, the advantage is readily apparent.

In addition, a retiring allowance may qualify, in whole or in part, for a transfer into a Registered Retirement Savings Plan (RRSP). Until late 1981, the amount that could be treated in this manner was *unlimited*. It bore no relationship to the ordinary maximum annual limit for RRSP investments, which before 1986 is only $5,500 (see Chapter Five). Under recent amendments, however, limits now apply to the amount of a retiring allowance that can be received and reinvested tax-free into an RRSP.

The current law provides for a tax-deferred transfer of retiring allowances into an RRSP of up to $2,000 for each year in which the employee was covered by a registered pension or deferred profit-sharing plan and $3,500 for each year of service with no pension coverage. Based on a recent proposal, however, the existing limits on tax-deferred transfers of retiring allowances will be replaced for 1986 and subsequent years by a single limit of $2,000 per year of service. For service prior to 1986, the current limits will continue.

If the vice-president in my hypothetical example retires at age sixty-five after thirty years with the company, around $90,000 could conceivably qualify for "rollover" treatment. One advantage of the RRSP transfer is that funds do not have to be withdrawn from such a program until the beneficiary reaches age seventy-one. In the meantime, the investment income earned by these funds accrues and compounds on a tax-deferred basis. Using current rates of interest, any amount put into an RRSP at age sixty-five would almost double by the time the executive reaches the age of seventy-one.

The Employer's Tax Position
You might ask why the government tolerates a non-statutory deferred-compensation program. The answer is that the company that pays retiring allowances does not get a write-off for tax purposes until the amounts are actually paid. Since the employer does not get a deduction that it would otherwise obtain for

salaries, Revenue Canada tacitly agrees that there is no necessity to tax the individual until such time as he or she actually receives payments.

The concept of non-statutory deferred compensation works best when an employer-corporation does not need a current deduction in the first place. Such situations would include non-profit or tax-exempt organizations such as universities and hospitals. In addition, there are many real-estate-development and oil and mining companies that, because of various tax write-offs, do not currently pay income taxes. If an employer doesn't need a write-off, one gets the best tax treatment. The employer will still get a deduction (if needed) in the year the amount is paid, and the retiring allowance does not have to be taken into income by the individual until he or she receives it.

For many large corporations, the question of when a deduction of this nature is received is perhaps immaterial. While the tax consequences of, say, $100,000 are certainly important for most individuals, the timing of such a deduction is not really of significance to a Bell Canada or a Canadian Pacific. Thus, although deferred compensation programs have been more closely regulated by recent tax amendments, such programs can be extremely useful, even for employees of large corporations whose profits *are* taxable.

Beware of Constructive Receipt
The only problem that you might conceivably encounter with respect to a retiring allowance program is the concept of "constructive receipt." Over the years, tax courts have held that where an individual unilaterally defers his compensation, he is still taxed as if he had received his payments. Thus, for example, if you receive a December pay-cheque but deliberately neglect to cash it until January, you are still taxed in the year that you actually get the cheque.

In order to avoid the doctrine of constructive receipt with respect to retiring allowances, a contract between an employee and the employer usually contains some contingency clause. There must be some element of doubt as to whether the retiring allowance will, in fact, ever be paid. Of course, the contingency cannot be a strict one, such as dismissal for incompetence or for immoral behaviour. If the executive *really* believed that there was an element of doubt as to whether he would receive his money, he would never accept this type of arrangement in the first place.

Thus, the standard contingency clause is usually tied into something unlikely, such as dismissal for giving away trade secrets to competitors. In the event of being fired for such cause, the retiring allowance would not be paid. This is sufficient contingency to avoid constructive receipt as each annual instalment is segregated from salaries in the retiring allowance fund. Most of us can live with this kind of contingency. If we give away trade secrets to competitors, the presumption is that the bribe or other payments will be more than sufficient to offset the loss of the retiring allowance.

How Much and When
The term "retiring allowance" is defined in the Income Tax Act to include three types of payments:

- a payment in recognition of long service;
- a payment in respect of loss of office;
- certain other termination payments.

Most of the discussion in this chapter involves only the first of these three types of payments. The other two will be dealt with last, in the section on payments for loss of one's job.

In spite of the many recent tax changes, there are still no guidelines in the Income Tax Act as to how much can be paid out by a corporation as a retiring allowance. The only restrictions in the Act pertain to the amount of a retiring allowance that qualifies for transfer into an RRSP. Thus, as mentioned previously, the first $100,000 does not necessarily have to be placed into an RRSP. If a taxpayer has no other income in the year he or she receives this amount, the effective tax rate is only 40%.

In 1981, however, Revenue Canada did issue an interpretation, which suggests that a payment of up to two and one-half years' salary would be reasonable in cases where the individual is not a member of a registered pension plan or deferred profit-sharing program.

In addition, there are no specific guidelines as to how old an employee must be in order to receive a retiring allowance. *A payment in recognition of long service does not tie in to either a specific age or to a specific length of service with the company.*

The significance of these points will be dealt with later, in the section on planning for non-residency.

Protecting the Employee
So far, we have only concentrated on the case of an executive employed by a large public corporation. The major drawback to the concept of a retiring allowance is that a corporation may not be able to fulfill its commitment at the time of the individual's retirement. If, for example, the employer goes bankrupt any time before an executive is due to retire, the employee does not have any protection beyond that of an unsecured creditor. For that reason, a retiring allowance may not be good planning for employees of medium-sized corporations.

However, the retiring allowance can be extremely useful in the case of a smaller owner-managed business—especially where the executives (owners) have confidence in their own ability to ensure that their company will be sufficiently solvent to meet its future obligations. In addition, a retiring allowance can be an excellent vehicle to assist in passing on the ownership of a small business to other persons, such as one's children or key employees. In recent years, the retiring allowance has become increasingly important for the owner-managed business. Several years ago, the Income Tax Act was changed so that corporations are no longer permitted to have large special pension-plan programs restricted for the benefit of owner-managers. Then, the 1981 tax amendments restricted deferred profit-sharing programs where a principal shareholder is a beneficiary. In other words, the owner-manager of the Canadian small business is limited to contributing to a personal RRSP each year (or participating in a modest pension plan) and cannot avail himself of the larger statutory plans available to most other taxpayers. Fortunately, the retiring allowance can make up for this inequity. The following example will explain how—even though the numbers would now require some revision because of the new rules.

Several years ago, I was asked by a Montreal chartered accountant to assist him in tax planning for one of his clients. The client was a construction company owned by two brothers, both of whom were in their early sixties. Each brother had been drawing a salary of $100,000 a year for the previous five years and the company had earned $500,000 of profits in its fiscal year that ended June 30, 1976. Without any planning, the first $150,000 of corporate profits would have been taxed (at that time) at approximately 25%, while the remaining $350,000 would have been subjected to taxes of about 50%.

The owners of the company were somewhat upset because construction starts in the Province of Quebec had dropped after June 1976, following the completion of the Olympics projects. Then, the industry collapsed completely a few months later when the Parti Québecois government came into power following the November election. By the time the accountant called me in as a consultant, it was already early December. I met with him and his clients, and at that meeting the two brothers expressed a desire to retire. They felt that it would be a while before the Quebec construction industry would recover and they really did not want to continue in the business. They decided, however, not to wind up the company but to sell it to a son of one of the brothers.

Given these facts, the first recommendation I made was that the company change its year end to December 31, 1976. (New ownership is one of the valid business reasons that the tax authorities accept for a change in year end.) It was as of that date that control would pass over to the buyer, and an audited financial statement was required in any event. There were no significant construction activities during the six months ended December 31, 1976, and for all intents and purposes, the operations showed a break-even position. However, as of December 31, I suggested that the company pay out $175,000 of retiring allowances to *each* of the two brothers. The brothers legitimately retired as employees, resigned their directorships and offices, and sold their shares.

The retiring allowances totalling $350,000 created a business loss for that fiscal period. The tax rules at that time provided for an automatic one-year carry-back of any business loss that could not be applied against other income in the current year. By carrying the loss back one year to the fiscal period ended June 30, 1976, the revised net profit became only $150,000—coincidentally the specific amount that then qualified for the 25% low rate of corporate tax. This resulted in a recovery of $175,000 of corporate taxes otherwise payable.

One of the two brothers took his retiring allowance, bought an income-averaging annuity (IAAC), and moved to San Francisco. (The income-averaging annuity purchase would no longer be possible after 1981.) The other brother transferred his funds into an RRSP. Both were able to defer significant amounts of tax.

In the case of an owner-managed business, such as in the preceding example, the retiring-allowance arrangement has one additional benefit. *It makes the corporation whose shares are being sold easier to sell.* In the preceding example, the payment of $350,000 reduced the tangible assets of the corporation by $175,000 ($350,000 minus $175,000 of corporate taxes recovered). Whatever price would otherwise have been paid by the son of one of the brothers to acquire the company consequently became that much less. For example, if the value of the corporation before the retiring allowances was $1 million, these payments reduced the value to $825,000.

A retiring allowance can thus be an integral part of *any* purchase and sale of a private business where the vendor shareholder-manager(s) will also be leaving the employ of the company. Retiring allowances can in fact make a private corporation easier to sell—they reduce the net tangible assets of the corporation.

Figure 4-1 **Simultaneous Retirement and Sale of Business**

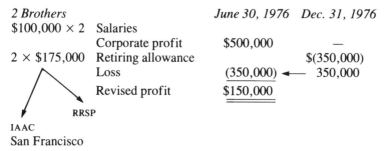

2 Brothers		June 30, 1976	Dec. 31, 1976
$100,000 × 2	Salaries		
	Corporate profit	$500,000	—
2 × $175,000	Retiring allowance		$(350,000)
	Loss	(350,000) ◄—	350,000
	Revised profit	$150,000	

IAAC
San Francisco

To update the numbers in the previous example, you should note that the IAAC rollover no longer applies and the maximum amount that can be transferred into an RRSP is limited to only $3,500 for each year of service. However, if we assume that each of these two brothers was with the company for thirty years before retirement, a total of $210,000 ($105,000 each) could have been "tax sheltered" in an RRSP—even under the new rules. Also, if the retiring allowance was set up on the books of the company as a liability on December 31, 1976, and was only paid on January 1, 1977, the tax cost of the remaining $70,000 per person could be minimized by the brothers having arranged to keep their other incomes for 1977 relatively low. Thus, the concept of retiring allowances is still as valuable as before.

Planning for Non-Residency

As I mentioned at the beginning of this chapter, a retiring allowance can be useful not only when you attain normal retirement age but also as a method of tax planning for non-residency. This is because a "payment in recognition of long service" does not tie in to any specific age requirement. To be effective, however, I suggest that there should be a minimum term of service of at least five to ten years *before* the employment relationship is severed.

At this point, it would be useful to review one or two tax-planning ideas that are generally applicable if you are contemplating leaving Canada. First, the Canadian tax system makes a sharp distinction between residency and non-residency. A resident of Canada is taxed on world income. A non-resident is only taxed (at normal graduated tax rates) on employment income from Canadian sources, self-employment income (i.e., business income), and certain Canadian capital gains. However, when property income (such as interest, rents, royalties, or annuities) is paid to a non-resident, it is subject to a special flat-rate tax of not more than 25%. A "part-year" resident of Canada is taxed on world income during that portion of the year that the person is resident. During the other portion of the year, there is no Canadian tax obligation as long as the individual does not have Canadian-source employment, business, or certain capital-gains incomes.

With this background, the first major tax-planning idea is to leave Canada, whenever possible, early in a given taxation year. The advantages can best be illustrated with another short case analysis.

In November 1977, an executive with one of the Calgary-based oil companies came to me for some tax counselling. He was being transferred by his employer to a related corporation operating in Australia. Among other things, the executive wanted to know what tax planning he should do before leaving the country. When he told me that he was booked to leave

Calgary in the last week of December, I immediately asked whether or not his departure could be postponed until the first week of January 1978. The man shrugged his shoulders and indicated that if there were tax advantages, a postponement could certainly be arranged.

I then asked him what benefits he was entitled to by virtue of severing his relationship with the Canadian company. He began to calculate his accumulated sick leave and vacation pay. In total, these came to approximately $8,000. His other income for 1977 was approximately $70,000—already sufficient to put him into a 55% marginal tax bracket in that year. I explained that adding a further $8,000 to the first $70,000 would produce effective taxes of 55% on the incremental income. However, by leaving during the first week in January, the $8,000 would then be taxed all by itself and the cost would only be about $1,200. Australian taxes would not apply to income earned before the executive takes up residence in that country. By leaving one week later, he could obtain an absolute tax saving of $3,200:

	1977	1978
Incremental income	$8,000	$8,000
Less: Taxes thereon (1977: 55%)	4,400	1,200
Net income	$3,600	$6,800

This particular executive then went so far as to suggest to his employers that they "accidentally" remove him from their payroll as of December 15, 1977. He also suggested that the "mistake" could be found in early January. In this manner, he hoped to move his last two weeks' salary from 1977 to 1978 in order to compound his tax advantages. The people in charge of payroll were receptive in theory, but they still rejected the idea. Apparently, this company is so large that it is "over-computerized." It was explained to my client that if he were removed from the payroll, the company would never be able to get him back on again. Using the old adage that a bird in the hand is worth two in the bush, my client agreed to receive his normal salary when it was to have been paid in the first place. However, the $8,000 of severance pay and other benefits were in fact moved into the following year because he delayed his actual departure from Canada.

This example also explains the importance of retiring early in a given taxation year, even if you are not planning to leave the country. Usually, your income in the first year of retirement will be much less than your income in the last year of full employment. Therefore, by retiring early in a given year, you can derive large tax savings with respect to severance pay, accumulated sick-leave payments, as well as the last year's vacation pay.

Let us now return to the opportunities to use retiring allowances in conjunction with non-residency. Assume that you are an executive employed in Canada by a company that either has or expects to have an affiliated (but legally separate) corporation operating in another country. For simplicity's sake, let's assume the other country is the United States. The president of your company calls you in and asks whether you would be interested in moving to Dallas or Denver in about two years, as a branch manager for the U.S. company. If you accept such a transfer, there are some excellent chances for tax planning.

You could ask that your present salary be reduced for the next couple of years by an amount equal to $2,000 or $3,500 for each year of service with your employer (depending on whether or not you were also a member of either a pension plan or deferred profit-sharing plan). The Canadian company could pay this to you as a retiring allowance in the year of departure and you could take the funds and purchase an RRSP.

RRSP Payments to Non-Residents

Having "rolled over" your retiring allowance into an RRSP, your worst exposure to Canadian tax would then be a flat-rate withholding tax of 25%. This is the requirement under the Canadian Income Tax Act whenever RRSP payments are made to a non-resident. This is significantly less than the marginal income-tax rates on executive salaries in Canada.

It is important to note that this idea will work only if you are ceasing to be employed by a particular company. If you are going to work for a foreign *branch* of the *same* company, the Revenue authorities will not accept the retiring allowance. This is because, in these circumstances, you would not have retired from a particular employer-company.

Even if you do not have time to plan for potential non-residency several years in advance, the retiring allowance is still feasible. Assume that you are an executive with a Canadian company and receive a salary of $60,000 a year. In January, your superior calls you into his or her office and asks you to accept a transfer to the U.S. affiliate in Chicago. To keep things simple, assume that your salary for the first year in the United States would be the same $60,000 and ignore the exchange-rate differences between the two currencies.

Again, opportunities exist for tax planning. You could ask the Canadian employer to pay you a $30,000 lump-sum retiring allowance. This would then be taxable all by itself in the year that you leave the country. Even without an RRSP rollover, your effective tax would be less than 25%! Then, during your first year of employment with the U.S. corporation, you would be prepared in such circumstances to work for a reduced salary of the remaining $30,000. This is because half of what would otherwise have been your salary has already been paid to you before leaving Canada.

Overall, the effective tax cost on a $60,000 income becomes virtually negligible. As long as the Canadian company and the U.S. company can make adjustments between themselves, there would be no real problem in setting up this kind of arrangement.

Definition of a Non-Resident
If you ever plan to become a non-resident, there are certain points that have to be considered. First, the Canadian Income Tax Act does not define the term "resident." Therefore, it becomes a question of fact whether or not an individual is or is not a resident for tax purposes at a particular time. In general, Revenue Canada takes the position that if an individual is not out of the country for at least two years, he or she will be deemed to have retained residency status if he or she was a Canadian resident before leaving. In addition, to substantiate non-residency, it is important that members of the taxpayer's immediate family accompany him or her out of the country. An immediate family would include dependent children as well as a spouse. While you are living outside the country, you are still entitled to visit. Nevertheless, the more time physically spent in Canada, the greater the risk that you will be deemed to have residency status.

In cases that have come before the courts, judges have often looked to the question of whether or not the individual maintains a home in Canada. Thus, whenever a client brings up the idea of "going non-resident," I strongly recommend that he or she sell his or her home to strengthen the tax position. If the individual is unwilling to sell, I recommend that the property be leased out on a long-term (minimum two-year) lease.

Next, you should have a reason for departing the country, such as another job or business opportunity, or perhaps the fact that you have decided to retire to a warmer climate. You should also have a valid residency status in whatever other country you are going to. In other words, if your status in that other country is only that of visitor, it becomes much easier for Revenue officials to deem that you have not ceased to be a Canadian resident.

You should also close out all bank accounts for regular operating expenses. This does not mean that you cannot have Canadian investments. However, you should not maintain bank accounts in Canada out of which everyday living expenses are paid.

Finally, club memberships in golf and country clubs should also be surrendered. In some cases, it may be possible to convert a normal membership into a special non-resident status.

While many clients and acquaintances have talked to me over the years about becoming non-residents, I have seen very few who have actually followed through—even where the tax savings would have been extremely substantial. One tends to think long and hard before uprooting an entire family and severing most ties with the past.

Death-Benefit Programs

Before leaving the topic of retiring allowances, a few comments on the tax consequences of "death benefits" would be in order. A death benefit is a payment made by an employer to a spouse (or in some cases to other dependents) of an employee who has died while in service. This type of payment can be likened to a posthumous award in recognition of long service.

For tax purposes, the *lesser* of $10,000 or the last twelve months' salary paid previous to the death of the employee is tax-free to the recipient of a death benefit. In most cases, the lesser amount will be $10,000. Although the funds are tax-free to the recipient, the employer still gets a deduction for the full payment as a business expense.

However, there is no reason to assume that a death benefit need be *limited* to only $10,000. It must simply be reasonable. Any payments in excess of the base amount would be income to the recipient but would be subject to very little tax if the recipient has no other income in the year or years they are received. Figure 4-2 illustrates this concept.

Figure 4-2 **Effective Taxes on Death Benefits**

Death benefit (in excess of $10,000 base amount)	$35,000	$50,000	$75,000	$100,000
Taxable income (net of $5,000 annual exemptions and other deductions)	$30,000	$45,000	$70,000	$ 95,000
Federal tax (approximately)	$ 6,000	$10,000	$18,000	$ 27,000
Provincial tax (assume 48% of federal tax)	2,900	4,800	8,600	13,000
Total tax	$ 8,900	$14,800	$26,600	$ 40,000
Effective tax percentage	25.4%	29.6%	35.5%	40.0%

You should note that the law permits a death benefit to be paid out *over several years*. As long as the total payment is reasonable from the employer's standpoint, the employer gets a deduction, while the recipient can take advantage of low tax rates each year—provided other income is not substantial in relation to the annual benefit payment.

Most people think of death benefits as payments that might be made by a corporation such as Bell Canada to the widow of an employee who had died while in harness. And yet, there is no restriction whatsoever limiting the right to pay death benefits to large public companies. In fact, a death benefit can be extremely useful in tax planning for owner-managed businesses as well. What better way is there to extract a minimum of $10,000 from a corporation and have that amount received tax-free? (To benefit owner-managers, the business must be incorporated, since the calculations are made with reference to salaries previously paid. The income of a proprietor of an unincorporated business is not considered a salary but is labelled as his or her business income.)

Within my own private seminar company, for example, there is a board of directors' resolution that provides that in the event of my death, the company will pay a minimum of $10,000 to my wife. Similarly, if my wife were to die (she is also an employee of the company), I would receive a death benefit of at least $10,000.

In the same way that a retiring allowance can be used as part of an arrangement to transfer the shares of a business from one taxpayer to another, a death benefit can also be used in conjunction with a buy-sell agreement. If the spouse of a deceased owner receives a large death benefit paid out over several years, it becomes that much cheaper for the surviving owners to buy out their late partner. The value of the business as a whole is decreased by the amount of the death benefit (net of corporate taxes recovered).

All private companies that pay salaries to owner-managers should adopt at least some kind of death-benefit program. There is everything to gain and nothing to lose.

Payments for "Loss of Office"

Although this chapter has discussed retiring allowances primarily in terms of payments in recognition of long service, you should note that the definition includes payments in respect of "loss of office" and certain other termination payments. Thus, where an employee is fired or asked to resign, a payment made by the former employer to the individual will be treated as a retiring allowance. Although such a payment is income, it also qualifies for reinvestment into an RRSP (within the limits discussed previously).

Note that where a former employee sues his or her employer for damages for wrongful dismissal, another recent tax change provides that all of his or her receipts (from the suit) will be considered taxable. Under the previous law, any award, whether made by a judge or by way of an out-of-court settlement, was *not* taxed to the extent that the payments exceeded an equivalent of six months' salary. Now, even excess payments are considered as taxable income.

CHAPTER FIVE

RRSPs, Pension Plans, and Other Statutory Deferred-Compensation Programs

In order to ensure the self-sufficiency of as many senior citizens as possible, the Canadian government encourages taxpayers to plan for their own retirement. The Income Tax Act sets out certain rules, which allow earned income to be exchanged for future benefits. This deferral of income is accompanied by specific tax concessions that make it easier for individuals to finance their retirement by themselves.

The tax rules do, however, draw a distinction between encouraging realistic savings plans and the tax-avoidance possibilities that would otherwise exist if the deferral allowances were overly generous.

1984–85 Proposals for Pension Reform

As part of his Spring 1984 Budget, former Finance Minister Marc Lalonde tabled two consultation papers outlining sweeping reforms to both public and private pension plans as well as Registered Retirement Savings Plans (RRSPs). Specific changes were recommended to both the Canada Pension Plan and the Old Age Security Act to extend coverage available to widowed and divorced persons and to strengthen these plans and improve total benefits. In 1985, Finance Minister Michael Wilson introduced legislation which will essentially implement his predecessor's recommendations.

New income-tax rules relating to deferred-income plans are geared to commence in 1986 and, after a transition period, are designed to become fully effective by January 1, 1990. These provisions are designed to eliminate the existing tax provisions for deferred-income plans discussed in this chapter and to replace them with a single set of rules that will allow individuals to earn pensions based on career earnings after 1985, regardless of employment or self-employment status.

The target pension is 2% of total career earnings to a maximum of $60,000, indexed by future changes in the average industrial wage. A new comprehensive deduction limit of 18% of pensionable earnings is proposed, with a maximum of $7,500 in 1986, increasing to $9,500 in 1987, $11,500 in 1988, $13,500 in 1989, and $15,500 in 1990. These limits will apply to all contributions to both registered pension plans and RRSPs. To the extent that an employer makes contributions on behalf of an individual, the individual's personal contribution level will be decreased. However, where an individual is not a member of a registered pension program, he or she will be entitled to self-finance a personal retirement program up to these new, very generous limits.

Because of complexities in record keeping, there will apparently be no provision to take pension or deduction entitlements prior to 1986 into account. In addition, the opportunity to roll over retiring allowances into an RRSP, discussed in Chapter Four, will be modified. This concession will be influenced by the fact that contribution limits to pensions and RRSPs will be targeted towards lifetime earnings. Thus, an individual who fails or is unable to contribute in a given year will be allowed to carry over the difference to up to seven subsequent years.

Other provisions within the proposed pension amendments provide for the portability of "vested rights" when an individual changes jobs. Delayed vesting will be limited to two years only and pension benefits will carry over between spouses. In the event that an employee dies prematurely, a spouse will become entitled to either a lump-sum amount or a percentage of the pension otherwise payable to the deceased individual. In addition, it is proposed that pension credits will be divided in the event of marriage breakdown.

While the government's efforts to provide extended pension coverage must be commended, the complexity of the program is somewhat ironic. Although the government has moved, as part of its more recent budgets, to simplify the small-business rules affecting perhaps 200,000 Canadian businesses, that same budget will eventually complicate the lives of literally millions of taxpayers—unless a simple system for streamlining the pension process can be devised. In this chapter, RRSPs and pension programs are discussed in detail.

Registered Retirement Savings Plans

Under the Registered Retirement Savings Plan program, an individual is allowed to set aside tax-deductible contributions if these are made in a given taxation year or within sixty days of the end of that year. For 1985, the maximum annual amount is 20% of "earned income" subject to a dollar limitation of:

- $5,500, where the individual is not a member of an employer-sponsored registered pension plan or deferred profit-sharing plan, or,
- $3,500 (less the individual's contributions to a registered pension plan, if any), where the individual is a member of an employer-sponsored registered pension plan or deferred profit-sharing plan.

"Earned income" is, basically, the sum of *net* receipts from employment, self-employment, pensions, rentals, and alimony. After 1985, it appears that rental income will no longer qualify as a component of earned income. Where an individual is not a member of a registered pension plan or deferred profit-sharing program in 1985, the "magic" earned income required for full participation in an RRSP is $27,500. This is because 20% of $27,500 is $5,500—the maximum amount that qualifies for an RRSP in any given year (excluding retiring allowances and other special transfers). In 1986, if the $7,500 maximum limit is adopted, along with an 18% limitation, the "magic" number will become $41,666 (18% × $41,666 = $7,500).

The theory behind the RRSP program is fairly simple. Contributions are made on a tax-deductible (or pre-tax) basis each year. As long as these amounts are invested in qualified investments, the income earned within an RRSP compounds on a tax-deferred basis. After several years of ongoing contributions, the available capital starts to snowball and the build-up of capital continues until retirement. At that time, the assets in the plan are liquidated and an annuity is purchased in order to provide a post-retirement cash flow. Although withdrawals from an RRSP are taxable, most individuals anticipate being in lower tax brackets after retirement than previously.

The benefits of an RRSP are substantial. If, for example, you invest $5,500 a year annually at an average of 10% compounded for thirty years, you would have almost $1 million at the end. This amount could purchase an annuity that would provide a *monthly* income of over $15,000 for the rest of your life. It is, of course, an open question of what $15,000 a month would buy if there is severe inflation—but that is beside the point, as you will see.

Qualified Investments
Historically, qualified investments of a Registered Retirement Savings Plan included things such as Canadian public-company stocks and bonds, Canada Savings Bonds, and mortgages. A small percentage of plan assets could be held in foreign securities. Starting in 1986, however, retirement income programs will be permitted to make *arm's-length* investments in the shares of private Canadian corporations. Up to 50% of plan assets will be eligible for such investments. The intent of this new legislation is to foster small-business development in Canada. It is questionable, however, whether too many people will be willing to risk their retirement savings by making investments in small businesses which they themselves do not control. Possibly, some people may conclude that they will invest in their friends' businesses if their friends invest in theirs. Nevertheless, the risk factor is substantial and only time will tell if this type of investment gains acceptance.

Should I Have an RRSP?
One of the most common questions posed to me by executives is whether or not an RRSP is advisable, especially because of investment restrictions. Real estate is still a non-qualified investment, as are precious metals such as gold and silver, and you cannot invest to any great extent in foreign securities. Notwithstanding the limitations placed on your RRSP portfolio, my general comment is that an executive doesn't have a choice—he or she *must* have an RRSP.

Let's examine the alternatives. For anyone in a 50% tax bracket in 1985, it becomes a choice of either having $5,500 earning income at a compound rate of, say, 10% each year or having half the capital ($2,750) with the tax paid and earning income at only 5% (since the unsheltered investment yield would be fully taxable). Having twice the capital returning twice the rate certainly makes an RRSP worthwhile.

To summarize then, in dealing with the question of whether or not an RRSP is attractive, simply ask yourself, what better choice is there?

Should I Borrow Money for an RRSP?

Until recently, an additional advantage of an RRSP was that an individual who did not have the necessary funds to contribute could borrow for RRSP purposes and deduct the interest incurred to make the investment. This encouraged many middle-income earners to participate in an RRSP program. However, the November 1981 Budget ended the deductibility of interest on loans taken out after that date to finance RRSPs as well as other income-deferral plans.

As a result, RRSP contributions dropped after December 1981—normally the peak time for such contributions. What few people realize even today is that borrowing money to buy an RRSP can *still* be advantageous as a forced savings program. Consider the alternatives. If an individual in the 50% bracket borrows $5,500 to buy an RRSP, and places his or her funds in the plan to earn 10%, after one year he or she will have earned interest income of $550. Even if he or she were to take all the earnings out of the plan and pay full taxes on this interest, the net yield would be $275.

On the other hand, borrowing $5,500 involves a commitment of $458.33 a month over a one-year period, not including interest. Given an outstanding loan of $5,500 at the beginning of a year and a balance that is reduced to zero by the end of the year, this is equivalent to owing $2,750 throughout the year (see the illustration on Figure 5-1). Even if the interest rate charged by a lending institution is 14%, the cost of the loan is therefore essentially 14% of $2,750, or $385 in total. Even though this interest is non-deductible, it is still not overly expensive when compared to the investment yield on $5,500 in the RRSP *throughout* the year. In fact, the actual cost in this example is really only $110 ($385 − $275).

Actually, the cost is substantially less. The previous example has assumed that the average loan outstanding throughout the year would be $2,750. If, on the other hand, a $5,500 RRSP contribution for 1985 results in a tax refund of $2,750 (for an individual in the 50% tax bracket) and these funds are used when received (generally in July or August 1986) towards an immediate reduction of the outstanding loan balance, the actual average loan throughout the year is much less. This means that the non-deductible interest expense is decreased accordingly. Therefore, in the final analysis, the cost of borrowing on a year-to-year

Figure 5-1 Borrowing to Buy an RRSP May Still be a Good Idea

Funds in RRSP		$5,500
Investment yield (10%)		$ 550

		Repayment over 12 months	
Funds borrowed for 1985 contribution	$5,500	Loan reduces to $	0
Average loan	$2,750		
Interest expense (14%)	$ 385		
If interest income is deregistered:			
Interest received	$ 550		
Less: Taxes (50%)	275		
Net interest income	275		
Less: Interest expense	385		
Cost of borrowing	$ 110		

Note: If a tax refund is received in July or August and is applied against the loan balance, the average outstanding amount becomes less than $2,750. There may, in fact, be *no* net cost of borrowing.

basis for the RRSP is virtually nothing. Keep in mind that after the first year, the plan-holder would then have $5,500 available to earn compound income in subsequent years. This procedure can be repeated year after year, taking into account the new limits discussed earlier in this chapter.

This discussion contains a valuable lesson. Any time the government makes a change in the rules, you must not only examine the theory but you must also take representative numbers and see what the impact of such a change really is. On the surface, a prohibition against interest deductibility on funds borrowed to buy an RRSP seems to be a severe restriction. And yet, in the final analysis, the cost, if any, is negligible.

Spousal Plans

If you agree that an RRSP is still a valid means of both tax sheltering and building up investment capital, there are additional refinements that should be kept in mind. The first of these is the "spousal" RRSP.

Ten years ago, the tax rules were amended to allow you to split RRSP contributions between yourself and your spouse. This does *not* mean that you can double up and contribute (up to) $11,000 for 1985. However, if your annual limit is, for example,

$5,500, you can channel this entire amount into your own plan, into a spousal plan, or you can allocate between the two in any proportions (for example, 50–50, 60–40, etc.). The only way that a married couple can have more than $5,500 added for 1985 to RRSP savings is where *both* husband and wife have earned income. Thus, if your spouse has an earned income of his or her own, he or she too can contribute to an RRSP, earmarking the funds either personally, to you, or in any combination.

Let us examine a situation where a husband has an earned income while his wife remains at home looking after the children. What are the advantages and disadvantages of setting up a spousal plan? One major advantage of splitting RRSP contributions is that over a period of time, two separate pools of capital are built up. Eventually, each pool will give rise to an annuity. Since tax rates for individuals are graduated, the tax bite will be substantially less if the annuity is split so that the husband only gets part of the income while the wife gets the balance.

The second advantage of a spousal plan relates to another important rule. As a concession for senior citizens who have had the foresight to save for retirement through deferred compensation plans, the Act provides that the first $1,000 of annual private-pension income is tax-deductible. The $1,000 tax deduction generally applies only where the recipient of the pension is over the age of sixty-five. (Receipts from the Canada Pension Plan or the Old Age Security Pension do not qualify for this deduction.) Thus, the second advantage of splitting your RRSP is to build up two annuities and to double up on the annual $1,000 pension-income deduction.

The only disadvantage to a spousal RRSP occurs in the event that a couple gets divorced. Where, for example, a husband has contributed into his wife's plan, the funds belong to her. This disadvantage does not, however, appear to be too serious. In recent years most provinces have adopted family-law provisions whereby assets acquired after marriage are divided 50–50 in the event of a marriage breakdown. Thus, a court would presumably take assets held by each party's RRSP into account as part of a property settlement.

My recommendation is that a spousal RRSP should be used— as long as your marriage is reasonably solid. I don't see much point in being paranoid about what might happen many years in the future. On the other hand, if your marriage is somewhat shaky, why look for trouble? It might then be best to forgo the tax benefits of this arrangement, keeping in mind, however, that the government's newest proposed legislation calls for a splitting of RRSP benefits in any event on marriage breakdown.

One word of caution. If you place funds into a spousal plan, you must be prepared to leave these dollars for a least a while. The tax rules provide that where a wife withdraws funds from an RRSP, her husband is taxed to the extent that he had made any contributions in his wife's name either for the current year or the two preceding years. This "attribution" of income is designed to prevent a high-bracket taxpayer from contributing funds (on a deductible basis) to his spouse's plan and her, in turn, withdrawing the money practically tax-free almost immediately thereafter. You cannot beat the system by causing your wife to withdraw "older" contributions first. Under the above rules, the most recent contributions are deemed to be the first ones withdrawn for tax purposes. Naturally, the converse also applies when a wife contributes to her husband's plan. The attribution concept does not apply, however, if funds are withdrawn from a spousal plan after a marriage breakdown.

No RRSP Annuity Before Age Sixty
In 1978, the tax rules were amended and now provide that you may not take an annuity out of an RRSP before you have reached the age of sixty. If you wish to withdraw funds before that time, you must make a lump-sum deregistration of your plan. You are, however, allowed to reregister those dollars on which you do not wish to pay taxes, subject of course to any handling fees that may be charged by the trustees of the plan.

If there is some possibility that you will require funds before you are sixty, because of unforeseen circumstances or a low-income year, you may be best off with one or two smaller RRSPS as well as a major plan that builds for your retirement. If you are in need of a few thousand dollars, you would simply deregister one of the small plans and make use of those funds after having paid your taxes.

Bequeathing Your RRSP to a Spouse
There are also some important rules that apply on the death of a taxpayer. Essentially, if you have an RRSP at the time of your death, the value of the RRSP is included in your income in the year

of death. This rule applies unless you have bequeathed your RRSP to your spouse. Lack of awareness of this rule can be rather expensive—especially if you die late in a year and have RRSP income over and above other income earned in that year. Generally, your will should provide for a spousal bequest of an RRSP. If an RRSP is bequeathed to a spouse, the spouse then has a choice:

- she can pay tax on all or part of that which she receives and then have a portion of the money left over; or
- she can transfer funds into her own RRSP.

If I were to die and my wife had very little income in that year, it would probably be advisable for her to take part of the RRSP that she inherits directly into her income. In fact, she might be willing to pay taxes on as much as $100,000. This concept was dealt with in Chapter Four. The total taxes on $100,000 would amount to approximately $40,000, and on an after-tax basis, she would have about sixty cents on the dollar available for reinvestment.

Additional RRSP funds could then be transferred into her own RRSP. While an annuity from an RRSP cannot be taken *before* age sixty, she can nevertheless wait until age seventy-one before making withdrawals. In addition, by placing an inherited RRSP into several separate plans, it is quite possible for the surviving spouse to make periodic withdrawals as funds are required. For example, if an inherited RRSP were rolled into ten separate RRSPs, there appears to be no restriction against deregistering one a year for the following ten-year period. The surviving spouse would be able to use the funds to meet ongoing living requirements at a relatively low annual tax cost.

Bequests of RRSPs to Other Beneficiaries
If you die without leaving a surviving spouse, there is still an RRSP rollover if you leave RRSP funds to dependent children or grandchildren under the age of twenty-six. The rollover is $5,000 for each year that the dependent child or grandchild is under twenty-six at the time you die. This particular rule was passed by Parliament in response to a lobby from unmarried or divorced taxpayers who felt that they were being discriminated against. Unfortunately, for most people this amendment is probably not worth the paper it is written on.

Think about how it would apply in your circumstances if you

were to die without leaving a spouse to receive your RRSP. In most cases, you would not have a substantial RRSP portfolio until approximately age fifty-five. This is because the compounding effect really only builds up in the last ten or fifteen years before retirement. When you are fifty-five, do you expect to have dependent children or grandchildren under the age of twenty-six? I, for one, hope that I will never have dependent *grandchildren*. In addition, by the time I am fifty-five, my youngest child will be twenty-five and the rollover, if any, would not be material.

Becoming a Non-Resident
Ironically, one of the best benefits that one can derive from an RRSP is reserved for the individual who becomes a non-resident of Canada. The maximum exposure to tax on RRSP withdrawals by a non-resident is a flat rate of 25%.

Temporary Residents of Canada
The RRSP can also be an excellent tax-saving device for temporary residents of Canada. Take, for example, the situation of a doctor coming to this country to obtain specialist training. Assume that he or she takes a hospital position paying $65,000 per annum and expects to stay in Canada for a three-year period. During those three years, the doctor should invest the maximum amount possible in an RRSP. He or she would get a deduction for tax purposes and would save about half the contribution in taxes each year. Then, when he or she leaves the country, the worst exposure to taxation would be a flat 25%. Any time one can recover fifty cents on the dollar when contributions are made and not pay more than twenty-five cents on the dollar a few years later, the saving is worthwhile.

What Kind of Plan Should I Have?
RRSPs are administered by trust companies, banks, and insurance companies. In addition, you are allowed to have a self-directed plan in which you appoint trustees (or a trust company) and the trustees make whatever investments that you as the plan-holder desire. Of course, all investments must fall within the acceptable tax guidelines discussed at the beginning of this chapter.

Traditionally, people tend to wait until the end of February to purchase their RRSPs for the preceding year. Many millions of dollars are spent annually by companies trying to promote their own particular plans. To attempt to compare all the different alternative investments is a full-time job for a qualified investment counsellor. Contrary to popular belief, most accountants and lawyers are not any better equipped to pick "the right" RRSP than you are. When it comes to selecting an RRSP, you cannot necessarily even rely on past performance. Remember that the performance of a particular plan is only a function of those people employed as fund managers. If a well-qualified investment analyst changes jobs, the plan that was number one last year might very well sink to number ten, while last year's poor performer can end up on top the following year.

The only concrete advice that I give to clients is that they invest conservatively. While purists will probably try to extract every last nickel of income, I tend to believe that a 1% or 2% difference in yield is not going to make or break the average middle-income and upper-income individual in the long run. It is true that compounding at a return of 8% instead of 10% can result in a significant difference over twenty or thirty years. However, plan performances will often balance out over the long run and you may not even be aware of what you could have realized had you invested differently many years ago. So don't worry about that extra 1% or 2% unless you have the time to pursue the top performers as the list keeps changing.

Insurance Companies Versus Banks and Trust Companies
Traditionally, insurance companies that administer RRSPs tend to charge the bulk of their fees for handling your money against the initial contributions. This is called a *front-end load*. By contrast, banks and trust companies tend to charge their fees all along in smaller amounts over the entire life of your plan. I once did a study comparing what I considered (at that time) to be an "average" insurance plan to an "average" trust-company plan. Over a period of twenty-five or thirty years, there was only a negligible difference in the assets that would be available to provide a post-retirement annuity.

Thus, when a client asks me to comment on the differences, I tend to say that in the long run, there is no real difference. However, if you are a short-term resident of Canada, or non-residency is imminent, I suggest that you stay away from any plan with a front-end load. This is because, on deregistration, you may find yourself getting less money than you actually put in. So if you plan on leaving Canada in a few years, your prime consideration should be directed towards an RRSP that will yield the largest possible income initially, with the smallest administration charges. In addition, you should obtain an undertaking from the trustees that your money will be refunded on demand and, if there are any reregistration charges, these should be clearly spelled out in your agreement.

Suggested RRSP Investments

Over the years, two schools of thought have evolved with respect to RRSP investments. The first group recommends investing money in interest-bearing securities or mortgages paying the best current yields. Other advisers suggest that you might be better off investing in equity funds involving Canadian public-company securities. The proponents of equities feel that capital growth will outstrip interest yields over the long run—as long as you pick the right securities!

However, equity investments are thought by many to be unattractive because of the fact that all withdrawals from RRSPs are taxable as ordinary income. In other words, you do not get the advantage of the favourable tax treatment accorded to Canadian dividends through the dividend tax credit (see Chapter Nine). In addition, capital gains become transformed into regular income.

At the time this is being written in mid-1985, the stock market is somewhat uncertain. Given the general slowdown of the economy, aggravated greatly by the restrictions of the 1981/82 tax changes, I, for one, do not recommend that RRSP contributions be put into stock-market investments. As long as there is no clear-cut indication that interest rates will stay down, I think that you should be conservative and invest in an RRSP which earns the prevailing rate of interest. After all, investment yields in an RRSP compound on a tax-deferred basis and anything better than the inflation rate is a positive return.

Using Your RRSP to Hold the Mortgage on Your Home

In Spring 1984, an important new development arose in conjunction with RRSP planning. Revenue Canada, for the first time, decided to permit a self-administered RRSP to hold a mortgage on a plan-holder's home.

As a general rule, an RRSP is not permitted to make a loan either to the annuitant or to a party that is not at arm's length. However, there is an obscure regulation within the RRSP rules that appears to permit these restrictions to be circumvented. Under this regulation, a mortgage loan becomes a qualified investment of an RRSP as long as it is insured by a public mortgage insurer and is administered by an approved National Housing Act (NHA) lender. Thus, as long as a mortgage is issued and administered under normal commercial terms, it appears that the Revenue authorities will allow this as a qualified investment.

If you are interested in investigating the possibilities of your RRSP holding your mortgage, you should be aware of what the requirements are. The first step involves transferring your RRSP funds to a self-administered plan. Next, you arrange to have the RRSP make you a loan secured by a mortgage on your home. The mortgage must be administered by an approved NHA lender, but this should not be a problem since most financial institutions qualify. Finally, you must arrange to have your mortgage insured by the Mortgage Insurance Company of Canada. Once this is done, you can withdraw the funds from your RRSP as a loan, completely tax-free.

However, before you rush out to do all this, you must take care to determine whether or not it all makes sense. Keep in mind that there are mortgage-insurance fees to pay and these range from 1% to 1 1/2% of the entire mortgage on your home. In addition, the plan administrator will probably charge a fee for arranging the various transactions.

Here is another situation in which an hour or two spent with your own accountant would be well worth your while. Keep in mind that this type of planning can be particularly attractive if you are unable to obtain alternate sources of personal financing. If the money which you withdraw from your RRSP is used for business or investment purposes, you may find that there are additional benefits. In this case, the interest that you pay to your RRSP will generally be tax-deductible even though it will accumulate within your RRSP on a tax-deferred basis.

"Cashing In" an RRSP for a Life Annuity
Until just a few years ago, there was only one way to "cash in" an RRSP. The Income Tax Act required an individual, prior to

reaching the age of seventy-one, to use the funds accumulated in an RRSP to purchase a life annuity from an insurance company. The annuity benefits were then taxable as and when they were received. The only available alternative was to make lump-sum withdrawals from the RRSP before age seventy-one and become liable for income tax on all amounts received. In order to protect your position against an early death, you were also permitted to modify the ordinary life annuity by adding a "guaranteed-term" rider. (A guaranteed term means that payments continue for at least that length of time even if the annuitant dies prematurely. However, any time a taxpayer lives beyond the guaranteed term, the payments will continue until such time as the individual dies.) The maximum guaranteed term permitted under an RRSP life annuity has recently been raised from fifteen to twenty years. In addition, you are also allowed to arrange a joint-and-last-survivor annuity program, in which payments would continue out of an RRSP until both husband and wife have died. Even the joint-and-last-survivor option may now be structured to have a guaranteed term of up to twenty years.

Over the years, the requirement that one deal only with a life insurance company at the tail end of a program did not appeal to many potential RRSP investors. Actually, the insurance companies have been somewhat unjustly maligned because of a very common misconception. If you are seventy years old and you go to an insurance company with $100,000 in your RRSP, you could probably find a company that would agree to pay you an annuity of approximately $13,000 a year if you do not opt for any guaranteed term. Of course, you would not ordinarily think that this is any bargain. If you are male, you are probably conscious of the fact that your average life expectancy is only seventy-two years. Thus, how would you feel about receiving only two years' worth of annuities, or $25,000 out of a $100,000 investment made initially?

If you agree with the above reasoning, you have fallen into the common trap. While it is true that the average life expectancy of a male would be seventy-two years, this is only for a person under forty. Once you pass the age of forty, life expectancy goes up. You will find, if you examine a standard table of mortality rates (see Chapter Ten), that a seventy-year-old male has a life expectancy of another twelve years, and that a female of the same age is projected to live another fifteen years. A male age seventy-three does not have a life expectancy of "minus one." Thus, an insurance company is not really mistreating you by offering $13,000 a year as an RRSP yield. In preparing calculations, the insurance company must budget for a twelve to fifteen-year payout, without any guarantees. Since most people are not aware of this, insurance companies have acquired "bad reputations" somewhat unjustly over the years.

Two Additional Options: Fixed-Term Annuities and
Registered Retirement Income Funds
In 1978, however, the government decided to allow trust companies to enter the RRSP annuity field and two further options were introduced:

- A fixed-term annuity may now be purchased to provide benefits to age ninety and/or
- RRSP savings may be transferred into a new kind of investment vehicle—a Registered Retirement Income Fund (RRIF).

Financial and other institutions that were previously eligible to issue RRSPs are permitted to offer the additional options. Such institutions include trust companies as well as insurance companies.

Typically, however, the government gave and took away at the same time. Earlier, I indicated that anyone issuing a life annuity to a seventy-year-old must be prepared to pay out over a twelve-year period. Under the fixed-term annuity to age ninety, the same initial capital is paid out over a twenty-year period. Thus, the penalty for taking a fixed-term annuity (over twenty years) is receiving smaller annual payments than under a life annuity. The fixed-term option may therefore only be attractive to those individuals with other incomes and other assets who wish to pass on estates as large as possible to their heirs. Of course, rates of return are subject to change from time to time and it is always necessary to shop around for the best possible deal before making a final decision.

Under the RRIF option, a specific fraction of your total RRSP assets—capital plus accumulated earnings—is withdrawn each year to provide an annual income until age ninety. The fraction is related to your age in the year and is simply equal to "1" divided by the number of years remaining to age ninety. As an example, for a seventy-year-old purchaser, an RRIF would run for twenty years. In the first year, with twenty years remaining, the holder would be required to take into income 1/20 of the total value of the plan at the beginning of the year. After another year, 1/19 of what is left would be withdrawn, a year later 1/18, and so on, until the final year, when the taxpayer reaches ninety, a last withdrawal would exhaust the fund. An individual is only permitted to own one RRIF. You may, however, if you so choose, allot only a portion of your RRSP accumulations to the establishment of an RRIF and invest the remainder in any number of fixed-term or life annuities.

You may also base the term of an annuity or RRIF on the age of your spouse, if the spouse is younger, thus securing benefits for the spouse to age ninety. Should you die before reaching ninety, the benefits under the new options, as well as under life annuities with a guaranteed term, could be bequeathed to a surviving spouse. Otherwise, as indicated previously, the value of any remaining benefits must be included in income in the year in which you die.

Presumably, the fact that each year you would ordinarily draw more out of the RRIF is intended to allow you to keep pace with rises in the cost of living. Thus, in theory, the RRIF is better than both of the other options. This is because there is a flexible rate of return, rather than a fixed rate, and increasing, rather than level, payments. However, in spite of some recent amendments in the legislation, the RRIF does break down somewhat in practice. This is because the payments made during the early years are much smaller than the yield which could otherwise be obtained under either of the two alternative options. In many cases, it is not until an individual is approximately age eighty that the RRIF would provide a better annual return than a life annuity.

Nevertheless the RRIF can be useful if you have other incomes and other assets. Generally, however, you would be more interested in maximizing your cash flow in the first few years after you retire. It is during this period that you might still be mobile and able to enjoy whatever comforts money can bring.

Registered Pension Plans

One of the most popular of the deferred compensation plans is the employer-sponsored registered pension plan. Essentially, a

96

pension plan can be one of two kinds. It can be a "non-contributory" plan, in which the company alone makes annual contributions on behalf of the participating employees; or it can be a "contributory" plan, in which both the employer and the employee make contributions.

Within the limits described later in this section, both employee and employer contributions are tax-deductible. The funds are placed in a trust and they are invested on behalf of the participants. As long as the trustees make qualified investments, the income generated on these contributions is not taxable. Thus, there is a compounding of both principal and income from year to year that builds up a lump sum that is ultimately used to provide retirement pension benefits.

Upon retirement, the amount accumulated on behalf of each particular employee is paid out, generally in the form of a life annuity, thereby providing funds towards future living expenses. Although the benefits received at that time are taxable, the employee is likely to be in a lower tax bracket after retirement than previously. As an additional tax incentive to participate in such a plan, there is the annual pension-income deduction, which makes the first $1,000 effectively tax-free each year.

There was a minor loophole in the Income Tax Act that has recently been closed. The pension deduction used to be available even in cases where an individual received a pension without retiring. For example, a typical case might be the retired employee who continued to be active as a consultant and who therefore "rolled over" his or her annual pension benefits (over and above $1,000 a year) into an RRSP. Under the new rules, such individuals will not be permitted to obtain the benefits of the pension deduction unless they are at least sixty years of age.

An Employee's Allowable Contributions
Most plans are structured so that employees will ultimately receive pensions of between 40% and 60% (usually based on 1½% to 2% for each year of service) of their average annual salaries for their "best" five years. In recent years, because of inflation, the best five years have tended to be the last five years.

The theory behind a pension of 40% to 60% of the best five years is that after retirement, an average individual's cost of living should be substantially less than it was earlier on (ignoring inflation). Presumably, this is because your children tend to be grown up and self-supporting by that time, and if you own a home, the chances are that the house has already been paid for.

Obviously, the benefits of a company pension are dependent in part on the length of time that the individual has been a participant in the plan. The longer you are a member, the greater the amount of annual contributions that have been put aside by the employee (in the case of a contributory plan) and by the employer.

For 1985, the maximum deduction permitted by the Tax Act for current service contributions is $3,500 per annum. It is rare, however, to find employees contributing this maximum each year, since most employees cannot afford to put aside that much money and still maintain a reasonable standard of living. Accordingly, most pension plans are designed so that an employee will only contribute from 4% to 7% of his or her annual salary. Using a 6% factor as an example, only employees earning approximately $60,000 a year or more would be contributing the maximum of $3,500 per annum. In such cases, the individual would not be able to contribute further amounts into an RRSP. As previously indicated, when an individual contributes less than $3,500 to a company pension plan for 1985, he or she is permitted to contribute the difference up to $3,500 into a (personal) RRSP.

The Income Tax Act is concerned with setting out basic rules, which are fair and equitable to both employees and employers but which do not provide for undue tax avoidance. Within each plan, there is a certain amount of flexibility and the parties involved can order their own affairs as circumstances dictate. For example, some plans provide for past-service contributions. Some might set smaller limits and some might provide an incentive in the form of supplementary payments on behalf of employees who make additional contributions.

Past-Service Contributions

In addition to current service contributions of up to $3,500 per annum, employees may also make payments in 1985 of up to an *additional* $3,500 for prior services rendered during years in which they were not members of the plan. These are referred to as "past services while not a contributor." There are two major reasons for these provisions. The first pertains to situations in which employees have been working for a company for a certain period of time before the company sets up a registered pension plan. Second, many pension plans restrict eligibility until employees have attained several years of service or a certain age.

In general, employers would like to see their long-time employees getting the same benefits as those who join the company at the time a plan is established. Accordingly, it is reasonable that some provision be implemented whereby the more senior employees can, if fact, "catch up" and not be penalized for having worked for a company before the introduction of a pension plan. Thus, the need for past-service provisions becomes evident.

In addition to the *annual* limit of $3,500 for past services while not a contributor, present income-tax rules also prescribe a *lifetime maximum* of $3,500 multiplied by the number of years of past service before becoming a member. For example, an employee who had been working for a particular company for five years before the company introduced a pension plan may contribute (in addition to current service amounts) a lifetime maximum of 5 × $3,500, or $17,500, between the time the plan is accepted by Revenue Canada and the time the employee retires. These contributions can be made in amounts of up to $3,500 in any *given* year. The employee may instead choose to contribute less than $3,500 per annum and make up his or her lifetime limit of $17,500 over a longer period.

Pension plans that are structured so that one is not permitted to join until a certain length of service has been completed automatically produce a period of past service while not a contributor and result in an opportunity to make additional contributions later on. There are several reasons why a company would restrict membership in its pension plan until a certain length of service has been attained.

Any contributions made by an employee are automatically refundable to him or her if the employee should leave the service of the employer. The refund might be immediate, deferred until a certain period of time has elapsed, or may be available only in the form of a smaller pension later on.

However, *employer* contributions to a plan are *not* necessarily payable to an employee who resigns or is fired. Present pension-plan regulations permit an employer to adopt "delayed vesting" for up to five years. This means that annual contributions made on behalf of a particular employee do not necessarily have to "belong" to that employee at the time the money is put in. Thus, contributions made by an employer in the first year only become the property of the employee at the start of the sixth year. Similarly, the second year's contributions may only vest at the beginning of the seventh year, and so on. Eventually, if the employee stays with the employer long enough, the contributions for the last five years become vested in time to provide a full retirement pension.

The fact that a plan can provide for delayed vesting is an important incentive for employers, since it can help in reducing staff turnover. This is because an employee knows that should he or she leave the employer, all unvested pension rights will be lost. For many executives, the amount can be substantial. If an employee leaves anyhow, or is dismissed, the employer may not recover amounts contributed into the plan on the employee's behalf—even if these amounts have not yet vested. Instead, the unvested contributions are reallocated to the remaining employees. This ultimately allows senior executives to derive even larger pensions than would otherwise have been purchased by their own contributions and amounts contributed directly on their behalf.

While most employers are pleased to provide additional benefits to loyal employees, they must also consider their own budgeting controls. Thus, companies often impose membership restrictions against new employees, who are likely to leave during the early (high-turnover) period. The past-service provisions then allow employees who have stayed on to catch up in later years.

As mentioned at the start of this chapter, the proposed reforms to the pension rules will limit delayed vesting to two years only. In addition, the new system will allow for increasing tax-deductible contribution limits between 1986 and 1990. Starting in 1991, contributions and benefit limits will be tied into the average industrial wage at that time.

Your Own Pension Plan
It is important for each individual to understand the pension plan of the employer with which he or she is associated (if the company does in fact have such a plan). Usually, there are various options available that are unique to each particular plan, and while I have discussed the general operation of company

plans, proper investment planning cannot be accomplished without an understanding of what the specific options are. For example, if your benefits are fixed at 2% for each year of service, you may not wish to make optional contributions—especially if you anticipate a lifelong career with the same employer.

However, if you are a member of a company pension plan and your total contributions are less than the allowable maximum, it would generally pay for you to make up the difference by contributing to a personal RRSP. In addition, if you are already involved in a company pension, you should be more inclined to use a spousal RRSP. This is so that both husband and wife can ultimately split post-retirement annuity incomes.

CHAPTER SIX

A Tax-Shelter Update

Tax Shelters

A tax shelter may result when a tax-deductible loss from a particular source is offset against other income. In Canada, there were three popular tax shelters in the 1970s: real estate investments, feature films, and oil and gas exploration ventures. Unfortunately, with changes in the tax rules and with the severe recession of 1982–84, many of these have disappeared.

In retrospect, it can be said that too many people placed shelter aspects ahead of investment considerations in the late 1970s. They forgot that a "tax loss" is not the same thing as a "tax shelter." An effective tax shelter only occurs when there are write-offs that produce losses for tax purposes, but where the *value* of the investment has not diminished and there has been no loss of cash. Just because a loss is deductible does not make it a tax shelter. Somebody in the 50% tax bracket who actually lays out one dollar is still out of pocket a minimum of fifty cents— even if the expenditure is deductible.

Recently, government programs to encourage research and development in high technology created a new tax shelter called the Scientific Research Tax Credit (SRTC). The SRTC was, however, short-lived. Certain loopholes were discovered and in his last budget, Finance Minister Wilson decided that any incentives for research and development should go directly to those entities carrying on such activities and not to investors.

Over the past few years, tax shelters have sprung up in businesses providing recreational and other services through the use of yachts, recreational vehicles, hotels, nursing homes, and other similar property. In Spring 1985, however, a proposal was made that the income tax regulations be amended so that individuals will no longer be allowed to shelter other income with losses created by depreciation from such property, even if it is used in a business that offers services combined with the use of the property itself.

The new rules do not apply if the investors are individuals who are *personally active* in the day-to-day operations of the business. In a case of a partnership, capital cost allowances (depreciation) will be restricted unless the partners who are personally active are entitled to share in at least two-thirds of the income and/or loss of the partnership for the year. The new regulations are designed to take effect beginning with 1986 and will apply to property acquired after May 22, 1985, unless there was a written agreement entered into before that date. There will be a special transitional rule for hotel or nursing home buildings acquired before 1987 as long as written agreements were entered into before May 23, 1985, and provided construction proceeds without undue delay.

This basically leaves the Canadian public virtually naked in the tax shelter arena—at least in the conventional sense. Nevertheless, there are some opportunities. In this chapter, I will first discuss the newest and perhaps biggest tax shelter of all—the proposed lifetime exemption from capital-gains taxes on the first $500,000 of such profits. I will then move to a discussion of real estate, including your principal residence, because of its importance to most people. Finally, I will deal with a "new" kind of insurance policy called "universal life."

The New Capital-Gains Tax Exemption

Perhaps the most encouraging provision in the 1985 Spring Budget, certainly for small-business owners and entrepreneurs, is a major initiative to encourage risk-taking and investment in both small and large businesses. Specifically, it is proposed that a new cumulative tax exemption for an individual's capital gains be introduced over the next five years leading gradually to a lifetime maximum of $500,000 (taxable capital gains of $250,000).

The exemption is geared to apply to all growth property owned by individuals—even stock market and other investments. It appears that husbands and wives will not be considered together, so that, for all investments including family businesses, up to $1 million of tax-free growth can conceivably be realized or passed on (after a phase-in period) between generations. The exemption will be brought in over six years beginning immediately. For 1985, the first $20,000 of capital gains in excess of capital losses is tax-free. This amount rises to $50,000 in 1986, $100,000 in 1987, $200,000 in 1988, $300,000 in 1989, and $500,000 in 1990 and subsequent years. For farmers, the $500,000 limit is available immediately. This will apply to farm land and buildings, shares in farm corporations, and interests in family farm partnerships. The existing principal residence capital-gains exemption (which will be dealt with later in this chapter) will not be affected by this new incentive.

Figure 6-1 **Phase-In of New Lifetime Capital-Gains Exemption**

	Capital Gains	Previously Taxable Capital Gains
1985	$ 20,000	$ 10,000
1986	50,000	25,000
1987	100,000	50,000
1988	200,000	100,000
1989	300,000	150,000
1990	500,000	250,000

The new capital-gains exemption represents a great opportunity for a more aggressive investment policy than before. In other words, your potential rate of return is considerably higher, making it, perhaps, more advantageous to engage in risk activity.

Throughout the balance of this book, reference will be made to capital gains and the new exemption where appropriate. For small business, which is covered in Chapters 12 to 15, there is now a larger than ever incentive to split ownership between husbands and wives. Moreover, there is a tremendous incentive to incorporate since the realization of goodwill of an unincorporated venture does not appear to qualify.

Vacation property now appears as a much more attractive alternative than previously. Although technically a husband and wife can no longer own between them two principal residences, a gain on a second property may still effectively be exempt from tax as part of the overall blanket capital-gains exemption.

Over the next few years, you are encouraged to watch the timing of your property dispositions carefully to maximize benefits during the phase-in period. Unfortunately, you may *not* extend your benefits by selling property on an installment basis and allocating your capital gains on a single disposition over several years.

By-Products of the New Capital-Gains Exemption

The new rules necessitate a large number of by-products most of which are rather technical in nature and will not be dealt with in this book. A few points should however be noted. First, the Indexed Security Investment Plan (ISIP) which was introduced just a short two years ago will be repealed effective January 1, 1986. If you have such a program, you will be allowed to extract your securities without any immediate tax bite. The brokerage house or houses with which you deal will presumably provide you with the necessary data for reporting.

The Registered Home Ownership Savings Plan (RHOSP) has also been repealed. Presumably, the government feels that this incentive is no longer necessary in light of lower interest rates over the past few years and as a result of the new capital-gains investment incentive. No contributions to an RHOSP may be made after May 22, 1985. Interest earned on existing plans is exempt from tax until December 31, 1985. Withdrawals may be made after May 22, 1985, tax-free *and may be used for any purpose whatsoever.* If you have withdrawn money from an RHOSP between January 1 and May 22, 1985, the money must be used towards the acquisition of an owner-occupied home or you will be subject to tax.

Other by-products to the new capital-gains legislation will be dealt with in subsequent chapters, where appropriate. It should be evident, however, that the opportunity to realize up to $500,000 of gains not subject to tax must now represent the biggest tax shelter of all.

Tax Shelters in the Real Estate Industry

Insofar as real estate is concerned, anything written before 1982 on the subject of tax shelters is no longer particularly useful. Under the previous law, investors in rental or commercial developments were permitted to obtain an immediate write-off of "soft costs" incurred prior to the completion of any construction project. These expenditures included items such as legal and accounting fees, costs of obtaining financing, interest expense during construction, and property taxes related to real property. Immediate write-offs for soft costs by investors are no longer permitted for construction projects initiated after 1981.

In the past, the total of these "first-time write-offs" often amounted to as much as 20% or 25% of the value of any construction project, and the tax savings served to greatly subsidize the amount of net cash required to purchase property. Under the new rules, such costs must be added to the capital cost of land and building. The amounts that are added to the building (i.e., "capitalized") will then be written off at the same depreciation rate as the building itself—5% a year. The need to capitalize these costs will also ensure that these amounts will be recaptured when the building is sold if, in fact, the property does not depreciate.

The new restrictions against deducting soft costs do not, however, apply to corporations whose principal business is the leasing, rental, development, or sale of real property. Thus, it now appears viable for large builders, and small builders who are still solvent, to resume operations. The tax shelters of the future may eventually be owned by the large development companies themselves. In order to attract investment, they will probably create arrangements whereby investors place funds into their projects through low-interest-rate loans to the development corporations. In exchange, the investors would then receive a percentage of the profits on eventual sale. In this manner, interest income that would otherwise be fully taxed if received could be exchanged for the opportunity to earn a capital gain.

Real Estate as an Investment

The drastic steps taken by the federal government in the last few years to reduce inflation removed many tax incentives and caught most Canadians by surprise. For example, the tax changes proposed in 1981 together with large increases in interest rates made Canadian real estate a very bad choice for investment in 1981/82. Now, however, we have a very different picture. Interest rates have decreased by almost half and if rents start to go up, the scene may soon change again for the better.

In 1980, when I wrote the first edition of this book, I suggested that you could borrow money at 13% (then the current rate) to acquire property even if at the start you received no rental return on your money. Given an after-tax cost of only 6½% (assuming deductibility of interest), I suggested that increases in the market value of property would more than offset this cost. This approach may again be valid and we will examine a case study which will show you in detail what I mean. Specifically, you will see that you do not need a substantial amount of cash in order to enter the real estate market. As long as you have borrowing power and can subsidize a negative cash flow out of excess earnings from your job, business, or profession, real estate might be just the right investment for you. The name of the game is leverage—making investments using other people's money. If interest rates stay down and/or the Canadian dollar is devalued over the next couple of years, there may soon be a quick revival of investor interest in the real estate market. This will especially hold true as we enter an era of severe inflation.

The important thing to realize is that former Finance Minister Allan MacEachen's proposed restrictions on the deductibility of interest expense on money borrowed for investment purposes *did not materialize*. Thus, investment interest continues to be tax-deductible even in cases where the related investments are not "profitable" on an ongoing basis. For many Canadians, therefore, the cost of borrowing money for investment translates to only fifty cents on the dollar. On the other hand, if you make a capital gain on eventual sale, the government never takes more than 25% of your profit and if you qualify for the new exemption, you may get to keep your *entire* profit.

A Real Estate Case Study

To illustrate the concept of examining real estate primarily as an investment, here is a specific study that I made a few years ago. While relevant interest rates have changed by a few points, the method of analysis is still valid. You will see that a "bad" investment can become a "good" opportunity when you take into account leverage and interest deductibility.

In October 1978, a group of friends came to me and asked if I wished to join in a small real estate venture. The idea behind this "partnership" was for each of us to put up $10,000 or $15,000 and to try to find properties that would carry themselves out of rental revenues with minimal downpayments. I liked the idea and so I agreed to participate.

Several weeks later, a real estate agent brought me a listing describing a small apartment building for sale in one of the nicer sections of Calgary. My friends had inspected this property and were impressed by its excellent condition and the fact that it was fully rented. I was asked to review the numbers. The first thing I did was prepare the schedule which appears in Figure 6-2.

What I wanted to do was determine the probable cash flow from the property before mortgage repayments. In my projections, I used a 3% vacancy allowance. Of course, a vacancy factor varies from time to time and place to place and the 3% is for illustration only—it should not be construed as being reasonable in all circumstances.

Figure 6-2 **Projected Statement of Income and Expenses for Proposed Apartment Building Investment**

Gross rents projected on an annual basis		$70,000
Less: 3% vacancy factor		2,100
		67,900
Less: Expenses		
Taxes	$5,000	
Insurance and heating	3,000	
Light and power	1,500	
Garbage	700	
Janitor	2,200	
Management fee	3,400	
Maintenance and supplies	2,400	18,200
Cash flow before mortgage		$49,700

My next step was to calculate how much financing the property could carry. There was an existing first mortgage of $282,000 which had recently been placed on the building at 10¾%. I determined the cash flow after first mortgage as follows:

Cash flow before mortgage	$49,700
First mortgage $282,000 at 10¾%—annual payments	
from amortization tables	32,400
Cash flow after first mortgage	$17,300

The next question was how much capital one should invest in order to earn $17,300. To answer it, I reasoned that either my friends and I had investment capital or we did not have the funds necessary to acquire the property. At that time, if we had cash, we could have invested in second mortgages at a 13% rate of return. Alternatively, we could have pooled our borrowing power to obtain a second mortgage at that same 13% rate. In either event, money was "worth" 13% at that time.

I consulted my mortgage tables and I then determined that a cash flow of $17,300 would provide a 13% yield on an investment of $130,000. In other words, if we invested our own money, $17,300 would provide a 13% rate of return to *us* while, on the other hand, if we borrowed $130,000 instead, the property could absorb this debt and still break even. I therefore computed the value of the property as a whole to be $412,000, being the sum of first and second-mortgage financing ($282,000 + $130,000).

The asking price was $589,000, and I told my friends to forget about this property as an investment since it was greatly overpriced. However, a few weeks later, I was informed that the property had, in fact, been sold for $567,000. My friends were somewhat upset and suggested rather drily that I review my calculations. I checked my figures and found that I had made no arithmetic errors. Being somewhat curious as to the buyer's motives, I went on to do some additional analysis. I first concluded that whoever had bought this property had overpaid by $155,000.

Actual selling price	$567,000
Break-even price	412,000
Excess cost	$155,000

I then reasoned that the purchaser must either have had funds of his own or substantial "borrowing power." If he had capital, I concluded that he was willing to invest $155,000 at a zero rate of return instead of the 13% that he could otherwise have obtained in second mortgages. Conversely, if he borrowed the additional funds at 13%, my tables told me that the annual cash-flow loss would be $20,500. My first inclination was to doubt the sanity of the purchaser. He was either giving up $20,500 a year that he himself could otherwise have earned, or he was willing to pay *out* this amount each year to a lending institution.

However, I decided to carry the calculations a little further. In the first years of ownership, whenever a rental property produces a cash-flow loss because of financing, most of that loss (as much as 99%) is as a result of interest expense. Accordingly, the loss is deductible. This loss *cannot* be made *larger* through depreciation, but in my example, the *after-tax* cash-flow loss would be considerably less than $20,500. In fact, if I assume an investor in the 50% bracket, the *after-tax* cash-flow loss is only $20,500 × 50%, or $10,250.

Against this loss, I would then have to balance a projected appreciation in value. Before the recent recession, real estate in Calgary tended to appreciate by 8% a year. Eight per cent of $567,000 is $45,000. Even after taking off (for simplicity) a 30% provision for real estate commission costs and taxes on the gain (since there was no exemption at that time), there was still an anticipated after-tax appreciation after only one year of $31,500. If you compare the after-tax cash-flow loss of $10,250 against $31,500 of probable appreciation, the investment starts to appear more and more attractive. The only problem, however, is that the cash-flow loss is *definite* while the appreciation in value is *speculative*.

The Risk Factor
A good friend of mine has what he calls a "greater fool theory" with respect to real estate, and recent events have proven him to be correct. In 1980/81, real estate became overpriced in many places in Canada because everyone appeared willing to lay out substantial amounts of money, figuring that there would always be a "greater fool" somewhere who would automatically overpay an *extra* 8% one year later! As long as there was no recession, everyone made money. However, when hard times arrived, many of those who were left holding overpriced properties found themselves in financial difficulties.

You should never pay too much for property unless you can accept the risk of a potential loss. Ironically, real estate investments tend to favour those who have made money in the past. If you are wealthy, you can afford to subsidize a property that is losing money and still hang on until market conditions improve. As long as there is no sacrifice in your standard of living, then the investment might be worth the gamble. However, if you buy property subject to heavy debt and you are relying on capital appreciation in order to quickly "bail out," then you are treading on dangerous ground.

I would be remiss if I didn't admit that the case study in the previous section is somewhat oversimplified. Anyone with a degree of sophistication when it comes to real estate analysis would not begin to chart a property over only a one-year term. Usually, five-year projections are made and the sophisticated analyst brings back all future cash flows or deficiencies (including after-tax profits on eventual sale) to a present value for purposes of his or her calculations.

If you are contemplating a specific real estate investment, you should deal with advisers who are capable of assisting in the preparation of these more technical calculations. Of course, keep in mind that the further you go from the present time in your projections, the more likelihood there is of significant errors entering into the picture.

Looking Down the Road

The new restrictions on soft-cost write-offs eliminate real estate construction projects as a tax shelter for most Canadians now that the last few pre-1982 projects have been sold off. On the other hand, in the next year or two, as rents increase, you may find that even middle-class investors will be able to re-enter the real estate market without having to resort to tax incentives. Only time will tell. As long as interest expense on money borrowed for investments remains tax-deductible, the opportunity to use leverage is certainly attractive.

The trick is to watch closely, since the real estate market never stands still. At the right time, a person who jumps in can do quite well. You must never forget, however, that real estate is an *illiquid* investment. It cannot be sold on the open market at a moment's notice in the same way as a publicly traded stock or bond. Nevertheless, if you approach the 1980s in the same way as I do—as being a period of "ups and downs"—you should begin to look at real estate as a relatively short-term investment. If interest rates drop further or the economy starts to rebound, you may want to consider buying. However, if high interest rates are then reintroduced, take whatever profit you can and get out before the next "bust."

Other Tax Changes

A discussion of real estate could not be complete without a brief review of some of the other tax changes which have come about in the last few years.

Capital Cost Allowance—First-Year Rate

The government has made modifications to the capital-cost-allowance system, which allows business and investors to deduct depreciation costs. The new law continues to prohibit investors from creating or increasing rental losses through capital cost allowance. In addition, however, tax depreciation on assets acquired is now limited in the first year to *one-half of the normal rate of write-off otherwise provided*. This change generally applies to assets acquired after November 12, 1981. For investments in multiple-unit residential buildings (MURBS), the change took effect in 1982. The multiple-unit residential building program has not been extended for construction starts after 1981.

Demolition of Buildings

The opportunity to claim a tax write-off (terminal loss) on the demolition of a building has also been eliminated for buildings torn down after November 12, 1981. The new rules essentially restrict the deduction for tax purposes to one-half of the loss, as if this were a capital loss instead of a business loss. The reason for this change is that in past years buyers of real estate who were acquiring property primarily for the value of the land used the old rules to pass on tax benefits to the sellers. The seller would demolish the building before the sale and use the (fully tax-deductible) terminal loss on the building to offset the capital gain on the land. To show his gratitude, the seller would then give the buyer a better price.

Instalment Sales

One area in which caution must be exercised pertains to instalment sales. If you sell property and you do not receive the full proceeds, you are required to report your entire profit over three years (if the profit is fully taxable as ordinary income) or five years (where the profit is taxed as a capital gain), even if you are paid over a long-term period. These rules make it difficult to structure long-term payouts without tax penalties.

There is, however, an exception for farmers and small-business owners who choose to sell their holdings to their children. In these cases, ten-year instalment sales are permitted.

Your Principal Residence

In general, the benefits of a real estate investment hinge on the deductibility of mortgage interest. Of course, when it comes to your own home, such interest is not deductible. Even so, a principal residence remains a good investment because a gain on sale is not subject to capital-gains tax—quite apart from the new exemption discussed earlier in this chapter. Besides, once you are faced with the choice between non-deductible mortgage payments and non-deductible rent, I feel that you are better off as an owner. In the long run *you* gain from the appreciation.

Is a Second Home a Good Investment?

Until recently, married couples could arrange a double capital-gains exemption on two principal residences. This provision has however been repealed for dispositions after 1981. Now, only one family residence will qualify for tax exemption.

The major difference between a "primary" principal residence and a "secondary" principal residence is the question of need. When it comes to a primary home, we all need shelter to come out of the rain and snow. A country home or cottage is an entirely different situation. One doesn't usually "need" a second residence.

If your lifestyle is such that you would personally make use of a cottage for a substantial portion of the year then, by all means, if you can afford it, go ahead and buy. Under these circumstances, if you are willing to use after-tax dollars to subsidize the ownership, this is a choice that only you can make. One of the key factors is whether or not you anticipate a gain on eventual sale to be taxable or tax-free. For example, if you have no other major investments (including your own business) and are therefore unlikely to otherwise make use of the $500,000 lifetime capital-gains exemption, you may then consider the second home as potentially a good investment. This is because your gain on sale will in fact be sheltered. On the other hand, if you are heavily involved in the stock market and are making profits or expect to sell your family business at a substantial profit, you would have to examine the second home in an entirely different light. Figure 6–3 shows how much capital growth you actually require just to break even, assuming you are in a 50% tax bracket and borrow money at 14% to invest in a second home in cases where a 25% capital-gains tax applies.

It is quite unlikely that a country house will appreciate by

Figure 6–3 **Capital Growth Required to Break Even in a Second Home If the Gain Is Taxable**

Cost of borrowing (non-deductible)	14.00%
Annual capital growth required to break even before taxes	18.67%
Less: 25% capital-gains tax (ignoring the new exemption)	4.67%
Annual capital growth required to break even after taxes	14.00%

almost 19% a year. On the other hand, assuming no capital-gains tax, you would only require a 14% annual appreciation to reach the break-even point.

If you are interested in recreational property for only a few weeks each year, you might be better off channelling your investment into a property that is purchased primarily for rental purposes and is only used personally on occasion. This will allow you to *deduct your interest expense* even if the property shows a "loss" for tax purposes. Your capital gain might ultimately be tax-free in any event, and you will have minimized your carrying costs.

If you and your spouse owned two homes at the start of 1982, and you would like to "preserve" your lifetime capital-gains tax exemptions for other investments, there are some other tax-planning opportunities that are worth noting. First, you should arrange an appraisal of a property that is *not* likely to be designated as a principal residence. The appraisal should be made as soon as possible and, obviously, if the appraiser is very generous (but realistic) in his or her figures, this will stand you in good stead. Second, the property not designated as a principal residence should probably be held by the family member (husband or wife) who is likely to be in a lower income-tax bracket at the time that the property is sold. The purpose, of course, is to pay the least capital-gains tax on sale. The person who holds the second property should not necessarily be the one who is in the lower bracket today. For example, if a husband is fifty years old while his wife is thirty-five, and both are working, it is probable that the husband will retire well in advance of his wife. Under those circumstances, the couple should consider structuring the ownership of the second property in the husband's name. Then, if the property is sold subsequent to his retirement, the tax may be substantially less than if the wife were to sell it in a year while she was still working.

A third area of potential planning is to transfer the second property as soon as possible (before there is any substantial post-1981 appreciation) or to acquire it initially in the name of a family member who has no principal residence and is in a low tax bracket. If that family member occupies the property from time to time, he or she could designate it as a principal residence and make a tax-free gift of the sales proceeds back to you upon ultimate sale. Alternatively, if that person dies and directs the property back to you under his or her will, there will be no taxes arising at the time of death (because of the capital-gains exemption for a principal residence), and you will then recognize a new tax cost for the house at its then-current fair market value. This is ideal planning in cases where an affluent couple who can afford two principal residences have parents who are apartment dwellers but who would spend time with their children in a country house during the course of the year. Of course, the children would have to trust the parents to bequeath the second property back to them and not to remaining brothers and sisters! You should note, however, that you may not make a transfer to an unmarried dependent child under the age of eighteen. In any event, these are matters to be explored together with your accountants and lawyers.

Life Insurance Policies as a Tax Shelter

All insurance policies other than pure term insurance offer an investment component in addition to the coverage. Under traditional arrangements, an insurance company takes the portion of the premium that is not required to maintain the yearly life insurance coverage (the total premium minus the "risk" premium) and invests these dollars to provide additional benefits for the policyholder. The policyholder's actual return takes into account:

- the investment earnings of the insurance company,
- the life insurance company's actual operating results, and
- any changes in mortality rates.

Customarily, however, there is no clear-cut disclosure of policy costs (such as commissions and administration fees), premiums applicable to the life insurance coverage itself, and the portion of the premium that is invested. Since policy "dividends" basically depend on the three factors mentioned above, insurance proposals invariably specify that the investment yield is "not guaranteed." As a result, many consumers have lost confidence in such insurance products over the years, primarily because they fail to understand all these concepts. The popular wisdom is to buy pure term insurance and invest the difference *elsewhere*.

In the last three or four years, however, a new insurance product has been developed and is becoming much more widely marketed across North America. Although each insurance company involved in selling this product has adopted its own unique description, the most common name for the concept is "universal life." While the different insurance companies have all introduced their own special "bells and whistles," I will describe what a universal life policy is and why it should be considered by Canadian investors.

Basically, universal life means flexible premiums and flexible coverage. The policyholder starts out with his or her own estimate of how much insurance he or she needs. The policyholder then makes a premium deposit that first covers the 2% provincial premium tax (3% in Newfoundland), as well as actual insurance costs and client fees. The actual insurance charges are based on the cost of maintaining the required insurance coverage at a rate based on the equivalent cost of a yearly renewable term policy. However, the key point is that *extra* premiums over and above the insurance element (in accordance with a government-approved formula) can *also* be deposited with the particular insurance company at the same time. These funds can then earn interest *on a tax-sheltered basis*—as long as the policy qualifies as "an exempt policy" under specified income-tax guidelines.

What makes the universal life concept somewhat unique is that the investment element is clearly spelled out under the terms of the contract. In addition, investors are usually offered a choice between a short-term interest account, which ties in to the prevailing interest rate as it fluctuates daily, and a guaranteed interest cash-value account, which enables investors to earn a fixed rate of return for between one and ten years. The net result is similar to the option of buying term insurance and investing the difference with, say, a bank or trust company.

The first major benefit, however, of a universal life program is that the investment income within the policy *compounds on a tax-deferred basis*, again, as long as the amount of insurance coverage is sufficient for the contract to retain its status as an "exempt" policy. This advantage becomes rather startling over a period of time. If we assume, for example, that interest rates stabilize for many years at a 9% level, it becomes a matter of comparing an accumulation at this rate against an after-tax rate otherwise available through a bank or trust company of only 4½% (for a policyholder in the 50% tax bracket).

In one case study that was prepared for me recently, the difference exceeded $165,000 after a twenty-five-year period on a policy with a first-year coverage of $200,000.

Under most of these universal life programs, a policyholder is entitled to increase or decrease the amount of his or her coverage on a frequent basis, usually annually. In some cases, coverage is adjusted automatically for changes in the Consumer Price Index. In other cases, medical evidence of insurability is required to increase coverage. Of course, if additional coverage is taken, the payment necessary to maintain the yearly renewable term-insurance element increases accordingly. But this, in turn, also increases the amount of *additional* funds that can be deposited into the interest-bearing account maintained by the insurance company for the policyholder, to earn additional tax-deferred interest income.

There are several other benefits of a universal-life plan. For example, once the cash account has built up over several years, it then becomes possible for the policyholder to maintain his or her coverage in whole or in part by simply allowing the insurance company to draw funds out of the investment account to pay annual premiums. This enables the policyholder to *pay premiums out of income that was tax-sheltered.* Note the contrast to other types of insurance policies, where premium payments are always made with after-tax income. The benefits of a universal-life arrangement become more pronounced as the cost of the yearly renewable term element becomes more expensive when the insured gets older.

There are two further benefits that should also be considered. First, setting a premium level within acceptable government guidelines and knowing exactly how much money is going into the investment account represents a good forced savings plan for most Canadians. This is especially true if arrangements are made with the insurance company to have payments deducted from the policyholder's bank account on a monthly basis.

Finally, and perhaps most attractive of all, is the opportunity to transform the tax deferral into an *outright tax savings*. This would apply in cases where the policyholder is prepared to leave his or her funds with the insurance company until death. At that time, a universal-life policy is structured to pay off the amount of coverage still in force *plus* the cash value build-up. The *full* amount is then returned to the policyholder's estate completely tax-free.

A universal-life program is suitable not only for individuals concerned with personal estate planning, but also in circumstances where insurance is required under a buy-sell (business continuation) program. If the insurance is held by a corporation, the cash accumulation can be used not only to provide for the buy-out of a shareholder at the time of death but can also be made available to fund an alternative buy-out in the event of a shareholder's retirement.

Today, it is virtually impossible for anyone to predict with any degree of certainty what interest and inflation rates will be in the future. A major advantage of a universal-life product is therefore the opportunity to adjust the amount of insurance and savings portion on a regular basis. Presumably, if an individual's income increases over time, he or she can afford to make additional payments and can compound the cash value accordingly.

You should note, however, that a universal-life contract should be treated as a long-range program. In other words, although coverage and premium payments are flexible, there must be a commitment to maintain the policy on an ongoing basis. This is because in the first few years the investment yield, while competitive, is still eroded by policy charges, including agents' commissions. It may take three or four years before the policyholder truly starts to benefit more from a universal-life arrangement than by buying term insurance and investing the difference elsewhere. However, once that initial phase-in period expires, the benefits of universal life compare quite favourably with other investment alternatives.

CHAPTER SEVEN

Maximize Your Investment Yields Without Incorporating

Planning Around Earned Income

The first step to maximizing investment yields is what I call "planning around earned income." In all probability, your earned income by itself is sufficient to put you into a fairly high tax bracket. You may find that it is not feasible for you to put off paying taxes on some of this income through a deferred compensation program and that your employer is not willing to accommodate you with a significant range of fringe benefits. You may also find that incorporating your own activities as a consultant (as outlined in Chapter Eleven) is just not possible.

If you find yourself in this position, you should at least direct your efforts towards effective tax planning for investments. My concept is very simple: from a tax point of view, the last thing anyone with a high *earned* income needs is investment income. If you are already in a 50% tax bracket because of your salary or business income, then one-half of your investment yield will immediately be eroded by large amounts of additional income taxes. How, then, do we go about planning effectively? The place to start is with the investment-income deduction.

The Investment-Income Deduction

In order to encourage middle-income and upper-income taxpayers to save more and spend less, the Income Tax Act provides a yearly exemption from tax of the first $1,000 of arm's-length Canadian interest and taxable dividends from Canadian securities. The theory is that it takes approximately $10,000 to $12,000 of investment capital to produce an annual return of $1,000 (at present interest yields). Thus, the middle-income and upper-income taxpayer is encouraged to save that amount of capital and to invest conservatively. Of course, the more you

119

save, the less you have to spend, and overall, the idea is to control inflation. (Before 1985, taxable capital gains were also eligible for the $1,000 annual deduction. However, in light of the new blanket capital-gains exemption discussed in the last chapter, taxable capital gains no longer qualify.)

The interest and dividends deduction (known here simply as the "investment deduction") is a feature of the tax rules that everyone should take advantage of. There is certainly no harm in investing conservatively when the yield is tax-free. If you invest in term deposits at 8% or 10%, you are still going to be ahead, even after considering the decrease in the purchasing power of your dollar, which is currently losing about 4% of its value each year.

Pay Off Your Home Mortgage

After having saved up enough capital to use the investment deduction to its full extent, the next step in proper planning is to discharge your home mortgage as quickly as possible. Assume for purposes of illustration that you have a mortgage of $50,000 on your home at an interest rate of 14%. Assume, as well, that you *also* have $50,000 in cash, which you have recently inherited. Your mortgage costs you $7,000 a year in interest, and this amount is not deductible. If, however, you take your $50,000 inheritance and invest it at the same interest rate of 14%, you will receive $7,000 of interest income. On the surface, there is an offsetting income and outflow. However (ignoring the investment-income deduction), the $7,000 received is fully taxable. If you are in a 50% tax bracket, you will only keep $3,500 on an after-tax basis. There is certainly very little merit in retaining $3,500 while paying out $7,000.

In fact, if your mortgage payable is at 14% and you are in a 50% tax bracket, you must earn a 28% pre-tax return on investment capital to make it worthwhile to carry the mortgage on your home. If anyone can show me how to earn a guaranteed 28% per annum on my money *with no risk*, I would appreciate a telephone call (collect) or a letter!

Thus, I recommend that a home mortgage be paid off as fast as possible. In the hypothetical case above, you should use the inherited capital of $50,000 to immediately discharge your debt. The only exception might be if you are one of the lucky ones with a low-interest "locked in" mortgage that dates back to the pre-inflation era.

Amortization

To amortize a loan is to extinguish it by means of payments over a period of time so that eventually the debt is reduced to zero. The most common amortization programs involve repayment schedules calling for identical monthly payments over the term of the borrowing, with each payment consisting of a combination of both principal and interest. Initially, most of the payments are used to pay interest. However, as the principal amount of the debt increases, more and more of the payments are used to reduce the capital amount.

This is shown in Figure 7-1, which illustrates a $10,000 loan at 14% interest compounded semiannually over twenty-five years.

Figure 7-1 **25-Year $10,000 Loan at 14%, With Interest Compounded Semiannually, Monthly Payment—$117.39**

Year	Payments Made $117.39 × 12	Interest	Principal
1	$1,409	$1,359	$ 50
5	1,409	1,319	90
10	1,409	1,239	170
15	1,409	1,079	330
20	1,409	739	670
25	1,409	99	1,310

Initially, each payment is almost all interest. Over the years, however, each instalment will contain less interest and more principal. This is because the borrower only pays interest on the outstanding principal balance of the loan at the time each payment is made.

If interest rates rise, the only possible way to keep monthly mortgage payments down is to lengthen the term over which the loan is amortized. As you will see, there may be some benefits, but there are also severe pitfalls.

For example, what if the twenty-five-year term on the above $10,000 loan were extended to thirty, thirty-five, or forty years? While the monthly payments would decline, the borrower is faced not only with a much longer payout period, but also with a *significant additional debt*. This is illustrated in Figure 7-2.

Figure 7-2 **Amortization of $10,000 at 14% Over Various Periods**

$10,000 at 14%	*25 Years*	*30 Years*	*35 Years*	*40 Years*
Monthly payment	$ 117.39	$ 115.40	$ 114.41	$ 113.92
Annual cost	1,408.68	1,384.80	1,372.92	1,367.04
Total cost	35,217.00	41,544.00	48,052.20	54,681.60
Total interest paid	25,217.00	31,544.00	38,052.20	44,681.60

Monthly payment over 25 years	$ 117.39
Monthly payment over 40 years	113.92
Difference	$ 3.47
Total interest over 40 years	$44,681.60
Total interest over 25 years	25,217.00
Difference	$19,464.60

The results of our analysis are somewhat mind-boggling. By spreading the debt over forty years instead of twenty-five years, there is a monthly saving of only $3.47 in the required monthly mortgage payments. However, the borrower must not only bind himself or herself to payments over an additional fifteen years, but is actually *increasing the total debt* by $19,464.60!

Mortgage-Acceleration Savings
While extending your debt obligation can, in the long run, be extremely costly, paying down your mortgage from time to time by making extra payments may be one of the best methods available to force yourself to save money. This is especially important planning for a principal residence, where the interest is non-deductible. Most mortgage contracts today will allow a borrower to repay up to 10% of the original amount of the debt each year as a special principal repayment.

Figure 7-3 shows the principal balance outstanding on a loan of $10,000 at the end of each year for twenty-five years where the interest rate is 14%. At the end of year one, the principal balance outstanding is $9,950, while at the end of year ten it is $8,990. Therefore, if the borrower were to repay $960 on the first anniversary of the mortgage, he or she would thus be eliminating almost *one-half* of the *total* annual payments that would otherwise be required. In other words, if the monthly payments stay the same (which they would) and the borrower makes *no further* special payments against principal, the debt would be completely extinguished only fifteen years later. Given a special payment of $960 at the end of the first year, he or she would then only owe $8,790 at the end of year two, $8,570 after year three, and so forth. Of course, if additional principal payments were made at the end of the second year (and subsequently), the debt would be eliminated that much more quickly.

Figure 7-3 **Balance Outstanding on a Loan of $10,000 at 14% (Rounded to Nearest $10), Monthly Payment— $117.39**

End of Year	Amount	End of Year	Amount	End of Year	Amount
1	$9,950	10	$8,990	19	$5,760
2	9,890	11	8,790	20	5,090
3	9,820	12	8,570	21	4,330
4	9,750	13	8,310	22	3,450
5	9,660	14	8,010	23	2,450
6	9,560	15	7,680	24	1,310
7	9,450	16	7,290	25	0
8	9,310	17	6,850		
9	9,160	18	6,340		

Perhaps the best opportunity a family has to pay down a mortgage is when a wife has been home for several years looking after young children and then rejoins the labour force. At this point, the family comes to a very important crossroad. It could choose to use the extra income to buy a new car, or treat itself to a vacation trip. However, if husband and wife can simply exercise a bit of restraint for *one year only* and apply the first $10,000 that the wife earns (after taxes) against their mortgage, they will have made a tremendous advance towards the security of owning a fully paid home. On a $100,000 mortgage at 14%, you have seen how it takes ten years for $10,000 of debt to be extinguished in the absence of mortgage-acceleration payments. I hope that the message is clear.

The Mortgage Term

You must always be careful never to confuse the *amortization* of a loan with its *term*. If you are told that a mortgage is to be amortized over twenty-five years, you must not assume that it has a twenty-five-year term. The term of a mortgage is the period of time that is given to the borrower before the lender can demand the principal balance owing on the loan. Until a few years ago, lenders did in fact make loans for long periods of time, such as twenty-five years, at fixed rates of interest. Today, however, mortgage terms rarely exceed five years. Thus, although the amortization schedule may reflect the payments necessary to discharge a debt over twenty-five years, the borrower, in most cases, must still repay the principal balance at the end of five years. Of course, the lender will usually renew the mortgage—at current prevailing rates. (Today, three-year, one-year, and even six-month term mortgages are becoming more and more common.)

Again, examine the schedule in Figure 7-3. If payments of $117.39 are made monthly over twenty-five years, a loan of $10,000 at 14% would be extinguished. However, here is the problem. At the end of five years, the lender will want his or her money and, on a twenty-five-year loan, you will still owe $9,660. To repay the loan you would probably have to commit yourself to another mortgage and borrow between $9,600 and $9,700. Assume that the new mortgage is for a further five-year period at the same rate and also with payments calculated to amortize over a twenty-five-year period. At the end of the second five-year period, your outstanding balance would be around $9,320. When you have to repay this loan, you can repeat the process.

Each new five-year term will result in smaller monthly payments because the principal amount at the start of each succeeding term will be less. However, instead of amortizing the loan down to zero over twenty-five years, it may take *over one hundred years to discharge the loan completely. There is only one way a twenty-five-year mortgage can be paid off in full over twenty-five years. The principal balance owing each time a mortgage is renewed must be amortized for a period that is not longer than the remaining number of years in the original amortization.*

The Mortgage Rate Protection Program

On February 15, 1984, former Finance Minister Marc Lalonde tabled a discussion paper entitled "Improved Security for Homeowners." The most innovative proposal contained in this paper was a Mortgage Rate Protection Program (MRPP), which was subsequently implemented. In this section, I will provide some of the more important details. Under the program, homeowners, upon payment of a fee, become entitled to protection of the interest rate on mortgages of up to $70,000 with terms to maturity of one year or greater. The interest rate to be protected is the market interest rate prevailing for the relevant mortgage term at the time the mortgage protection is taken out.

The program is not designed to protect homeowners against all fluctuations in mortgage rates. Rather, the basic purpose is to provide security against severe disruptions resulting from extraordinary increases in rates. Thus, the legislation provides that increases in mortgage rates of up to two percentage points above the mortgage reference rate are not covered by the program. The protection does, however, cover three-quarters of any cost increase resulting from an increase in mortgage interest rates greater than the 2% threshold—to a maximum of ten percentage points over this threshold. The amount of protection available is referenced to the amount owing on the mortgage at the time of renewal. Thus, if a partial prepayment has been made, the payments would then be based on the amount still owing after this prepayment.

Here is an example. If the original mortgage is at 12% and the interest rate at the time of renewal is 18%, the homeowner would not receive any relief for the first 2% of increase. However, three-quarters of the remaining additional interest of 4% (18% − 14%) would be insured. This would limit the homeowner's interest burden to 15% in total during the renewal period.

Under the rules, the protection period is equal to the term of the original mortgage and begins when the original mortgage term expires. Thus, an individual would have the flexibility of choosing the period of protection that he or she desires when choosing the term of the original mortgage. For example, if, on January 1, 1986, an individual takes out a one-year mortgage that expires on December 31, 1986, the protection period would become January 1, 1987, to December 31, 1987. On the other hand, if an individual takes out a five-year mortgage on January 1, 1986, he or she would be protected from January 1, 1991, to December 31, 1996.

Existing homeowners are eligible to join this program at the date of their next mortgage renewal. Only the principal residence of a homeowner is, however, covered, and rental properties and those owned by corporations are not eligible.

The fee for protection is $1\frac{1}{2}\%$ of the face value of the mortgage to be insured up to a maximum of $1,050 ($1\frac{1}{2}\% \times$ $70,000). This fee is payable at the time the insurance agreement is entered into but could also be included as part of the amount of the mortgage loan to be amortized over the period of the mortgage.

Another feature of this plan is that the interest-rate protection is transferable upon sale of a home. If the purchaser assumes a mortgage on which a protection fee has been paid, then mortgage-rate protection can be transferred along with title. Any claims arising from the MRPP would be paid to the new owner on renewal of the current mortgage. To the extent that transferability is perceived to be of benefit, this would allow the seller to negotiate with the purchaser to receive some portion of its value in the form of a higher sales price.

While the program is to be commended and certainly makes residential real estate a much more attractive investment by limiting risk, you should also note, however, that the government is telling us something very interesting between the lines. Specifically, the government is admitting that it has absolutely no control over future interest rates. While most people think that the Canadian interest rate is set by the Bank of Canada, this is not necessarily the case. We are very much influenced by what happens in the United States and, in fact, changes in world economic and political conditions can also affect future interest rates. The inability of business in Canada to guarantee itself a long-term fixed interest rate on borrowed money is one of the main impediments to a strong economic recovery. However, the concerns of business will not necessarily spill over to those buying real estate if you choose to take advantage of the MRPP legislation.

Borrowing Money from Private Sources
With today's high cost of residential housing, more and more young people are finding it difficult to acquire their homes without some sort of family subsidy. Perhaps you may be fortunate to have a "rich relative" who would be willing to lend you money. First of all, your relative would probably be earning slightly less on his or her capital if it is in term deposits than you would have to pay if you were to approach a lending institution. Perhaps your benefactor might be persuaded to pass this differ-

ence on to you. In other words, if he or she is receiving 9% interest on a term deposit, he or she may be willing to accept a similar rate on a private loan secured by your residence. Moreover, your relative may also be willing to allow you to pay interest only until your income increases sufficiently for you to start discharging principal. In many cases, a private lender is quite content with an interest yield on capital only. The lender does not necessarily *want* to receive blended payments of capital and interest. There is the satisfaction of keeping his or her capital intact and not having to worry about reinvesting small payments of principal, which you would otherwise pay from time to time.

Sometimes, people will take advantage of the fact that interest income is taxable while the corresponding expense is not deductible when funds are borrowed for personal purposes. For example, if an individual in a 50% bracket is earning interest at 9%, he or she is only netting 4½% after taxes. That same individual might be willing to lend money to a friend or relative at only 6% or 7% to assist the latter in buying a house, provided the interest is paid in cash. Often, the borrower won't object to such an arrangement because he or she will pay a substantially lower rate and the payments cannot be deducted anyway. Thus, the borrower pays substantially less than the prevailing mortgage rate, while the lender ends up keeping more than what he or she otherwise would have retained, had "conventional" taxable interest been received.

Because any practice involving undeclared income is fraudulent, you are cautioned to stay away from such an arrangement. However, I have seen cases where mortgage loans are made at *no interest* but where the borrower makes an annual (noncompulsory) gift each year to the lender that is (coincidentally) equal to 6%–7% of the original loan. This procedure is acceptable. You should note that gifts made are not deductible and gifts received are not taxable.

After Burning the Mortgage...

Once your home is paid for, you have some room to manoeuvre. If you find an appealing investment, you may *then* borrow the capital that you need against your paid-up home. If you borrow *specifically for the purpose of making investments*, your interest expense becomes tax-deductible.

Note that there is no shortcut to be taken. If you use an inheritance or your savings for investment purposes without having first paid off the mortgage on your home, you will *not* be permitted to argue that you *could have* paid off the mortgage in the first place and then borrowed for investment capital. In tax cases that have come before the courts, the judges have insisted on a proper "tracking." If you take a shortcut, be prepared to suffer tax penalties.

Transactions with Family Members

Once you have maximized your investment-income deduction by setting aside $10,000 or $12,000 of investment capital, and once your home mortgage has been paid off, the next step in effective planning is to try to split investment income with family members. The idea is to take advantage of other persons in the family who are in lower tax brackets than yourself.

While this section will consider transactions both with a spouse and with children, you should note that the Income Tax Act simply differentiates between a spouse and anyone else. Consequently, any references in either this chapter or Chapter Nine to a taxpayer's "children" can be interpreted as broadly as you wish. A "child" can therefore mean a grandchild, niece, nephew, brother, sister, or even close friend. The same tax rules also apply to transactions with your parents.

The purpose of this chapter is to discuss how to maximize the yield from reasonably finite sums of investment capital. The examples given will use figures of up to $100,000. The point is that a *direct* transaction with another party can often result in significant tax savings when you deal with a certain amount of investment capital. In other words, it may not be necessary for you to overcomplicate your affairs by setting up corporations, trusts, and other similar vehicles.

Transactions involving substantially greater investment capital are discussed in Chapter Nine. In such cases, the use of corporations and trusts is not only advisable, but in many cases, is practically mandatory.

Husbands and Wives
One of the many differences between the Canadian tax system and that of the United States is that Canada taxes a husband and

wife separately, whereas the United States permits the filing of joint tax returns. Since Canada treats husbands and wives as separate taxpayers, the Tax Act is therefore somewhat concerned with the potential that might exist for income splitting between spouses. We have already seen that tax rates for individuals are graduated. Accordingly, the tax on a single taxable income of, for example, $40,000 would be significantly higher than the tax otherwise payable on two taxable incomes of $20,000.

In order to prevent splitting of investment income, there is a tax rule that states that where a taxpayer transfers property to a spouse, or to a person who subsequently becomes a spouse, the income generated by the transferred property reverts back to the transferor. In addition, the rules also provide that if the transferee disposes of the property and substitutes something else, the income on the substituted property *also* reverts back to the transferor. These "income-attribution rules" apply as long as the transferor is alive, resident in Canada, and the transferee is his or her spouse.

The attribution rules apply whenever property is either given or sold to a spouse. (Loans will be discussed a bit further on.) Note, however, that an actual gift of cash does not have any tax consequences at the time the gift is made. This is the case no matter whether the recipient is a spouse *or* anyone else. The donor does not get a tax deduction, nor is the donee taxed. While at first glance this may be surprising, the rationale is apparent if you stop to examine the nature of cash. Cash is simply income on which taxes have already been paid.

For example, if I give my wife $100,000, the gift itself will not have any tax implications. However, if she invests the money at 10%, the interest income of $10,000 will be taxable in *my* hands notwithstanding the fact that my wife received the actual funds. Moreover, if my wife takes "her" capital of $100,000 and acquires shares in a public company, receiving a dividend of, say, $7,000 in a subsequent year, then I will be taxed for that dividend as well. In this case, the public company shares would be considered "substituted property."

There are, however, some interesting omissions in the tax rules that apply to transfers between spouses. The courts have held, for example, that the income-attribution rules only apply to income generated from the transferred property itself (or from substituted property). The rules have no bearing, however, on what is referred to as "second-generation," or compound income. Thus, if my wife were to take the $10,000 of interest earned in the first year and invest this sum separately, deriving additional interest of $1,000 in the second year, this latter amount will be taxed in her hands and not in mine.

Of course, if we put the dollars into proper perspective, it becomes evident that in spite of the "second-generation-income" advantages, a gift between husband and wife will not result in significant savings. Even if I am in a top tax bracket of 50%, and my wife is not otherwise taxable at all, the most I can save out of having made the gift of $100,000 at the beginning of the first year is 50% of $1,000, or $500, at the end of the second year. Certainly, the tax saving is not material when compared to the initial gift.

Updating the Rules

Over twenty years ago, an important tax case came before the courts. In this specific situation, a husband *loaned* a substantial sum of money to his wife. In exchange, the wife gave her husband a note payable, promising to repay the loan on demand but without any interest. The funds were invested by the wife, who then reported the income earned on her own tax return.

At that time, as is true today, there was no legal or tax requirement that interest be charged on any loan between one individual and another.

In this case, the Department of National Revenue applied the income-attribution rules in assessing the transaction. The husband appealed. The judge held that the term "*transfer* of property" as used in the Income Tax Act includes transactions involving sales or gifts, but that a "transfer" does not include a loan. Furthermore, the court concluded that there was no restriction against one spouse lending money to the other in order for the recipient to earn income.

For many years, therefore, it was recommended tax planning to split income between spouses by simply making *loans* of investment capital. Such loans would generally not be interest bearing and would usually be repayable on demand. The after-tax income that was built up by the spouse in the lower tax bracket was then used for various purposes such as the repayment of a home mortgage or just to provide funds for further investments.

Unfortunately, Finance Minister Wilson chose in his Spring 1985 Budget to put an end to such planning. Income attribution with respect to transfers of property to a spouse (or a minor) has been extended to apply to loans outstanding on May 22, 1985, or made after that date. There are, however, some transitional rules. For term loans already outstanding before May 23, 1985, there is no attribution of income as long as the loan is repaid on or before the *later* of December 31, 1985, and the date the loan matures. For demand loans made before May 23, 1985, there is no attribution until 1988. The new rules apply to direct transactions as well as trust arrangements accomplished by any means whatsoever.

Income attribution will not apply, however, to funds reinvested out of a salary paid by a taxpayer to a spouse who is an employee of his or her unincorporated business or partnership. In addition, as I will explain in Chapter Eight, if a wife and husband enter into a legal separation or get divorced, income attribution will cease.

While the new rules put a damper on future tax planning, you should note that if you already have a demand loan in place, you still have a two-and-a-half-year reprieve. Another possibility for planning is to calculate a low-income spouse's after-tax earnings during the early years of marriage. Presumably these funds would have been used at that time to cover living expenses. If the high-income spouse now repays this amount and the low-income spouse uses the funds for investments, it appears that future investment income can be sheltered in this manner.

Of course, other arrangements come to mind such as a loan to your friend's spouse on the condition that the friend makes an equivalent loan to your spouse. Needless to say, however, if Revenue Canada catches on to such a series of transactions, there are sufficient anti-avoidance rules in the Income Tax Act to upset such a plan.

A major point, however, is that you may still lend money to a low tax bracket spouse to acquire *growth property* on which there is no significant ongoing income. In this way, it may be possible to beat the system by doubling up on the new capital-gains exemption. This is the next topic for discussion.

Transfers of Capital Property Between Spouses

Having dealt with the income generated from property transferred by one spouse to the other, there are now some important capital-gains implications to consider in such a transaction. If you transfer capital (growth) property such as stocks (in both public and private companies), corporate bonds, or real estate to a spouse, the transfer of property is deemed automatically to have taken place at the transferor's tax cost. In other words, no matter what the current value of that property is, no capital gain or loss is recognized at that time. (The most recent federal budget has made no changes in this area.)

However, when the transferee subsequently sells the property, the capital gain or capital loss reverts back to the transferor. The computation of this gain or loss is based on the transferor's original cost for tax purposes. Basically, you accomplish absolutely nothing in the way of reallocating capital gains or losses by making gifts or sales of capital properties between spouses. There is a full capital-attribution rule whenever the gain or loss is ultimately realized on a sale to a third party. This can be illustrated by an example in which:

- the cost of capital property (e.g., land) to the husband is $10,000.
- the fair market value at date of gift or sale to the wife is $20,000.
- the property is subsequently sold by the wife for $70,000.

Regardless of the fact that the fair market value of the property is $20,000, the husband will be deemed to have disposed of it at his cost of $10,000. However, when his wife subsequently sells the property, the entire capital gain of $60,000 (one-half of which is taxable) will revert to the husband.

When dealing with capital property, you could not overcome the system even before the May 1985 Budget by lending this property to a spouse who was in a lower bracket. The courts have held that if a transaction cannot be accomplished on a commercial basis, it cannot be done for tax purposes either. There is no such thing as "lending" real estate or lending stocks or corporate bonds to another person.

(A taxpayer is permitted to transfer capital property to a spouse at fair market value under certain circumstances. While the recipient will benefit from any future growth in value, the transferor will pay taxes on accrued gains at the time of transfer. This election is, however, only of use where there is a division of property in preparation for a separation or divorce. This is discussed in the next chapter.)

Beating the System
With proper planning, however, the rules can still be beaten—
even without a divorce. All it takes is a little bit of foresight. If a
husband, for example, wishes to transfer growth to his wife
(who is in a lower tax bracket), he would first have to lend her
cash. The cash would then be take by the wife and invested in the
capital property in question—whether it is land, shares, or
corporate bonds. In this manner, the capital growth would accrue
to her benefit for tax purposes. However, any income generated
on the property during the ownership period would be taxed in
the lender's hands. As mentioned earlier, a wonderful opportunity exists to double up on the new capital-gains exemption and
this planning still has merit especially for investments yielding
very little income on an ongoing basis.

If you want to take advantage of these tax-planning provisions, it is important that no shortcuts be taken. It is insufficient
to simply register the ownership of a property in whole or in part
in the name of a (low tax-bracket) spouse. You would have to be
able to show Revenue Canada that a loan was made in the first
place and that these funds were used for purposes of making the
investment. In addition, you should stay away from backdating
transactions. Creating documentation to evidence a loan after the
fact is fraudulent, and if the taxpayers are found out, the
penalties can be very severe. To summarize, *make loans first and
buy the property after*.

Transactions with Persons Other Than Spouses

There are other significant provisions in the Income Tax Act that
are also designed to prevent income splitting. Whenever a
taxpayer transfers property to a minor, the income from the
transferred property reverts back to the transferor until the
minor reaches the age of eighteen. This provision is designed to
prevent anyone from splitting income with his or her children or
grandchildren while they are still below the age of majority and
then making use of the income generated from the property for
the taxpayer's own advantage.

If you wish to transact with minors, you should go through
the formalities of using an investment corporation, for reasons
that will be discussed in Chapter Nine. In general, this would
only be suitable if you have substantial investment assets.

In passing, I raise the somewhat rhetorical question of whether or not it would really be advisable to make large gifts to children under the age of eighteen, regardless of the tax consequences. Even if there were no income-attribution rules, would you really want your children to have sizeable investment capital of their own at the age of eighteen?

Even before the recent budget changes, you could not circumvent the rules by making loans to children or grandchildren when the recipients are under eighteen. The restriction again stems from legal problems. A child under the age of eighteen has no legal power to contract anywhere in Canada. When something cannot be done under common law, the courts have held that it cannot be accomplished for tax purposes either.

There are, nevertheless, some opportunities to split income with minor children that you should consider. First, let's consider family allowances. Family allowances are taxed in the hands of the person who claims a child as a dependent. However, since the funds are technically to be used for the child's benefit, Revenue takes the position that if the money is invested in the child's name, the income belongs to him or her. If you can afford to do so, you should bank your children's family allowances each month in separate accounts. Over a period of time, the amount standing to the credit of each child, including reinvested income, will become substantial.

Another point to consider is that if you are carrying on a business (either incorporated or unincorporated) there is no legal restriction against paying salary to a minor child. This is as long as the child is truly rendering services in exchange for pay. This planning will be discussed in more detail in Chapter 13.

The Registered Education Savings Plan

A Registered Education Savings Plan is a trust that you may set up for the benefit of your children or grandchildren to defer tax on investment income. The purpose of the program is to provide funding for college and university education. Although the contributor must invest tax-paid money, income earned on funds within a Registered Education Savings Plan can accumulate free from tax until paid over as ordinary income in the hands of children or grandchildren for educational purposes. At any time, the original investment can be withdrawn tax-free by the contributor.

There can be a disadvantage if a Registered Education Savings Plan program is set up for the benefit of one child only and that child does not continue his or her education beyond the high school level. The income earned in such circumstances could be forfeited. On the other hand, if a discretionary trust arrangement is entered into for the benefit of any or all of the children (or grandchildren) of the contributor, it is then possible to obtain the economic advantages of the program as long as at least one of the contingent beneficiaries continues his or her education.

A Registered Education Savings Plan must have at least 150 subscribers. At the present time, a lifetime limit of contributions per beneficiary is set at $25,000 but this amount is indexed annually in accordance with the cost of living. This increase only applies to the unutilized balance, if any, that has not as yet been contributed to the plan. In other words, if you contribute $15,000 on behalf of one beneficiary and inflation is 10%, you may in the next year contribute as much as $11,000 (110% × $10,000) for a total of $26,000.

While the income from a Registered Education Savings Plan is taxable when distributed to beneficiaries, you should note that each beneficiary is likely to be in a low tax bracket at that time and, as well, can deduct tuition fees as an offset against the income. This program is targeted to individuals who have tax-paid capital and who intend to eventually subsidize their children's post-secondary education.

The opportunity to compound investment income without ongoing taxes for an extended period of time and to use these funds to provide support for your dependents is something that certainly merits closest attention. This is especially true in light of the recent restrictions imposed on loan arrangements to spouses, which I discussed previously.

Loans to Older Children
Where children (or grandchildren) are eighteen or over, it can be extremely advantageous to split income by making loans. Figure 7-4 depicts a typical situation where a parent, by making a $55,000 loan to a child, can save up to $1,840 using 1985 exemptions.

This saving, which results from capitalizing on the child's lack of income, is certainly significant in comparison to a total

135

Figure 7-4 **Example of Tax Savings Resulting From a Loan to a Child**

Assumptions:
- Parent has $55,000 of investment capital, bearing interest at 10%, *over and above* the $10,000 needed to utilize the annual $1,000 "investment-income deduction." Parent is in the 50% tax bracket.
- Parent has a child over age 18 attending university. The child has no income and the parent uses the after-tax investment income to pay tuition fees ($600) and to provide support.

Alternative 1: No loan to child.

Interest income to parent (10% × $55,000)	$5,500	
Less: Income taxes thereon (50%)	2,750	
Net interest income		$2,750
Add: Tax savings from		
Personal exemption for child (in 1985)	$1,420	
Transfer of education deduction (assume		
8 months × $50)	400	
	$1,820	
$1,820 × 50% tax saving		910
Net cash flow		$3,660
Cash flow utilized:		
To pay tuition		$ 600
To pay expenses		3,060
Net cash flow		$3,660

Alternative 2: A $55,000 loan is made by the parent to the child. (The loan is non-interest-bearing, and is repayable on demand.) A term deposit is purchased by the child.

Child's tax position:	
Interest income (10% × $55,000)	$5,500
Less: Tuition fees paid by child	600
Net income for tax purposes	4,900

Note: Tuition fees are only deductible by a student, although the $50-a-month education deduction is transferable to a supporting individual whenever the student does not need it to reduce his or her own taxable income to nil.

Personal exemption (1985)	(4,140)
Investment deduction	(1,000)
Education deduction (8 months × $50)	(400)*
Taxable income	Nil
Taxes payable	Nil
Cash flow utilized:	
To pay tuition	$ 600
To pay expenses	4,900
Net cash flow	$5,500
Advantage of loan ($5,500 - $3,660)	$1,840

*The $400 education deduction could be transferred to the parent. This would result in additional tax savings of $200, thus increasing the advantage of the loan.

investment income of $5,500. Multiply this benefit by the number of years that the child attends university, and there is a substantial advantage. The savings can be used to provide additional support for the child *or* for the benefit of the family as a whole. The demand-loan feature should protect the parent in the event that the child decides to use the dollars for anything other than the purchase of a term deposit or similar investment. Presumably, one's bank manager would witness the note, and in the event that the child tried to "cash it in," it would be incumbent upon the manager to inform the parent of these developments. Of course, if your child is unreliable, you would not jeopardize your asset position even for the tax advantages.

Family Planning
If a person has planned a family so that one child is finishing university just as the next one is starting, you can see that the benefits of the above plan can be compounded. As one child graduates, the parent can demand that the money be returned, and the funds are then available to lend to the next child. Of course, if several children are in university at the same time, then a parent would need more money in the first place to compound the advantages.

Transfers of Capital Property to Children and Others
With respect to capital gains, as opposed to the cash transactions just discussed, there is a significant difference between transfers made to a spouse and transfers made to anyone else. A transfer of capital property to anyone else must take place for tax purposes at *fair market value*. The following illustration shows how this is the case whether the property is sold or given.

Figure 7-5 **Example of Capital Property Transfer to Child**

Cost of capital property to the parent (e.g., land)	$ 10,000	Parent's capital gain
Fair market value at date of transfer	$ 20,000	
Sale by child subsequently	$170,000	Child's capital gain

As indicated in the example, there is a tax trade-off. Where the parent's land has a cost of $10,000 and a fair market value of $20,000, giving or selling that property will result in an immediate capital gain. The advantage of the transaction, however, is that the child receives the benefits of future growth.

Before the end of 1981, it was possible to defer the recognition of a gain on sale by arranging to postpone the receipt of proceeds of disposition over as long a period as desired. This feature of the "old" tax system has been eliminated for dispositions of property after that date.

Proceeds of a sale can still be deferred, but the rules now generally require the vendor to pay tax over three to five years. A ten-year instalment sale is, however, permitted for farms and small businesses transferred from parents to children.

In some cases, it may be possible to reduce the impact of the new rules. Suppose the parent in the example just illustrated sold only a few acres of his or her land at a time, over twenty years. This would create an effect similar to that of a long-term instalment sale.

General Tax Planning for Capital Gains

In future, planning for capital gains will be largely a factor of the extent to which any individual has already used up his or her lifetime exemption. Note, however, that if there is no disposition of property, there is no capital gain to be reported. One of the most popular methods that sophisticated investors use to postpone gains is simply *not selling*, but *borrowing* instead against increases in values of investments in order to build up their holdings. Borrowing with a pledge of property as collateral has no implications for tax purposes.

The ability to borrow is also useful since you can often borrow dollar for dollar against full increases in value. This is better than selling property and having your reinvestment potential eroded by taxes payable. If you own real estate, such as vacant land, and are considering a sale, another good tax-planning technique might be to rent out the property instead. Consider the following situation, where an annual pre-tax cash flow of $7,750 would result if a property were sold and the after-tax dollars were invested to yield 10%:

Cost of property	$10,000
Anticipated selling price	100,000
Capital gain on disposal	90,000
Taxable capital gain	45,000
Taxes at 50% (assuming the exemption has been exhausted)	22,500
Cash available to reinvest ($100,000 − $22,500)	77,500
Available pre-tax return at assumed rate of 10% (per annum)	7,750

As an alternative, a purchaser who is willing to pay $100,000 might be willing to pay a rental of, say, $15,000 per annum under a long-term lease. The agreement could also incorporate an option for the purchaser to buy the property at *today's fair market value* in twenty-five years.

From the vendor's position, however, an annual rental of $15,000 per year provides him or her with a substantially larger cash flow than if he or she were to reinvest the after-tax proceeds of sale ($15,000 versus $7,750). The vendor is also guaranteed to get the agreed-upon purchase price in any event at the end of twenty-five years.

Planning for Capital Gains on Personal Residences

As mentioned previously, a special tax exemption applies to a gain on the sale of a principal residence. A principal residence is an accommodation owned by a taxpayer (either alone or jointly), which is ordinarily inhabited by him, his spouse, a former spouse, or a dependent child at any time during the year—as long as the taxpayer designates the property as his principal residence. As discussed in Chapter Six, a family owning two residences may designate only one of them as a principal residence for any given year after 1981.

The accommodation can take any form such as a house, apartment, farm, condominium, or even a share in a cooperative housing corporation. A principal residence will also include not only the building, but the land on which it is situated, up to a limit of one acre. For any additional land to be treated as part of the principal residence, the owner must establish that it is "necessary to the use and enjoyment of the housing unit as a residence."

So far, there have been a few tax cases on the topic of excess land, and it would appear relatively certain that if you live in a community where the minimum lot size is, say, five acres, the extra land would fall under the exemption as well.

Technically, your capital gain must be calculated in the same way as gains on other assets. However, there is a formula exempting a portion of the gain based on the number of years during which the property was designated as a principal residence as a proportion of the total number of years of ownership. For purposes of these calculations, only years after 1971 are taken into account.

Since your entire gain is normally exempt, Revenue officials do not require any designation of property as a principal residence to be filed from year to year. It is only when property is disposed of and where a *taxable* gain results, that a designation must be filed with your tax return for that year.

There are still rules that will allow an individual to have up to two sales of principal residences in the same taxation year. Thus, if an individual moves from Montreal to Toronto, and then on to Vancouver, all in the same year, it is possible for the disposition of both the Montreal house and the Toronto house to be tax-free. (Actually, there is no requirement that these houses be situated in different cities.)

A Word of Caution to Habitual Renovators
From time to time, there are newspaper and magazine articles about people who have a rather interesting hobby. They buy older homes, move into them, fix them up, and resell them at a profit. If someone undertakes such a venture only sporadically,

he or she can still expect to qualify for the principal-residence exemption for the gain on sale. However, if an individual develops the habit of buying, fixing, and selling a different house each year, Revenue officials will consider these transactions to be a business. *As such, the entire gain could become taxable.* There have been a number of tax assessments of which I am personally aware that resulted from investigations initiated from information in newspaper articles. Thus, anyone who practices this rather interesting hobby should either maintain a low profile or be prepared for the possible adverse tax consequences that may result from human-interest stories.

Changing the Use of a Principal Residence
To accommodate people who are subject to temporary transfers, the Income Tax Act permits a taxpayer to move out of a home and still designate the property as his or her principal residence for up to four years. In order to make this election, the individual must remain resident in Canada and must not designate some other property as a principal residence during that period. If the designated property is rented out during that time, capital cost allowances may not be claimed to reduce rental income.

There is an extension to this rule, which permits a principal-residence designation to continue beyond four years in cases where the individual (or a spouse) is transferred by an employer and later reoccupies the home. This is provided that reoccupation occurs no later than one year following the year in which employment with that employer terminates.

These rules are designed to provide tax relief where a property is first a principal residence and then later becomes a rental property. Before 1985, no similar alleviating provisions existed for a reverse situation. If a property started off as a rental property and *then* became a principal residence, the owner had a problem. The rules of the Act provided that at the time there was a change of use, there was a deemed disposition of the rental property at current fair market value. *This triggered recaptured depreciation and capital gains even though there was no change in ownership.* The taxes payable had to be paid without any corresponding inflow of cash. The only consolation, of course, was that *future* growth in the value of the property was exempt from tax under the principal-residence rules.

Fortunately, the rental property conversion problem no

longer exists. The tax rules were recently amended so that no capital gain need be calculated until ultimate disposition on property originally acquired as a rental property and later converted into a principal residence. However, if you would like to obtain such relief, you are not permitted to claim capital cost allowance (depreciation for tax purposes) after 1984. If you own a rental property and you are contemplating moving in, any prior years' capital cost allowance will be subject to recaptured depreciation at the time you change the property's use. However, the postponement of being forced to realize a capital gain should provide you with a tremendous benefit.

Whenever an individual occupies part of a property and rents out the other part, the "housing unit" will consist of the portion occupied, and the rental portion is subject to capital-gains treatment when a disposition takes place. If a housing unit is used for non-residential purposes, such as where a doctor carries on practice using part of the home, only that portion occupied by the owner as a housing unit will be eligible to be treated as a principal residence. Any gain on disposal of the non-residential portion will be subject to normal tax calculation.

At some point in time, most Canadians must make a decision about whether to buy a home or to rent. Certainly, there are many factors that must be taken into account. However, in defence of home ownership, it should always be considered that a personal residence is the only major asset on which profits can be realized without a part being caught up in the tax collector's net, if your lifetime capital-gains limit has been reached.

CHAPTER EIGHT

Tax Planning for Separation and Divorce

My purpose in this chapter is to deal with four specific topics:

- the tax consequences of alimony and lump-sum settlements to both the recipient and the payer;
- transfers of property from one spouse to the other in contemplation of separation and divorce at the time of marriage breakdown;
- allowable personal-exemption claims for the two parties both in the year that a divorce or separation takes place and subsequently; and
- some general tax tips governing the receipt or payment of alimony.

The Tax Treatment of Alimony

Under the Canadian income-tax rules, alimony and separation allowances are tax-deductible to the payer in the year that these amounts are paid and they are included in computing income of the payer's spouse or former spouse in that same year. However, for this tax treatment to apply, five specific requirements must be met:

1. The amounts must be paid as alimony or as an allowance for the maintenance of the spouse or former spouse, children of the marriage, or both.
2. The spouses must be living apart at the time each payment is made and throughout the remainder of the year pursuant to a divorce, judicial separation, or written separation agreement.
3. The amounts must be paid pursuant to a decree, order, or judgement of a court *or* pursuant to a written agreement between the parties.

4. Each payment must be one of a series of payments payable on a periodic basis.
5. The amounts must be paid to or for the benefit of the spouse or former spouse (as explained in the next section).

While the rules may appear, at first glance, to be quite straightforward, there are many important technical points and grey areas that require clarification. Let's therefore go back to the five conditions that I just outlined and deal with them one by one.

Alimony Is an "Allowance"

First, let's explore the concept of alimony paid as an allowance for the maintenance of a spouse or former spouse. The tax authorities consider an allowance to be a sum of money determined in advance by a court or by the parties themselves, as being the required, recurring payment to be made by the payer in order to maintain the payee and/or the children. To be deductible, the use of the allowance must be at the complete discretion of the recipient who must not be required to account for it.

In some instances, however, the Income Tax Act and the administrative practice of Revenue Canada do permit a payer to deduct payments made to a third party on behalf of a spouse or former spouse. These include medical expenses, educational fees, home-heating costs, mortgage payments, or utility bills. Of course, if they are deductible on the one side, they are taxable in the hands of the beneficiary for whom these payments are made.

In order for third-party payments to qualify as alimony or separation allowances, it must be very clear that there is an agreement between the parties and that these payments have been deducted from the amount otherwise payable to the beneficiary spouse, with the express concurrence of that spouse. Alternatively, the amount must be paid to a court or an agency of the court pursuant to a court order. The only exception is any expense that represents either the purchase price of a house or mortgage payments, where the principal and interest amounts exceed 20% of the original principal balance owing on the mortgage. Such payments are considered as lump-sum and will not be deductible to the payer nor taxable to the recipient.

You should note that the Revenue authorities do consider an amount subject to adjustment in accordance with the Consumer

Price Index or a similar formula, or any other indexed series of payments, to qualify as an allowance. This is the case even though the exact future amounts payable are not specified in the order or agreement.

As I explained, the allowance must be for the purpose of maintaining the spouse or former spouse as well as children of the marriage or both. Under the income-tax rules, payments made to someone who was previously a common-law spouse do not qualify as alimony. Similarly, maintenance payments would not be deductible to the payer if they are made on behalf of children who are not children of the marriage. For example, payments made to support children from a former spouse's previous marriage would not be deductible by another husband or former husband unless these children had been legally adopted.

Spouses Living Apart

Now let's turn to the second criterion, the rule that the spouses or former spouses must be living apart at the time each payment is made and throughout the remainder of the year pursuant to a divorce, judicial separation, or written separation agreement. The concept of living apart is extremely important. The government is naturally concerned about income-splitting arrangements between a husband and wife that are artificial. For example, in the absence of special rules, consider the following. Assume that I am earning $40,000 a year while my wife has no income and is at home looking after our children. It would pay us to get divorced or enter into a legal separation arrangement under which I would agree to pay her an alimony of $20,000 a year. This way, when the smoke clears, I would pay tax on $20,000, and she would pay tax on $20,000, and we would be able to take advantage of the low tax brackets twice. Of course, if we continue to live together, this arrangement is clearly a sham. Therefore, the Income Tax Act guards against this potential abuse by imposing the requirement that the parties live apart.

One key factor, as well, is the concept of living apart not only at the time each particular payment is made but throughout the balance of the year. In other words, if a couple reconciles, either legally or merely by mutual consent, late in a given year, this will have the effect of negating all alimony and separation-allowance payments made previously during that particular year, as far as taxes are concerned. In other words, the payer will not get a deduction for the payments and the recipient will not be taxable for them.

Remember my reference to a divorce, judicial separation, or written separation agreement. Generally, payments made pursuant to a divorce or judicial separation become merely a question of fact. However, many court battles have been fought over the years on the subject of *written* separation agreements. Before 1984, support payments made before the date of a court order or written separation agreement were not deductible by a payer nor were they included in calculating the recipient's income. Recently, however, the government changed the rules for payments made before a court order or written agreement, where the deductible and taxable treatment would have applied if these payments were made after that date. Starting in 1984, payments are now deductible to the payer and included in the income of the recipient, if the order or agreement *eventually* entered into so provides and the amounts were paid in the year the order or agreement was made *or* in the immediately preceding year.

Thus, if a couple separates in mid-1985 and a written agreement or court order is not obtained until late 1986, the payer will still be able to deduct any 1985 and 1986 support payments in full, provided that these are referred to in the eventual agreement or court order.

Again, I cannot stress how important it is to have a written separation agreement in place on time in the absence of a court order or judicial decree. To cite some cases, the tax courts have held that payments pursuant to an oral agreement do not constitute alimony for tax purposes. In addition, an agreement between the lawyers representing both parties was held not to be a proper written agreement between the parties themselves. Also, evidence of cancelled cheques alone issued by the payer and endorsed by the payee did not constitute a valid written agreement. In simple language, you must be careful. You've got to dot your proverbial i's and cross your t's.

Alimony Is a Series of Payments
Let's now deal with the concept of a series of payments payable on a periodic basis. The concept of periodic payments is another one of these vastly contentious areas and has been the subject of many courtroom battles. Periodic payments are interpreted as

146

payments that are made periodically; recurring at fixed times, not at variable periods; not at the discretion of one or more individuals, but from some prior obligation.

The big bone of contention is evaluating payments as periodic on the one hand or lump-sum settlements on the other. A lump-sum settlement is not deductible to the payer nor is it taxable to the recipient. Let's look at some of the potential pitfalls in dealing with Revenue Canada. First, if an individual makes a lump-sum payment to a spouse or former spouse in place of several periodic payments not yet due, but imposed in future under a court order or agreement, this lump-sum payment will not qualify as the equivalent of periodic payments. Also, where an amount is paid for a period prior to an order or agreement, and the order or agreement requires that the payment be made after the date of such order or agreement, this amount will also fail to qualify because it was not payable on a periodic basis.

The only tax relief that is apparently offered is in cases where a lump sum can be identified as being on account of periodical payments due after the date of a court order or agreement but which had fallen in arrears. In such a case, the lump sum will generally be considered as "qualifying periodic payments."

But, again, you must be careful. There was an interesting tax case that was heard by the courts recently. A woman received a lump sum of $6,000 in settlement of $12,000 for which her former husband was in arrears under a separation agreement. When Revenue Canada attempted to tax her on this amount, she took the position that this was merely a lump-sum payment in settlement of a legal action and was not taxable to her. The court agreed because the amount was not paid under the original order for support. We can assume that the payer did not get a corresponding deduction.

Even in cases where lump-sum payments of arrears are considered income when received, you should note it is certainly conceivable that the tax bite to the recipient will be significantly higher than if payments had been spread out over several years.

Then again, be aware that you have some flexibility. A lot depends on how a court order or separation agreement is drafted. For example, the parties may agree that a specified amount of money is to be paid in total. Settlement may then be made wholly or in part by means of regular periodic payments over a specific length of time. Generally, if the agreement or order states that these payments are an allowance for the support and maintenance of the spouse or former spouse and/or the children, as long as each regular payment is consistent with that purpose and the payments are spread over an extended period, they will be treated as alimony or maintenance.

You should also note that periodic allowances would still qualify as such even if they are paid only through part of each year. For example, assume that an agreement states that the children will reside with the wife for ten months of the year and with the husband for the remaining two months. Thus, if the monthly allowance for the maintenance of the children is payable by the husband only during those months that the children live with their mother, the tax treatment as alimony will not be disqualified. The husband in my example will be able to claim a deduction and the wife will be taxable even though, for two months out of the year when the children are residing with the payer, no such allowance is actually paid.

You should be aware that where payments continue to be made after the death of the payee, they are not deductible by the payer whether they are made to the payee's estate, to the children directly, or to anyone else. However, if the payer is not permitted a deduction as alimony or maintenance, he might still be entitled to a personal exemption for the child or children. Also, if custody of the child or children reverts back to the payer, he may, under certain circumstances, be eligible to claim child-care expenses as well.

As I mentioned earlier, there have been literally hundreds of tax cases that have come before the courts over the years dealing with the question of whether or not payments should be treated as alimony or separation allowances. Let me just refer to a few recent cases to emphasize how careful you must be in seeking the proper advice and in structuring your planning in an appropriate manner.

In one recent case, a separation agreement called for three payments spaced a year apart. The payer was not permitted to claim a deduction, since the three-year payout was not considered to be periodic.

In another case, a husband made extra payments to help out his former wife and children in circumstances where these payments were not required under the existing separation agreements. He was not permitted to claim any deduction for these gratuitous amounts.

To summarize, therefore, there are several important planning steps which must always be considered. First, be aware of the tax consequences of any payments made before a written separation agreement is signed by both parties or a judicial order is brought down by a court. Unless an agreement is formalized by the end of the following year, the payer will not get a deduction nor will the recipient be required to take these amounts into income.

Second, payments that are in excess of the amounts called for under the agreement or order will not be treated as alimony or separation allowances.

Third, lump-sum settlements in lieu of financial commitments for alimony or support are not deductible to the payer or taxable to the recipient.

Fourth, be very careful in trying to determine the tax consequences of payments that vary from time to time, such as educational expenses, camp fees, or medical costs. In spite of recent changes to the law, it would be much more prudent for anyone seeking a deduction to make the ordinary payments high enough to cover these more sporadic costs.

One further point that should be noted governs the benefits that you can derive from this chapter. While my orientation has been towards structuring the types of arrangements that will provide tax deductibility to the payer, keep in mind that if you are someone who is receiving money or is about to receive a financial settlement of some kind, it may be in your interest to have the arrangement structured so that you need *not* pay taxes on all or part of that which you will receive. It is just as important for the potential recipient of funds or benefits to know the tax consequences as it is incumbent on the payer to know where he or she stands. For example, if you are given the choice between receiving a lump-sum settlement of $10,000 or alimony for one year only of $1,000 a month, you cannot make an intelligent choice unless you carefully assess your after-tax position.

Property Transfers in Contemplation of Divorce or Separation
Before looking at property transfers between husbands and wives in contemplation of separation or divorce, it is important

for you to review the general rules that apply whenever property is transferred between husbands and wives, which I discussed in Chapter Seven.

If property had been given by one spouse to the other, general income-attribution rules do not apply when the spouses are living apart and are separated pursuant to an order of a court or a written separation agreement. This is an *automatic* exception to the general rule and it means that income attribution will cease at the time of separation. Taxes on this income will be paid by the recipient of the gift, not by the person giving it. Of course, a formal divorce negates income attribution as well. But, there is one catch. The problem arises where individuals who are separated cease to live apart within twelve months from the date on which they entered into a written separation agreement. A quick reconciliation will have the effect of bringing back the income attribution rules *retroactively*. Presumably, both parties would be required to file amended tax returns to reinstate the general income-attribution rule.

It is interesting to note that the retroactive adjustment only applies if a separation evidenced by a written agreement between the two parties is terminated. There is no retroactive adjustment if the spouses cease to live apart within twelve months after a separation order is granted by a court.

So far, I think that these rules are relatively simple to apply. In fact, there is really no specific tax planning involved. It appears only proper that attribution should cease in situations in which one spouse is receiving income from property transferred by the other spouse and the transferor no longer lives with the recipient.

What are more complicated, however, are situations under which capital or growth property is transferred between spouses either before, during, or after a separation. Good examples of growth property include real estate, shares in both public and private companies, and even corporate bonds, which tend to fluctuate in value, as well as investments in precious metals such as gold and silver.

Again, as I explained in Chapter Seven, the general thrust of the Income Tax Act is to guard against attempts made to artificially split income, and the general rule is quite straightforward. Whenever a taxpayer transfers growth property to a spouse after 1971, the transfer is deemed to take place at the transferor's cost for tax purposes. In the case of depreciable property such as a building, the transfer is deemed to occur at cost minus the accumulated depreciation claimed for tax purposes in prior periods. In other words, under this general rule, the transfer does not give rise to any income in the hands of the transferor at the time the property changes hands. However, the Income Tax Act then goes on to state that when the recipient eventually disposes of the acquired property, the entire capital gain or capital loss and, in the case of property such as a building, recaptured depreciation revert back to the transferor. In the final analysis, it is as if the transfer had never been made. No tax advantage is achieved.

There are a number of important exceptions to this particular rule, which apply in situations where marriages break down. For example, if a transfer of growth property takes place pursuant to a written separation agreement or in accordance with a court order governing a separation, the transferor may elect to have the property deemed sold to his estranged spouse at fair market value. Presumably, such an election is made by simply reporting the disposition on the personal tax return as if it were a sale at fair market value. This will trigger capital gains and/or recaptured depreciation in the year the transfer is made. Then, if the property is subsequently sold by the recipient spouse, any *additional* capital gain and/or recaptured depreciation will be the responsibility of the person who received the property. This is provided that *both* spouses together file a written agreement with their income-tax returns for the year during which the separation took place.

Even if capital or growth property had been transferred from one spouse to the other before a separation ever occurred, and the recipient spouse continues to hold that property at the time of separation and afterwards, the attribution of capital gains to the transferor can be prevented, if that same joint election is filed in the year that a separation takes place. If this is the case, the spouse who sells the property becomes responsible for both capital gains as well as, in the case of depreciable property, recaptured depreciation.

Without question, the foregoing rules are somewhat complicated and you might be asking yourself, what do they really mean? Actually, these provisions are relatively new and have only been part of the Income Tax Act for a few years. The impact of these rules can best be illustrated by means of a simple "real life" example.

Back in the early 1970s, a friend of mine and his wife separated. Under the terms of their separation, he transferred to her a real estate investment that he had held in his own name. My friend and his wife were separated for about a year before they decided to go through with a divorce. Then my friend's wife got some good advice. The advice was to sell the real estate before the divorce went through so that her husband would be stuck with both the recaptured depreciation and the capital gain. This is because no election to transfer at fair market value was available at that time and there was only the very simple rule, which stated that attribution of income *and* capital gains applied as long as a couple was legally married.

My friend came to me and asked me whether he had any recourse, but I was unable to help him with his tax problem. I pointed out, however, that had his wife waited until after the divorce, she would have been stuck with the entire tax bite, even the tax on recaptured depreciation for the period before she actually owned the property.

In a nutshell, the recent changes make it possible for a husband and wife to effectively settle up their accounts at the time that a separation takes place. You might ask why a husband might be willing to elect to transfer property to his wife or vice versa at fair market value in the year of separation if it means prematurely triggering taxes payable. If you stop to think for a moment, however, the answer does become clear.

Under the general matrimonial provisions of most provinces, property held by husbands and wives is presumed to be divided equally at the time that a marriage is dissolved. Generally, if assets are held primarily in the name of the husband, a reasonable proportion is thus transferred to the wife anyways. Of course, if assets are to be allocated in equal proportions, it only stands to reason that liabilities should be allocated in this manner as well.

In other words, it should be possible to calculate and isolate the taxes payable as a result of any property transfer. Half of the taxes then become the responsibility of the recipient of the property. Assume, for example, that a husband holds $200,000 in term deposits in addition to a real estate investment. Half of the term deposits, and all of the real estate are to be transferred to his wife. The taxes payable as a result of the real estate transfer are, let's say, $30,000. Instead of transferring the real estate investment as well as half the term deposits, the amount of term deposits transferred should be reduced to take into account the tax liability. He would give her half of $170,000 instead of half of $200,000.

For many middle-income and upper-income individuals, this particular set of rules is perhaps the most important set of provisions governing marriage breakdown. Failure to understand them can result in extreme penalties. Also, it seems fairly obvious that if someone gets bad or inadequate advice from his or her own advisers, that there is legal recourse against these advisers.

For example, assume that a husband transfers growth property to his wife in contemplation of divorce and there is no election made to deem the transfer to take place at fair market value. The wife then sells the property during the term of the separation but before the divorce goes through and the husband gets stuck with the entire income-tax liability. If his advisers had failed to tell him about this potential problem, I would suggest that he could take legal action.

On the other hand, what happens if the wife delays and sells the property only after the divorce goes through? Under these circumstances, she must cope with the entire tax bite. In this case, I think she would have recourse against *her* advisers for not having informed her about the available elections that could have been filed. You can see that this whole matter is a potentially explosive situation.

You should note, however, that the preceding problems do not arise when an interest in the family home is transferred from one spouse to another. This is because of the general income-tax exemption from capital gains on the disposition of a principal residence. As I explained, however, you must use caution in dealing with other real estate holdings. This includes vacation property that does not qualify as a principal residence.

Personal Exemptions in the Year of Marriage Breakdown and Subsequently
Let us now deal with the topic of personal exemptions and the rules that apply to the break-up of a husband-wife family unit. First of all if, in the year that a separation takes place, a husband

pays alimony or maintenance support to his wife, he has the choice of either claiming a deduction for the alimony or maintenance actually paid or the standard personal exemption otherwise available with respect to a dependent spouse. The personal exemption is indexed annually and is actually $3,630 in 1985. However, this exemption is reduced by the net income of the supported spouse while married, in excess of a $510 base amount. This base amount is also indexed annually. In other words, the first $510 that a supported spouse earns while married in 1985 does not affect the claim for a personal exemption of the supporting spouse.

So, what do you do? Clearly, if the amount of your deductible alimony and/or maintenance exceeds the available spousal exemption, by all means, claim your actual payments. On the other hand, if you separate late in a given year and before that time your spouse had no income or very little income, you may be better off claiming the spouse as a dependent. You should note that this is the choice of the payer and does not involve the recipient of alimony or maintenance at all. What the payer does will also have no impact on the recipient's tax position.

After the year in which a divorce or separation occurs, a payer is only entitled to deduct alimony or maintenance payments.

If you were separated and you reconcile in a given year, your spouse's income for the whole year must be considered in determining your married exemption. In addition, as I mentioned earlier, you are not permitted to deduct any separation allowances, even for the period before you were reconciled.

In some cases, both parents may claim exemptions for the same children in the year of separation or divorce but not in the years following. For example, if one spouse was supporting the family before a marriage breakdown and the children become dependent on the other spouse for the remainder of the year, both parents may claim deductions. However, if the parent having custody of the children claims the "equivalent-to-married exemption" for a particular child, the other parent may not make any claim whatsoever for that same child.

The Equivalent-to-Married Exemption
If you are divorced or separated and support a relative related to you by blood, marriage, or adoption, who lives with you and is

wholly dependent on you, you may be eligible for this special exemption. The reason that it is called an equivalent-to-married exemption is because the dollar value is the same as an exemption for a spouse. In addition, the same net income limitations apply. In other words, you may claim as much as $3,630 in 1985 (this amount is adjusted annually for inflation) provided that your dependent relative did not have a net income over $510 (this is also indexed).

The most common situation for such an exemption is that of a divorced woman who is living with her dependent children. She may claim one of the children as equivalent to a spouse instead of the ordinary exemption for a child. It is generally best to claim this special exemption for the youngest child. This is especially true where some of the children are under age eighteen and some are older. Since you must exchange exemptions, you would rather give up an exemption of $710 than a deduction which is about twice as large. (The exemption for a child eighteen or over is $1420 in 1985.) If you claim a child as equivalent to married, you must still take family allowances received for that child into income.

If an individual pays maintenance allowances for a particular child, he or she may not claim that child as a dependent. Also, as I mentioned earlier, if a spouse or former spouse to whom alimony or maintenance is paid dies, the payer may not continue to deduct support payments paid directly to the children or to someone else on the children's behalf. However, depending on the circumstances, the children might then be claimed as dependants, with perhaps one of the them qualifying for the equivalent-to-married exemption.

General Tax Tips Concerning Alimony

Before concluding this chapter, I want to acquaint you with a few general tax tips governing the receipt or payment of alimony. First, from a recipient's point of view it is always important to budget for taxes that will eventually fall due. This is especially serious if the recipient of alimony also has other income, for example, from employment.

Assume that a woman is working and is earning $15,000 a year. On top of that she receives alimony or support from a former husband. The fact that her employment income is in the

$15,000 range puts her into approximately a 30% income-tax bracket. This means that the alimony will be subject to taxes of at least 30% from the first dollar. Of course, if the alimony is large, the effective tax could conceivably be somewhat higher. Failure to budget for this tax cost can be rather stressful when it comes time to filing a tax return the following April.

If you are in the position of receiving alimony or maintenance payments over and above other income, it would be well worth your while to sit down and calculate your eventual tax exposure at the beginning of each year. Then, it becomes important for you to save the necessary dollars to pay your tax liability. One way that this might be accomplished, at least to some extent, is through a forced-savings program. For example, perhaps you go to your employer and ask him or her to increase the taxes withheld at source against your regular salary. One way to do this is to have taxes deducted as if you were single, not taking into account your potential claim for your children, including the equivalent-to-married exemption that might otherwise be available. In this manner, part of your tax liability arising from the receipt of alimony or maintenance can be settled through additional tax payments throughout the year.

It is important for *anyone* who receives alimony and/or maintenance to recognize that this income is treated as "earned income" for tax purposes. The significance is that it therefore qualifies for a potential transfer to a Registered Retirement Savings Plan (RRSP), as explained in Chapter Five. The opportunity to shelter at least part of alimony or maintenance income within an RRSP is something that should be explored.

If you are employed and are therefore subject to tax deductions at source, you may have a potential cash-flow problem if you pay large amounts of alimony. This is because the benefits of a tax deduction are not usually received until you file and receive a tax refund. However, to cope with this timing problem, the Income Tax Act gives you the right to have your deductions at source reduced, as long as you certify that failure to allow a tax reduction will present an "undue hardship."

Finally, let me turn once again to the topic that I started this chapter with, the subject of comparing alimony or maintenance to lump-sum payments. I suggested that, in general, a payer would like to have the payments classified as alimony or maintenance in order to obtain a deduction while a recipient might prefer to receive lump sums. Of course, there is always the possibility that the payer is, for one reason or another, in a lower tax bracket than the recipient. For example, what if the payer has substantial tax write-offs or a deductible loss from a business? Under these circumstances, the payer might be well advised to structure a financial settlement with a spouse or former spouse as a lump-sum payment, *especially if the payer can get a discount off the amount otherwise payable*.

One potential opportunity is for the payer to turn over all or most of the proceeds from the sale of the family home or for the payer to surrender his or her equity in the home for a reduced consideration. As I explained earlier, a transfer of an interest in a family home from one spouse to the other does not carry with it any of the income-tax implications that I dealt with in the section of this chapter concerning property transfers.

Marriage breakdown tends to be a contentious issue, to say the least! While I have tried to highlight tax strategies that may fit certain situations, I strongly recommend that you seek professional advice before implementing any specific tax-planning steps should you be confronted with this issue.

CHAPTER NINE

Maximizing Your Investment Yields Through Incorporation

For those Canadians with substantial investment assets, the tax saving that results from income splitting can best be achieved through the use of family-owned holding companies. Before exploring this avenue in detail, however, a short review of the tax rules for corporate-earned investment income would be useful.

Overview of the Corporate Tax Structure for Investment Income

Investment income, such as interest, rents, royalties, and the taxable half of capital gains, is initially taxed at approximately 50% (the actual rate varies slightly from province to province) when earned by a corporation. The Income Tax Act permits the remaining 50% to be reinvested. You should note that a corporation will not be eligible for the new $500,000 lifetime capital-gains exemption, which will be phased in between 1985 and 1990.

The theory behind this tax structure is that as long as a 50% tax is paid initially, the government does not mind if a shareholder would have paid a slightly higher percentage in personal taxes. (Before 1982, when personal tax rates often reached as high as 65%, the opportunities to use investment companies to defer tax were much greater than they are today.)

In most cases, where an investor is in a tax bracket below 50%, it is unlikely that he or she would have enough capital to form an investment company in the first place. For investors in the top bracket, the main benefit of an investment company is the opportunity to collect income and then *deflect* it to family members in lower tax brackets.

Although a privately owned investment company can only "keep" 50% of what it earns, at any time dividends are paid out to shareholders, 16⅔% of the investment income is then *refunded* back to the corporation. In other words, the net *perma-*

nent corporate tax is only 33⅓%, and 66⅔% of each dollar's earnings is eventually available for distribution. These rules are summarized as follows:

Investment income	$100.00
Corporate tax	50.00
Net corporate retention (maximum)	50.00
Refundable tax (16⅔% of $100)	16.67
Available for dividends	$66.67

The Taxation of Canadian Dividends Received by an Individual

As odd or complicated as the above rules may seem, the tax treatment of dividends received by a Canadian individual from a Canadian company seems even stranger. When an individual receives a Canadian dividend, the dividend is included in the taxpayer's income. In addition, he or she is then required to include in income a *further* 50% of the amount actually received. This extra 50% is called the "50% gross-up."

The grossed-up dividend (150% of the actual dividend) is then taxed at the individual's marginal rate for that year. Initially, this appears to create a penalty situation where more than what is actually received is taxed. However, in arriving at the individual's taxes payable, there is a dividend tax credit that is *equal* to the 50% gross-up. (The federal dividend tax credit is approximately 75% of the gross-up, while a provincial dividend tax credit covers the balance.) These rules are illustrated in Figure 9-1.

Figure 9-1 **Schedule of Tax Payable on $100 Canadian Dividend**

	$23,000	$36,000	$60,000
Taxable income level			
Individual's marginal tax bracket	40%	45%	50%
Cash dividend	$100	$100	$100
50% gross-up	50	50	50
Additional taxable income	$150	$150	$150
Tax in marginal bracket	$ 60	$ 67	$ 75
Dividend tax credit (combined federal and provincial)	50	50	50
Net tax payable	$ 10	$ 17	$ 25

If you examine the schedule, it becomes apparent that the tax treatment of dividends does not result in a penalty to the shareholder who receives them. Although the shareholder initially pays tax on an amount greater than what is actually received, the dividend tax credit *more than compensates* for this inequity. If, for example, you are in a 40% tax bracket and you receive $100 of additional income from any other source *except* Canadian dividends, you would expect to pay $40 on the *incremental* income. However, on a Canadian dividend, the tax is only $10. Similarly, an individual in the 45% bracket only pays $17 tax on a $100 dividend, while someone in a 50% bracket pays only $25.

The favourable tax treatment of dividends from Canadian companies takes into account the fact that a dividend is a distribution out of profits on which *a corporation has previously paid tax. The dividend tax credit is intended to compensate the individual shareholder for at least a portion of the corporate tax previously paid.*

Actually, the "gross-up and credit" system is designed to exactly compensate a shareholder for a permanent corporate tax of 33 1/3%. Thus, when anyone receives a dividend of $66.67 out of $100 of investment income initially generated through a private corporation, this provides the shareholder with the *same after-tax retention* as would have been the case if he or she had received the entire investment income ($100) directly.

As mentioned previously, if the shareholder of a corporation is in a tax bracket slightly higher than 50%, he or she can use the corporation to obtain some tax deferrals. At some future time, when the individual decides to draw out dividends, he or she is *no worse off* than had the investment been owned *personally* in the first place. There is an illustration of the two alternative approaches in Figure 9-2. (You should note that this example ignores the effects of the $1,000 investment-income deduction.)

Figure 9-2 **Comparative After-Tax Retention on Investment Income**

Alternative 1

Investment income (e.g., interest, rents, royalties, taxable capital gains) is earned personally

Investment income	$100	$100	$100
Marginal tax bracket of investment holder	40%	45%	50%
After-tax retention on $100	$60	$55	$50

Alternative 2
Investment income is earned by a private Canadian corporation

Investment income	$100		
Less: Approximate effective federal and provincial corporate tax	50[1]		
Retained earnings	$ 50		

	40%	45%	50%
Shareholder's tax bracket	40%	45%	50%
Tax prepayment under Alternative 2	$10[2]	$ 5[2]	Nil[3]

Effect when dividends are eventually paid out

Retained earnings in corporation	$ 50.00		
Add: Refundable tax	16.67		
	66.67		
Less: Dividend in cash	(66.67)		
Corporate net retention	Nil		

	40%	45%	50%
Shareholder's tax bracket	40%	45%	50%
Dividend in cash	$ 66.67	$ 66.67	$ 66.67
50% gross-up	33.33	33.33	33.33
Income for tax purposes	$100.00	$100.00	$100.00
Tax at marginal rates	$ 40.00	$ 45.00	$ 50.00
Less: Effective dividend tax credit (equal to gross-up)	33.33	33.33	33.33
Net tax	$ 6.67	$ 11.67	$ 16.67
Net retention (dividend in cash – net tax)	$ 60.00	$ 55.00	$ 50.00
Net retention without corporation Alternative 1	$ 60.00	$ 55.00	$ 50.00

Notes:
1. The company has a potentially refundable dividend tax on hand of $16.67. This amount is refundable at the rate of $1 for every $4 of dividends paid.
2. Where the investor is in a tax bracket below 50%, it is very unlikely that he or she would form an investment company in the first place.
3. In some provinces, personal marginal rates will reach 52%–54%. For residents of these provinces, there may be a 2%–4% tax *deferral*. For residents of Quebec, the tax deferral may be even greater.

The Investment-Income Deduction

The previous example does not take into account the annual $1,000 investment-income deduction, which was discussed in Chapter Seven. The investment-income deduction only applies where qualified income is received from *arm's-length sources*. Thus, using an investment company may have one small pitfall. If you channel *all* of your investments into a private corporation, and then proceed to extract dividends, what was previously arm's-length income becomes non-arm's-length. You must therefore "hold back" at least $10,000 to $12,000 of investment capital, which should be invested in your own name. This amount should be sufficient to yield $1,000 of arm's-length investment income from Canadian sources annually.

Therefore, you would not usually consider an investment company until you are in a 50% tax bracket and also have significant *additional* capital beyond what is required to maximize the use of your annual $1,000 deduction.

The Use of Investment Companies

The gross-up and credit system has a very interesting by-product, which is a major factor in tax planning for Canadian corporations and their shareholders.

Specifically, up to $36,000 of Canadian dividends can be received in 1985 by an individual *totally tax-free* as long as he or she has *no other income*. This is illustrated in Figure 9-3, which uses average tax rates applicable across Canada.

The example shows a dividend of $36,000 that is grossed up by an extra $18,000. However, after applying personal exemptions and other deductions, the tax otherwise payable is completely offset by the $18,000 dividend tax credit. The net effect is to reduce taxes to nil.

Remember that the concept of tax-free dividends only applies where an individual has no other income. If the individual in our example had an *extra* $1,000 from *any source whatsoever*, the taxable income would become $51,000 instead of $50,000. In this case, since the individual is already in a 48% combined federal and provincial tax bracket, the extra $1,000 of income would attract $480 of taxes. There would be no further dividend tax credits available to offset this additional burden.

Thus, if you receive dividends as well as other income, the other income "floats to the top" and gets taxed at your highest marginal bracket with no relief. If you have substantial other income, you should be aware that the tax advantages of Canadian dividends are reduced considerably. You should also note

Figure 9-3 **If a Taxpayer Has No Other Income, $36,000 of Canadian Dividends Are Tax-Free**

Dividend	$36,000
50% "gross-up"	18,000
Net income	54,000
Less: Estimated personal exemptions (rounded)	4,000
Taxable income	$50,000
Estimated federal and provincial taxes	
On $36,000	$11,300
On $14,000 (tax bracket 48%)	6,700
On $50,000	18,000
Less: Dividend tax credit (combined federal and provincial)	(18,000)
Net tax payable	Nil

that there is no direct relationship between dividends and other income. Therefore, you could *not* receive, for example, $16,000 of salary and a further (tax-free) $20,000 of dividends. The interaction of various dividend and other income mixes must be determined on a trial-and-error basis with the aid of your own accountant in your particular province.

Opportunities for Income Splitting Through a Corporation

The tax rules for investment income were designed to produce an equitable treatment where income is earned and is then passed on as dividends *to the person who injected the capital into a corporation in the first place.* It is probable that the legislators failed to adequately consider the opportunities that would exist to use a corporation as a vehicle to collect income and then *channel it to family members in low tax brackets.* This is illustrated in the form of a diagram, Figure 9-4, and in the example on Figure 9-5, which outlines the magnitude of the tax

163

advantages obtainable by simply putting together the investment-income rules explained previously.

In the example shown, Father incorporates a private company to hold the investments that he would otherwise retain personally. He exchanges his investments for a non-interest-bearing loan to the corporation or for shares bearing a very low dividend yield. If shares are used, they are also structured so as not to provide any substantial growth potential.

Figure 9-4 **Income Splitting Through a Corporation**

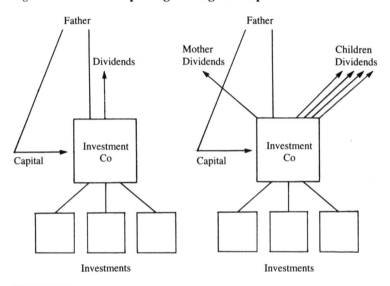

INTENTION OF RULES   OPPORTUNITIES FOR TAX PLANNING

At the time of incorporation, Mother and the four children simultaneously invest a relatively nominal amount of money in the company and subscribe to the common shares. Growth and dividend benefits would be attached to these shares. In order to avoid "income attribution" (as discussed in Chapter Seven), it would be important for the family members to invest their own funds or use money borrowed from outsiders. If necessary, Father could guarantee their loans without creating an adverse tax situation.

Since the investments are now held by the corporation, the company would begin to earn the interest income that would otherwise have been Father's. Initially, the corporate tax rate is approximately 50%. However, beyond the fact that the corporation can retain 50% of its investment earnings, the company also has the ability to pay out 66²/₃% of its profits by way of dividends. This is because of refundable tax considerations. In this case, at the time dividends are paid, $45,000 out of the (previously paid) corporate tax of $135,000 is refundable to the company. This would enable the company to pay Mother and the

Figure 9-5 **Advantages of a Family-Owned Investment Company**

Assumptions:
Father is in the 50% bracket and has $2.7 million of investment capital earning interest at 10%. He is married and has four dependent children. His wife and children have no income.

Alternative 1—Investment income is earned personally

Interest on $2.7 million at 10%	$270,000
Less: Income taxes thereon at 50%	135,000
Net retention (50% of total)	$135,000

Alternative 2
- A corporation is formed and $2.7 million is transferred by Father to the company in exchange for a non-interest-bearing loan or for non-dividend-paying shares.
- Father subscribes to additional shares with voting powers sufficient to control the corporation, but with no "growth potential."
- Mother and the children subscribe to common shares.

Interest on $2.7 million at 10%	$270,000
Less: Corporate tax at 50%	135,000
Retained earnings	135,000
Add: Refundable tax to corporation when dividends are paid (16²/₃% × $270,000)	45,000
Cash available for dividends	180,000
Less: Dividends to wife and four children	(180,000)
Remaining cash available for dividends	Nil
Dividend to each of wife and four children ($180,000 ÷ 5)	$ 36,000
Net tax payable by each	Nil
Net retention by family (5 × $36,000)	$180,000
$180,000 ÷ $270,000	66.6%

four children dividend payments of approximately $36,000 each. If none of them has other income, the net tax payable after gross-up and credit will be nil. Thus, $180,000, or 66.6% of the total earnings, is available for reinvestment purposes. This is $45,000 more than Father would have retained on his own.

To reiterate, a corporation is therefore a vehicle for people with at least $200,000 to $300,000 in investments to collect income that would otherwise be taxed in one person's hands at high marginal rates. The income is then recycled and reallocated to other family members who are in low tax brackets, and significant absolute tax savings are achieved.

Sheltering Capital Gains

While the previous examples in this chapter assume an interest yield, income splitting through a corporation is viable for all sorts of investment activity. If, for example, the family corpora-

Figure 9-6 **Treatment of Taxable Capital Gain Made by an Investment Company**

Assumptions:
- Father makes a (non-exempt) capital gain of $100,000 of which $50,000 would be taxable. He is in the 50% tax bracket. Without the benefits of a corporation, his tax would therefore be $25,000.
- Father is married and has four children—none of the other family members has any income.

If a family investment-holding company had made the gain instead:	
Taxable gain	$50,000
Less: Corporate tax at 50%	25,000
Retained earnings	25,000
Add: Refundable tax to corporation when dividends are paid ($16^2/_3\%$ × $50,000)	8,333
Dividend to other family members	$33,333
Dividend to each ($33,333 ÷ 5)	$ 6,666
Net tax payable by each	Nil
Final corporate tax ($25,000 – $8,333)	$16,667
Father's tax—if no corporation	$25,000
Corporate tax	16,667
Tax saving	$ 8,333

tion holds marketable securities, the tax burden of capital gains can also be reduced greatly. The taxable half of the capital gain is taxed as investment income, while the tax-free half of a gain is not only tax-free to the corporation, but also can be extracted by the shareholders personally, with *no tax payable*, on a special-dividend basis. Figure 9-6 illustrates how a *taxable* capital gain of $50,000 may be sheltered where investment assets are held through a family corporation.

In future, sheltering capital gains through an investment corporation can be extremely useful planning in cases where an individual has already used up his or her lifetime capital-gains tax exemption.

Sheltering Public-Company Dividends

Investment yields in the form of public-company dividends can also be sheltered by funnelling these earnings through a private corporation. When a private holding company receives dividends from Canadian public companies, these dividends are taxed at a flat rate of 25% *instead* of the regular 50% tax that applies to other forms of investment income. This 25% tax is completely refundable as soon as the holding company in turn pays out these dividends to its shareholders. Thus, where Canadian public corporation dividends are received by a private company and are simultaneously paid out, there is *no tax whatsoever* at the corporate level.

Again, given a spouse with no other income and four children, the opportunity exists for each one to receive $36,000 of dividends tax-free. On a combined basis, this amounts to $180,000 per annum. If the average Canadian public company pays a dividend of 5% (computed as a percentage of the cost to acquire the shares in the first place), it is therefore possible to *completely shelter* the income yield from $3.6 million of share investments! (5% × $3,600,000 = $180,000).

Of course, the potential to tax shelter all kinds of investment income will vary from case to case and depends primarily on the number of family members that one has available for this purpose. The opportunities are, however, astounding. *In spite of recent federal budgets, the idea that taxes are paid by those who are best able to absorb them is clearly a myth.* Ironically, if one has several hundred thousand dollars or more of accumulated capital, the (net) tax rate on investment yields may be less than the rate applicable against a small pay increase received by a grocery clerk!

Our fiscal policy does not hurt the rich; it simply makes it much more difficult for anyone else to become wealthy.

Control of the Investment Corporation

The previous examples have assumed that Father would control investment policies and dividend-payment decisions through his voting preferred shares in the family company. The family members would own the common shares, which would participate in growth and which would facilitate income splitting.

How can Father ensure that his family members will reinvest their dividends in the company, short of using violence or other unsavoury methods of coercion? Actually, he has several alternatives. First, he can have the corporation capitalized with a special class of shares—non-voting redeemable preferred shares. Then, instead of having the company pay cash dividends to trigger a refund of taxes, he could have the company pay stock dividends to his family members in the form of these non-voting redeemable preferreds. The corporation would still obtain its $16^2/3\%$ refund of tax, but all that the family members would receive would be pieces of paper. Although a stock dividend from a private company is technically taxable, as long as the amount is not more than $36,000 per person, the tax payable would be nil. Since Father would always have voting control of the company, he would decide if and when these special preferred shares would be redeemed.

The Formation of Discretionary Trusts

An alternative would be to create a trust to hold the shares of the children, while Father continued to control the flow of income and all investment decisions. Although establishing a trust is the most complicated method of ensuring dividends are reinvested in the company and it involves the greatest amount of legal and other documentation, it is the preferred route to take—especially if the children are minors.

Usually, a family trust involves three trustees, including Father, Mother, and a close family friend, relative, or adviser.

Generally, if Father is providing his capital to the investment corporation, he would have the right to replace either of the other trustees, although they would not be able to replace him.

The trust would use borrowed funds to subscribe to the common shares of the investment corporation. This is done to avoid income attribution—especially where one or more of the children are minors. Dividends would then be paid by the corporation to the trust as illustrated previously.

When a trust receives a dividend, the trustees have two options. First, they could have the trust pay taxes on the entire dividend. Obviously, this would not be a good choice since there are significant taxes payable on dividends in excess of $36,000. As a second option, however, the trustees are permitted to enter into what the Tax Act calls a "preferred beneficiary election." The preferred beneficiary election is simply a decision to *allocate* the dividends to the children for tax purposes. The allocation makes the children's income taxable instead of the trust's. Of course, as long as the allocation per child is under $36,000, there are no personal taxes payable. In fact, however, no amounts need be paid out unless Father actually wants to give the children some money. The trustees can instead be in the position of holding money on which taxes have been paid. They can reinvest the funds back into the holding company to compound future growth.

If a trust is set up as being "discretionary," this provides even further scope for tax planning. The discretionary feature means that the trustees are permitted to eventually distribute capital (generally upon the dissolution of the trust) to whichever of the preferred beneficiaries (and in whatever proportions) the trustees, at their discretion, may at *some future time* see fit. Thus, Father may freeze his estate and pass on growth, even if he is unsure of exactly where he wishes such growth to go! Perhaps the children are relatively young and their capabilities and personalities are still not known.

The key point is that at present there is no requirement that the preferred beneficiary election (which allows for equal allocations of income between the children) be tied in to ultimate distribution ratios. As an extreme example, even though income may have been allocated to four children for many years, Father may decide that only one child should eventually receive *all* the funds. In fact, the rules permit a decision on distributions to be deferred for up to twenty-one years.

In order to discourage long-term *inter vivos* trusts (that is, trusts formed by living persons), there is a deemed disposition of trust property at fair market value if the trust is still in existence on its twenty-first anniversary. The deemed disposition would ordinarily trigger capital gains and this should be avoided. A deemed disposition can be avoided by simply winding up the trust shortly before its twenty-first anniversary and distributing the assets (the common shares of the investment corporation) to some or all of the children. Of course, if Father is still alive, he could continue to control the company and its portfolio through his voting preferred shares. However, within twenty-one years, he should be in a position to know which of his children he wants to give an (eventual) inheritance.

Discretionary trusts giving the trustees the power to make annual preferred beneficiary elections are becoming more and more popular in tax and estate planning. Care must always be taken to comply with the particular laws of the jurisdiction in which the trust is being set up. Accordingly, it is always advisable to have the arrangement for such a trust documented by lawyers and accountants who have had experience in such matters.

Capitalization of the Investment Company

A question usually arises in setting up an investment corporation as to how much money each of the shareholders must contribute in exchange for their shareholdings. For example, can a family member invest only one dollar in the common-share capital of a company and thereby receive dividends of up to $36,000 a year?

So far, there has been only one reported tax case on this subject. The case involves two Alberta optometrists who incorporated a management company in 1970 to administer their practice. The company was controlled by these two individuals through voting, non-participating shares, but their wives also held shares, which were non-voting but fully participating. The company paid management fees to the doctors and declared dividends to the wives that were very substantial in relation to their original investment. In fact, it appears that the wives literally invested pennies and, over a three-year period, received over $90,000 in dividends.

The Minister of National Revenue contended that an indirect

benefit had been conferred by the doctors on their wives and that the whole set-up was a sham. The Tax Review Board upheld the Minister's treatment of the situation on the basis that although there was a business purpose for the incorporation of the company, the declaration of these dividends to the wives was not a sound business practice.

The judge showed no distaste for income splitting and estate planning as a *concept*, but, in his judgement, he gave the opinion that acceptable limits had been exceeded. He concluded that the scheme was simply intended to avoid income tax and that the dividends were rightly assessed as being income of the doctors. This case was appealed and eventually settled out of court.

In spite of this one case, many accountants and lawyers are still not overly concerned and investment companies are often set up with only nominal share capital. However, I personally recommend extreme caution in this area. If, for example, you are forming an investment corporation with the expectation of paying $36,000 a year of dividends to family members (either directly or through a trust), I think that the capitalization per person should be at least $10,000.

Thus, in a family corporation involving a wife and four children, common shares should be issued for a total consideration of, say, $50,000. To avoid income attribution, the father should not give these funds to the family members. Rather, they should take a bank loan, which, if necessary, could be *guaranteed* by him. The interest on the borrowed money would be tax-deductible, since the borrowings would be incurred for the purpose of earning income in the form of dividends from the corporation. In addition, the infusion of an extra $50,000 of capital into the corporation would result in additional income being earned by the company. There would be no economic loss. Finally, the bank loan could always be repaid by the family members out of dividends over a period of one or two years.

The advantage of taking all these steps is that the Minister of National Revenue would probably be hard pressed to allege that a transaction is a sham when $10,000 is invested for the purpose of earning $36,000. Unfortunately, there are no guidelines within the Canadian tax structure and any final decision as to capitalization of an investment company is a matter that must be resolved by the taxpayer together with his or her own advisers.

Interest Versus Dividend Income

Retreating somewhat from the rather rarified atmosphere of investment corporations with portfolios of $2–$3 million, let's look at the tax implications of receiving either interest income or dividend income in Canada. There are two distinct comparisons that should be made:

1. The relative yields of both interest-bearing and dividend-bearing investments, and
2. The effectiveness of both kinds of investments in counterbalancing the ravages of inflation.

As of fall 1985, it would not be unreasonable for an investor to expect a return of around 10% where funds are placed to earn interest. On the other hand, if you invest in Canadian public-company common stock, you might encounter great difficulty in finding investments that pay dividends of more than 5%. On the surface, therefore, there would be a 5% differential in yield between interest-bearing securities—such as term deposits, mortgages, or Canada Savings Bonds—and many Canadian public-stock investments.

Although most people are aware that an investment in term deposits, mortgages, or bonds may produce what appears to be a superior yield, part of the advantage is offset by the decreasing value of the dollar, which accompanies the inflationary process. However, many people are still somewhat security-conscious and feel that a 5% spread in yields is too large to warrant an investment in the stock market. It is recognized that over the long term, stock-market investments could appreciate and may therefore be a reasonable hedge against inflation, but there is still the "down-side" risk of potential declines in value.

Unfortunately, most people lack sufficient information when it comes to making proper investment decisions. Much of the problem stems from exposure to our American neighbours. In the United States, there is no difference between the receipt of interest and the receipt of dividends by an individual. Both are taxed at regular personal rates. In Canada, however, there is a very important distinction between these two kinds of income. Dividends are subject to the gross-up and credit treatment, while interest income is simply taxed at ordinary marginal rates. A comparison of after-tax retention for individuals in various brackets is shown in Figure 9-7. The example ignores the first $1,000 of annual investment income, which is tax-free whether the $1,000 comprises interest, (grossed-up) dividends, or any combination of the two.

As the comparison shows, the after-tax retention on dividends for taxpayers in *all* brackets is one and one-half times as high as the corresponding retention on interest. Thus, for anyone who is taxable, a 5% dividend will yield as much after tax as a 7½% (pre-tax) interest yield. Similarly, a 6% dividend is comparable to interest at 9%.

Therefore, the difference between earning interest at 10% or dividends at 5% is really only a difference of two and one-half percentage points (10% – 7½%). In addition, the 2½% difference is really a *pre-tax* difference. *For a taxpayer in the 50% bracket, a 2½% difference in pre-tax yield translates to only 1¼% after tax.*

Let's put this into proper perspective using realistic numbers.

Figure 9-7 **A Comparison of After-Tax Retention**
Canadian Dividends Versus Interest Income
(Ignoring the $1,000 investment-income deduction)

	40%	45%	50%
Individual's marginal tax bracket			
Alternative 1—$100 Canadian dividends			
Cash dividend	$100	$100	$100
50% gross-up	50	50	50
Taxable income	$150	$150	$150
Tax in marginal bracket	$ 60	$ 67	$ 75
Dividend tax credit (combined federal and provincial)	50	50	50
Net tax	$ 10	$ 17	$ 25
Net retention (cash dividend – tax)	$ 90	$ 83	$ 75
Alternative 2—$100 Canadian interest			
$100 interest	$100	$100	$100
Tax in marginal bracket	40	45	50
Net retention	$ 60	$ 55	$ 50
Ratio of after-tax retention			
Dividends: Interest	3:2	3:2	3:2

Assume you have $20,000 to invest and have a choice between a 10% term deposit or a Canadian blue-chip stock paying a dividend of 5%. If you opt for the share investment, you must be prepared to sacrifice 1¼% of $20,000, or $250 per annum. Then you must ask, what are my chances of the securities appreciating by at least an amount offsetting my $250 loss? Of course, there is some risk involved. The securities could decline in value because of poor market performance overall or because you just happened to pick the wrong stock. On the other hand, if you invest $20,000 in interest-bearing securities, you can be *sure* that your $20,000 capital will only be worth about $19,000 at the end of one year given current inflation rates!

I must stress that the foregoing example is only valid where an individual is taxable in the first place. If you are in a 50% tax bracket, there just doesn't seem to be much value in earning 5% *net* interest income when the inflation rate is also 5%. On the other hand, I have no objections if my twenty-year-old son invests his summer earnings in a term deposit. The reason is that my son hasn't reached the point where his income is taxable. If that is the case, a 10% *gross* return on a term deposit is the same as his *net* return. For him to invest in dividend-bearing securities would, in fact, involve a difference in yield of about 5%.

I also would not be too upset if my eighty-year-old grand-mother had her life savings invested in term deposits. Even if her income is taxable, she would be much more concerned with the security element of having the money available at any time than she is about the devaluation of the dollar.

Finally, I am not adverse to interest-bearing investments when they are held by pension plans, Registered Retirement Savings Plans, or deferred profit-sharing plans. *As long as the investment income is tax-sheltered, the after-tax yield and the pre-tax yield are one and the same.* I would not, however, recommend an interest-bearing investment for anyone whose income is taxable unless the after-tax yield was at least equal to the annual inflation factor.

CHAPTER TEN

Tax and Investment Planning for the Retirement Years

This chapter outlines specific strategies to help you assure yourself of a comfortable retirement, regardless of the age you choose to retire at.

To determine whether you are ready for retirement, you must be able to answer yes to four specific questions:

1. Am I in a financial position to maintain a standard of living that is adequate for my needs and those of my spouse?
2. Am I mentally prepared to move away from the environment of a structured working day to the unstructured life that follows retirement?
3. Will I be able to use my time in an effective manner so that I will get satisfaction from what I do and avoid boredom and depression?
4. Are my goals and objectives compatible with those of my spouse?

This chapter is restricted to dealing with the first question, ensuring a successful retirement from a financial and investment standpoint. It examines inflation and life expectancy; how the government assists retired Canadians through pension programs; the importance of a Registered Retirement Savings Plan as a means of providing retirement capital; income splitting between husbands and wives; effective money management and how to evaluate various investment alternatives; and finally, tying up the loose ends through proper estate-planning techniques. Some of these topics are dealt with in greater detail in other chapters of this book as well.

Understanding Inflation

Perhaps the biggest problem facing people close to retirement age is the spectre of renewed inflation. At the time this is being written, in mid-1985, the Canadian inflation rate is quite low, but no one knows what the future will bring. All too often, however, the impact of the Consumer Price Index on our lives is blown way out of proportion. In my opinion, inflation is not nearly as deadly an enemy as you might think.

Let's consider for a few moments how inflation works. If we look back at 1981–82, a period of high inflation, the numbers will prove that you need not be too concerned with inflation—as long as you have planned properly. At this point, you may want to take a look at Figure 10-1. It shows the changes in the Consumer Price Index from April 1981 to April 1982, at a time when the inflation index was in double digits.

Figure 10-1 **Major Components of the Consumer Price Index**

	% Change April 1982 from April 1981		Statistics Canada Weighting %		Weighted Changes (Column 1 × Column 2)
Housing	13.8	×	35.4	=	4.9
Food	6.1	×	21.1	=	1.3
Transportation	16.3	×	16.2	=	2.6
Clothing	6.0	×	9.6	=	.6
Recreation, reading, and education	8.7	×	8.6	=	.7
Tobacco and alcohol	15.7	×	5.4	=	.8
Health and personal care	10.3	×	3.7	=	.4
All items			100.0		11.3

Here's how the Consumer Price Index works. There are seven items that are included in the statistical computations. The categories are housing; food; transportation; clothing; recreation, reading and education; tobacco and alcohol; and health and personal care. Statistics Canada measures the percentage changes in the cost of a basket of goods and services from the end of one month in comparison to the same month in the previous year. Then, a percentage increase is calculated. For example, the food index would take into account the price of a loaf of bread a year ago compared to the price today. As you can see from Figure 10-1, in all cases, prices rose between April 1981 and April 1982 by between 6% and 16%.

Then, Statistics Canada applies a weighting formula. The

formula takes into account the fact that all of us tend to spend more of our disposable incomes on certain components rather than others. On average, our biggest expenditure is for housing, 35.4 cents out of each dollar. Then come food; transportation; clothing; recreation, reading, and education; followed by tobacco and alcohol (almost double what we spend on health and personal care). If we then take the actual percentage increases multiplied by the weighted averages, we get figures that, when added up, give us changes in the Consumer Price Index.

If you now stop to look at the third column in Figure 10-1, you can see that at a time when inflation was in double digits, only two items in the entire Consumer Price Index were meaningful. They are housing and transportation; at that time, 7.5% out of the 11.3% total increase.

There is one important lesson that you must learn from this. Specifically, *as long as you can stabilize your own housing and transportation costs, you really don't have to be particularly concerned about how consumer prices move.* No matter who you are, no matter how aggressive or non-aggressive in your investment policies, there are two things that you must target for by the time you retire. First, you must have your house paid for by that time. If you choose to continue to live in that home, you will still be subject to annual increases in your taxes and utilities, but these probably won't go up by more than a few hundred dollars a year. Alternatively, if you choose to sell your house, the fact that it's paid for will provide you with capital. If you take that money and invest it conservatively, taking advantage of some of the income-splitting techniques with which I deal in this book, you should be able to generate sufficient investment income to pay your rent.

The second point is that by the time you retire, you must target to have a late-model car fully paid for. In fact, if your family consists of a husband and wife, you might consider two late-model cars both fully paid for. Then, if you have to, you can probably keep those same vehicles serviceable for much of the remainder of your lifetimes. Again, you may not be able to "fix" your entire transportation costs. After all, insurance, gasoline, and even licence fees are subject to change, but a good portion of your transportation costs will be stabilized. In fact, depending on your lifestyle and where you reside, you may find that you don't want or need a car subsequent to retirement. If you have had two cars previously, you may find that one car now suffices.

What I'm really trying to show you is that, as I mentioned before, general changes in the Consumer Price Index can be quite misleading. The CPI is an overall calculation, but each family's individual inflation factor is somewhat unique.

Consider as well some of the other components of the Consumer Price Index. Food, for example. Obviously, the cost of feeding a family of two is significantly less than the cost of feeding a family that is supporting children. Tobacco and alcohol is another interesting category. Take another look at Figure 10-1. At the time that inflation was 11.3%, the consumer price increase attributable to tobacco and alcohol alone was almost 1%. If you and your spouse didn't smoke or drink, this would have reduced your family's susceptibility to inflation. And the list goes on. It costs less to provide clothing to a family of two than it does to clothe a large family with growing children. Also, by the time you retire, you should not be paying education costs and, if necessary, you can tailor your recreation expenditures to fall within your means.

So, the first concrete plan that I suggest to you in dealing with retirement is to control your housing and transportation costs as much as you can. Then inflation need not be seen as a mortal enemy.

Understanding Life Expectancies

That's the good news. What's the bad news? Well, the bad news, if you can call it that, is that you will probably live a lot longer than you expect. Most people are hung up on the fact that men ordinarily live to age seventy-two, while women live perhaps three years longer. This is true. These are the overall statistics for life expectancy. However, the older you get, the longer you can expect to live in total. Take a look at Figure 10-2, which is an extract from the Standard Canadian Life Expectancy Table.

You can see that if you're sixty-five years old, you have a life expectancy of seventy-nine if you are male, and eighty-two and a half if you are female. At age seventy, you can expect to live to eighty-one if you are male, and eighty-four if you are female. This is fairly easy to explain. Picture a room filled with people all seventy years of age, all reasonably healthy at this point. On

Figure 10-2   **Mortality Table—Male and Female Life Tables**
                Canada 1970-72—Expectations of Life in Years

Age	Male	Female	Age	Male	Female	Age	Male	Female
60	16.95	21.39	70	10.90	13.85	80	6.41	7.88
61	16.27	20.58	71	10.38	13.17	81	6.05	7.39
62	15.61	19.79	72	9.88	12.51	82	5.70	6.93
63	14.96	19.01	73	9.39	11.86	83	5.36	6.48
64	14.33	18.25	74	8.92	11.24	84	5.04	6.06
65	13.72	17.47	75	8.47	10.63	85	4.74	5.67
66	13.12	16.72	76	8.02	10.03			
67	12.54	15.98	77	7.60	9.46			
68	11.98	15.26	78	7.19	8.91			
69	11.43	14.55	79	6.79	8.38			

average, they will live more than another decade. In other words, the fact that a person is seventy years old does not necessarily mean that he or she will die within two years.

So, whatever you accumulate by the time you retire has to be sufficient to meet your needs for an extended period of time. This means that over and above paying for your house and car, you have the responsibility of setting aside some additional capital.

What Can I Expect From Government?

Before we look at what *you* have to do, let's see what you can reasonably expect from the government. At age sixty-five, you become eligible for the Old Age Pension, which at the beginning of 1985 was approximately $275 a month. In addition, if you have worked in Canada since 1966, you should be eligible for the maximum Canada Pension Plan, which is a further $350 a month in round figures. Figure 10-3 provides a calculation of what a husband and wife can reasonably expect to receive in 1985 if both of them are age sixty-five or over and only one of the two had been working before retirement. You can see that the pension-income level is well in excess of $10,000 a year for a couple. This does not take into account potential income under the Guaranteed Supplement, which I will ignore for purposes of this chapter. After all, if you take reasonable steps to plan for your retirement, you shouldn't need the Supplement nor be eligible to receive it.

179

Figure 10-3 **What Can I Expect From the Government?**

Reasonable expectation in today's dollars:
Husband and wife both over age 65—if only husband had been working

Old Age Security 2 × $275 =	$ 550
Canada Pension Plan 1 × $350 =	350
	$ 900 per month
	$ 10,800 per annum

Note: A single person who had been working before retirement could expect $275 a month in old age pension as well as $350 a month from the Canada Pension Plan. This amounts to $625 a month or $7,500 annually.

One of the decisions that you may have to make is whether or not to apply for the Canada Pension Plan at age sixty-five. You don't have to apply at that age, but if you don't continue to earn pensionable income, it is certainly in your interest to do so. If you continue to be employed or to carry on an unincorporated business, it may be better for you to delay your application and continue paying premiums until age seventy, in order to increase your monthly pension. One reason to do this would be if you had very low earnings in earlier years, which could be replaced by higher earnings after age sixty-five. If you're unsure what to do, I suggest that you visit the nearest Canada Pension Plan office and ask for some assistance. In fact, a visit to that office can be well worth your time so that you may check that you have made sufficient contributions so that your spouse will qualify for survivor's benefits in the event of your death. A detailed analysis of the Canada Pension Program as well as the Old Age Security Program is beyond the scope of this book, although my key point is that a couple can probably rely on an income of around $10,000 a year, which will be indexed for inflation, while a single individual might receive around $7,500.

There are various other tax-related considerations that come into play at age sixty-five. For example, provincial health and hospital-insurance premiums are generally reduced or even eliminated. You get an additional personal exemption of around $2,500 that you may claim on your income-tax return. This is also indexed annually. Thus, between husband and wife, the additional tax exemptions over and above basic personal exemptions are approximately an extra $5,000. You also become eligible for the annual $1,000 pension-income deduction, which

I dealt with in Chapter Five when I discussed Registered Retirement Savings Plans and employment-related pensions. Finally, you are exempt from the requirement to pay Unemployment Insurance premiums if you continue to work.

To summarize what I have said so far, I have suggested that you target to have your house and car (or cars) fully paid for by the time you retire. In addition, you may comfortably rely on the Canadian government to provide you with an annual income of between $7,500 and $10,000, depending on whether you are single or married.

After these factors are considered, saving sufficient capital to meet the remainder of your living expenses and provide a little bit of luxury is not an insurmountable task. For many people contemplating retirement, there are benefits from a pension-plan program resulting from prior employment. In some instances— for example, if you were a government employee—your employment-related pension may even be indexed. Some pension-plan programs are geared to provide up to 70% of your final year's income while in full-time employment. About half of pension plans provide a widow's pension, which is usually about 50% of what the deceased spouse was getting.

Whether or not a pension will be paid to the surviving spouse may depend on whether the contributor dies before or after retirement. Some private plans only provide for a return of contributions if the contributor dies before retirement. Or they may guarantee payment of a pension for a specified number of years, if he or she dies after the pension begins to be paid. As I explained in Chapter Five, if you are eligible for an employer pension plan, you owe it to yourself to learn about your entitlements and options.

The Registered Retirement Savings Plan (RRSP)

For many people, however, the cornerstone of a successful retirement is the Registered Retirement Savings Plan program. For a complete discussion, I again refer you back to Chapter Five.

You should be aware that, in addition to regular RRSP contributions, you are also permitted to make special transfers of certain lump sums received at the time of retirement and subsequently. If you get a payment in recognition of long service, perhaps comprising accumulated sick leave and vacation pay not taken during your term of office, or if you receive payment from your former employer for loss of office (in other words, because you have been asked to take early retirement), these payments may be eligible for special transfers into an RRSP. The maximum amount is $2,000 for each year of service while you were also covered by an employer-sponsored pension or deferred profit-sharing plan, and $3,500 for each year of service before 1986 while not covered by such a program. In addition, you may "roll over" at least part of both government pensions and employment-related pension receipts each year until age seventy.

One key point is that you are not required to draw money out of your RRSP until that same age seventy. Thus, if you find that your other income is sufficient to meet your post-retirement needs for several years, you can leave your RRSP funds alone to earn income on a tax-sheltered basis, and even add pension rollovers to your RRSP. At age seventy, you would start to draw an annuity, which could be used to provide income for yourself and your spouse for the remainder of your lives.

You have probably been subjected to a tremendous amount of advertising over the years on the subject of RRSPs. You are probably conscious of the fact that if someone starts saving at age thirty-five, there is no reason, given current interest rates, that such an individual shouldn't have a million dollars in his or her RRSP by the time he or she retires.

However, for many people, to start saving in an RRSP at such a young age is quite difficult. Also, the contribution levels used to be a lot lower than they are today. What if you have never invested in a Registered Retirement Savings Plan and you are only five or six years away from retirement? It still isn't too late to start, especially if you now no longer have any dependent children. Assuming you are earning $30,000 a year or more and a reasonable interest rate, you should be able to save at least $50,000 by the time you retire. This will certainly be enough to give you an annual income of between $5,000 to $7,000 a year, which, when added on to the amounts you can expect to receive from government programs, can be of substantial benefit.

Many people, in fact, cannot really start to put aside significant RRSP funds until their mid or late fifties. This is because their disposable incomes are tied up in paying off home mortgages and in providing education and living costs for their children. Once the family unit is down to two people, the goal of saving money can be a lot easier to achieve. If you use the RRSP, take advantage of spousal programs and try to double up on the $1,000 pension-income deduction that I discussed previously in Chapter Five.

What if you are already retired and never contributed to an RRSP or company pension? Since all your Canada Pension and Old Age Security income can be contributed to your RRSP—and a deduction claimed for the full amount for that year—you have an opportunity to convert some currently taxable income into what could be tax-free income for life.

Let's assume you are between sixty-five and seventy-one and are not receiving income qualifying for the pension-income deduction. You might use this strategy: open an RRSP and transfer an amount equal to this year's Canada Pension Plan and Old Age Security payments into the RRSP. Then use the RRSP funds to purchase a life annuity to pay you up to $1,000 in qualifying pension income each year.

Other Tax-Planning Techniques

Let's now take a look at some more tax-planning techniques. There is a good chance that if you are serious in your desire to build a comfortable retirement, you will already have some capital saved, over and above money in an RRPS and a house and car that are paid for. You could conceivably sell your house and invest your money to produce an income large enough to cover your rent as well as many of your other living expenses. For some people, the sale of a house can be very attractive, since the capital gain on the disposition of a principal residence is tax-free under Canadian law. However, maximizing investment yields then becomes an extremely important concept. What I would suggest is that you arrange to split your investment income with your spouse. I have discussed this in Chapter Seven.

At a bare minimum, you should try to structure your savings so that you and your spouse each have at least around $10,000 invested conservatively in Canada Savings Bonds, term deposits, or similar investments. This is because the first $1,000 of Canadian investment income earned annually is tax-free. This $1,000 investment-income deduction is over and above the

$1,000 annual pension-income deduction that I mentioned previously. So, if we consider the additional personal exemptions to which people age sixty-five or over are entitled as well as the available pension and investment-income deductions, you can see that the tax rules are not all that unfavourable.

Effective Money Management

Let's now discuss money management. In general, I suggest that anyone approaching the retirement years take steps to avoid substantial business or investment risks. This is unless you have sufficient assets so that a loss of capital won't affect your position. One area in which I suggest extreme caution is in conjunction with bank guarantees. I personally have seen a number of situations over the last couple of years in which parents approaching retirement age have guaranteed the bank indebtedness of their children who were involved in businesses. When the businesses failed as a result of the recession, the parents were forced to make good on their guarantees—in one or two cases, at a cost of their entire accumulated savings. Sometimes it may be tough to say no, but you may have no choice.

Generally, most people approaching their retirement years want their assets to stay as liquid as possible. Consequently, most monies are kept in investments such as term deposits or Canada Savings Bonds. There are, however, a couple of alternatives that you may want to consider and I'll discuss these in the next few pages. Before I do, though, I suggest that you avoid a common mistake and that is keeping too much money in your personal chequing account. Usually chequing accounts do not bear any interest at all or, if they do, the interest rate is negligible. Keep your chequing accounts only as high as you have to in order to cover whatever payments you are required to make from time to time. Keep the balance of your funds in a daily-interest account until needed. Then you can make transfers to your chequing account to cover amounts that you have to pay out.

Another important point is to always be aware of what your tax bracket is. This will tell you how much the government will take away from basic income over and above pensions or RRSPs. For example, if your taxable income from pension sources after your personal exemptions is, say, $11,000, you are already in a 30% income-tax bracket. This means that if you earn interest income over and above the basic annual $1,000, which is tax-free, the government will take away thirty cents out of each additional dollar. So, if you are earning, say, 10% interest on a term deposit or Canada Savings Bond, you should realize that your net yield is only about 7%.

You will also find that an understanding of tax brackets is useful if you wish to assess the impact of holding down a part-time job subsequent to retirement. For example, let's assume that you are reasonably well off and have investment and pension income that puts you into a 40% bracket, with a taxable income of around $22,000. If you take a part-time job that pays you $6 an hour, you will really only be earning 60% of that, or $3.60—in other words, a net amount approximately equivalent to the minimum wage. If you are thinking of taking the job in order to keep busy or because the job has some appeal to you, by all means go ahead, but if it's purely a financial decision, the high tax cost that already comes into play at your taxable income bracket should be taken into account.

The Pros and Cons of Annuities

A big decision that you may have to make is whether or not you want to live on income only or whether you are also willing to dip into your capital. A lot depends on whether or not your income is adequate to support your lifestyle and your own personal circumstances. For example, what if you don't have any children or other beneficiaries to whom you wish to leave an eventual estate? After all, you know the old saying, "You can't take it with you."

If you are willing to spend capital, the big question is how much can you use up each year so that you don't run out of money during your lifetime. You could solve this problem quite easily if you knew exactly how long you were going to live, but most of us just don't know. Fortunately, your solution might simply be to purchase an annuity from an insurance company, which deals with the problem of uncertain lifespans by pooling many lives together in its calculations of how much it can afford to pay out in exchange for lump sums of money received. There are a number of annuity options that are available. One thing to consider is your health. If your health is bad, you may get a better deal than if your health is good! This is because if you have a shorter life expectancy than average, the issuing company might give you a greater annual income for the same purchase price.

You should explore the types of annuities that are available to you. First, there is the ordinary life annuity, which pays you an agreed sum at stated intervals for the rest of your life. Upon death, all obligations to make these payments cease. An ordinary life annuity is not usually too popular because people are concerned that they might die prematurely. So, unless you have an iron constitution and are pretty sure that you won't get hit by a bus, an ordinary life annuity should not generally be considered unless you have no spouse and absolutely no heirs whatsoever.

A second option is a joint-and-last-survivor annuity for you and your spouse. This means that payments would continue until the last of husband and wife die. You could build in a guaranteed-term option as well. For example, if both you and your spouse die prematurely, the payments could be structured to continue for the balance of the guaranteed period.

Another option is a term-certain annuity, which will pay you money for the rest of your life or for a specified number of years. Term-certain annuities of fifteen or even up to twenty years are not uncommon. The advantage of such an arrangement is that, if you were to die prematurely, the payments would continue for the balance of the guaranteed period. Trust companies as well as insurance companies provide these kinds of annuities.

Finally, there is the concept of an escalating annuity, under which the payments increase annually. At the start of the payout period, the amount that you would receive would be lower than from a regular annuity but the payments would become greater within a few years. The purpose of such an annuity is to compensate for the impact of inflation and the fact that as time goes on, you may require a greater income flow to meet your living expenses.

What About the Stock Market?

So far, in dealing with investment yields, I have concentrated on interest income. I would like to provide a few thoughts, however, on the stock market as a potential consideration. Usually, one tends to think of the stock market as involving risk and I am not suggesting that you may want to use your savings subsequent

186

to retirement in order to speculate. However, there are a number of Canadian blue-chip stocks that bear fairly substantial dividends. Some of these are common shares but most are preferred shares.

The interesting thing about a Canadian dividend is that it qualifies for a dividend tax credit, a concept that is unique to Canada. This has been discussed in Chapter Nine. You should recall that, if you are in a taxable position, no matter what bracket you are in, the yield on a Canadian dividend is always one and a half times the equivalent yield from interest. In other words, if a stock bears a dividend of 6%, that is equivalent to interest at 9% on an after-tax basis. Similarly, an 8% dividend will provide you with the same after-tax dollars as if you were earning interest at 12%. I strongly suggest that, if you have a reasonably large amount of investment capital, you discuss the market with a qualified investment counsellor at your convenience.

Life Insurance Considerations

Another topic that must be considered is life insurance. If you are like most Canadians, you have at least some coverage. If you have permanent insurance as opposed to a term policy, you should try to ensure that your coverage is paid up by the time you retire. I wouldn't like to see anyone in a position where he or she is bound to pay premiums after the earned-income years are ended. If you have a whole life policy, the chances are that it has a cash surrender value. The cash surrender value can be drawn out and used to pay premiums or to buy additional paid-up insurance, it can be turned into an annuity, or it can be used as security for a loan.

In some instances, if you draw the cash surrender value out, you will be taxed. Also, if you surrender your policy, your coverage ceases. On the other hand, you may be able to borrow against a policy under very favourable conditions. If you have life insurance, especially policies with cash surrender values, you can see that it is necessary to make an important decision. This should only be done after careful consideration and with a full understanding of all the options. Once you make your decision, it is probably irrevocable. By all means, speak to your own insurance agent, but I also suggest that you get some independent advice as well from an accountant, lawyer, or other financial adviser.

Effective Estate-Planning Techniques

Finally, consider your estate planning. This topic is covered in detail in Chapter Sixteen. If you are married, your concern should generally be directed not only to your own retirement, but also to the financial needs of your spouse. If you have a large estate, no doubt you will be somewhat concerned about passing assets on to your children, or maybe even grandchildren, at as inexpensive a tax cost as possible. Again, I counsel you to sit down and discuss estate planning with your own advisers.

Fortunately, the tax rules relating to husbands and wives are quite generous. Very simply, under Canadian tax law an entire estate can pass from husband to wife or wife to husband without triggering any adverse income-tax implications whatsoever. In other words, you don't have to pay any taxes on the transmission of an estate until the last of husband and wife die. This is unless you want to trigger taxes earlier by passing certain assets on to other beneficiaries.

In some cases, you may not want to pass assets directly to your spouse but might instead prefer to use a trust. This would apply if you want to direct the ultimate disposition of your property so that it passes on to the beneficiaries that *you* so intend. A good example of when a trust will is appropriate is if you or your spouse is in your second marriage and either of you has adult children by previous marriages. You may want to ensure that your spouse is protected but, in the final analysis, you may want to take steps to guarantee that your assets pass to your children and not necessarily to those of your spouse. Again, family circumstances are always different and your accountant and lawyer are there to advise you.

I recommend that before you retire, you make calculations of the projected income from your assets both in your lifetime and in the event that you die. In other words, even if you and your spouse could live together comfortably at present, the big question often is can your spouse maintain a lifestyle if you predecease? For example, when you die, your Old Age Pension will no longer be paid. Your spouse, on the other hand, will continue to receive any pensions that he or she may be entitled to by virtue of being age sixty-five or over. Payments from the Canada Pension may be substantially different as well and, as I already mentioned, the provisions with respect to private employment-related pensions vary dramatically, depending on circumstances. In some instances, there is a substantial reduction if a former employee dies, and in other cases, there is even a complete discontinuance. Sometimes, ongoing payments would only be made as long as the surviving spouse does not remarry.

Effective in 1987, the Pension Benefit Standards Act is to be amended to significantly alter existing pension legislation. The new rules will provide increased portability, transferability at the time of a job change, and several measures designed to improve pensions for women. Specifically, survivor pensions will no longer be terminated if the survivor remarries and the value of pension credits and pensions already being paid will be split equally between spouses upon marriage breakdown. While welcome change is apparently around the corner, I suggest that you still be conservative in dealing with the question of maintaining your spouse's lifestyle after your death.

Perhaps to some extent, life insurance will balance against potential income reductions in these circumstances. If you maintain an insurance policy that pays off at the time of death, keep in mind that the full proceeds are tax-free. The investment yield from your insurance can certainly be used by your spouse to offset reductions in income from other sources.

Normally if you die, the fair market value of any RRSP would be included as part of your income in the year of death. However, if you bequeath your RRSP to your spouse, he or she can roll it into another RRSP and delay payment of taxes until money is actually received. In order to have such a "rollover," however, it's extremely important for you to have a proper will.

Making a Will

It appears that at least half of all Canadians who die in any given year don't have wills. Believe me that the problems and expenses caused by not having a will can be astronomical. I cannot stress how important it is for you and your spouse to have up-to-date wills.

In preparing your will, keep in mind that circumstances change from time to time. For example, what if you sell your home? Instead of having real estate as perhaps your major asset, you might now have cash. Make sure that your dependent family members are well provided for. In some instances, if there are more than enough assets to adequately maintain your spouse, I think you should consider bequests to your children at the time of your death and not necessarily when the last of husband and wife dies. In my opinion, it is possible to overprotect a spouse and that is almost as bad as underprotecting. Why make the children wait until they are in their fifties or sixties to inherit property? This is often the case if one of the spouses lives into his or her late seventies or eighties.

In putting your affairs in order, make sure all your documentation is easily accessible. For example, your birth certificate, social insurance number, prior years' tax returns, marriage certificate, description of all securities that you own and their locations, and a list of safety deposit boxes, key numbers, and where they are, should all be easy to find. Your insurance policies should also be readily accessible as well as your current will. If you have made prior wills, I suggest that you destroy them so that there is no confusion.

Summary

If you plan properly for your retirement, you will find that a tremendous load will be lifted from your shoulders—the necessity of scrounging to earn money to pay your living expenses will be gone. You will find that, perhaps for the first time, your income will be permanent and not dependent on keeping a job. Pension income and income from investments will come in without any further requirement to work or perform. You will be able to spend your days in a manner that you desire and your money will continue to roll in. The work of the past will provide the income of the future, leaving you free to enjoy the rest of your life.

CHAPTER ELEVEN

Incorporating Your Earnings—
The Ultimate Solution?

Advantages of Personal-Service Companies

By definition, a personal-service corporation is a company that earns fees or commission income. Generally, the income arises as a direct result of the activities of one or a few individuals. Personal-service corporations set up in the past include:

1. Professional corporations (in the province of Alberta only) for doctors, dentists, lawyers, and accountants;
2. Management companies for professionals; and
3. Corporations for athletes, entertainers, executives, commissioned salespeople, and business consultants.

Personal-service companies can be used for tax-planning purposes in a variety of situations. Perhaps their most common application is for professionals and other individuals who are in a position to contract their services through the use of a corporation. In most provinces, only *individuals* can lawfully carry on certain activities, such as the practice of law, medicine, dentistry, or public accountancy. The exception is in the province of Alberta, which passed legislation in 1976 allowing taxpayers in the professions the right to incorporate in full. In other provinces, professionals can incorporate part of their practices through the use of a management company.

The advantages of personal-service corporations stem from the fact that "active business income" of a Canadian-controlled private company qualifies for a small-business tax rate of around 25% on the first $200,000 of profits each year (the actual rate varies from province to province). Although any profits over $200,000 are taxed at approximately 50%, it is unlikely that the profits of most service companies in any given year (after salaries are paid out) would be in excess of $200,000 in any event. Thus, the high rate of tax is not really applicable.

Management companies have also been used by taxpayers in an attempt to transform what was previously employment income into income from a business.

To summarize the advantages of management companies (where they have been successful in avoiding the attack of Revenue Canada):

- They provide the ability to split income between members of one's family—as long as salaries paid are for services rendered and are reasonable in the circumstances. Income splitting by way of dividends is also available.
- They create the existence of a new taxpayer (the corporation itself), which may qualify for a low rate of tax of approximately 25% on business income. After-tax dollars retained by the company can then be invested on behalf of its "owners."
- As retained earnings accumulate, depending on how the management company is set up as to shareholdings, estate freezing and income splitting can both be achieved. These topics were discussed fully in Chapter Nine.
- A management or service company earning business income may be subject to much more liberal deductions for expenses than would an individual's employment income. The corporation could pay for such costs as conventions, business-promotion expenses, and owning and/or operating an automobile.

In the past, one of the major reasons for incorporation has been the inability of a taxpayer carrying on an unincorporated business to pay a salary to a spouse. In 1980, however, this restriction was eliminated and such salaries now constitute valid deductions for tax purposes. Of course, the remuneration will have to be included in the spouse's income and the payments must be reasonable in relation to services rendered. The spouse paying the salary must also be carrying on a bona fide *business* activity.

Professionals and others who employ spouses in their businesses may now find that the advantages of incorporation are reduced considerably. It will now be useful to incorporate only where profits are in excess of their families' spending requirements and where the corporate rate is to be preferred relative to higher personal marginal tax rates, or if there is an advantage in paying dividends. These matters will all be discussed in the next three chapters, which include tax-planning techniques for any Canadian private corporation, large or small.

Incorporated Executives and Senior Employees

One important recent tax change means that incorporated employees are no longer able to avail themselves of low corporate rates of tax. An incorporated employee is defined as an individual whose relationship with the person to whom services are rendered can "reasonably be considered to be that of an officer or employee and his employer." Such corporations are also prohibited from claiming *any* business expenses.

The new rules apply for taxation years commencing after November 12, 1981. Professionals, independent sales agents, entertainers, and bona fide consultants are *not* affected by these new rules.

Professional Corporations

As I mentioned previously, Alberta is the only province that allows professionals to incorporate their practices in full. A professional corporation is somewhat of a hybrid between an individual and a corporation. By law, the only shareholder is the professional himself or herself. In other words, no splitting of shareholdings among spouses or other members of the family is permitted. In addition, the professional remains personally liable for all the debts and obligations of the corporation. The "unlimited liability" factor gives the public the same security as if it were dealing with the professional directly. This applies with respect to professional matters, trade debts, and any other obligations. In all other respects, the professional corporation is, however, a validly constituted entity. As such, corporate, and not personal, tax rates apply.

In general, tax planning for the professional corporation is rather simple. The corporation is set up to handle all billings, and it pays all expenses. The professional is paid a salary equal to his or her (pre-tax) living requirements. Wherever possible, the corporation also pays salaries to members of the profession-al's family for their assistance. Naturally, where such salaries are paid, the professional can thus afford to draw less money, thereby remaining in a lower tax bracket.

Corporate tax rates then apply to surplus profits. Usually, the corporate tax rate is significantly less than the marginal rate that would otherwise apply to the professional. Consequently, the corporation becomes an investment vehicle for after-tax profits. Some of the profits are used to finance the costs of business expansion, to pay for equipment, and to carry receivables from clients or patients. The balance can be invested in whatever types of investments the "owner" so desires.

Management Companies for Professionals

Outside Alberta, where professionals may not legally incorporate, many doctors, dentists, lawyers, and accountants have formed service companies that perform many of the management functions connected with a professional practice. Revenue Canada has indicated that corporations may be used by practising members of the professions in certain circumstances. The services that such corporations can provide would include:

- Negotiating and signing leases for the premises from which the practice is carried on, and handling monthly rental payments.
- Hiring and training of staff and maintaining payroll and other personnel records.
- Purchasing supplies and acquiring or leasing all necessary furnishings, including equipment that may be required by the practitioner to carry on his or her professional practice.
- Providing accounting services, including billing and collection of accounts receivable.

In a typical situation, most of these services are provided by the corporation on a cost-plus basis. The corporation computes its costs of performing these services and adds a profit factor, which is charged back to the professional. Rates ranging from 10% to 15% have not been considered unreasonable. Ironically, the higher the overhead of the professional's operation, the greater the dollar amount of profit that can be transferred to the corporation.

Payment of an agreed fee to the corporation has the effect of reducing the professional's income by the amount of the profit factor. Where the individual is already in a high tax bracket, the result is an immediate tax deferral equal to the difference between his or her marginal tax bracket and that of the corporation. This is illustrated in Figure 11-1.

Figure 11-1 **Management Companies Reduce a Professional's Personal Taxes**

Without management company:

Gross income of professional	$120,000
Less: Expenses to operate practice	50,000
Professional's net profit subject to tax	$ 70,000

With management company:

Gross income of professional	$120,000
Less: Management fees paid	65,000
Professional's net profit subject to tax	$ 55,000
Fee income of corporation	$ 65,000
Less: Expenses "taken over" from professional	50,000
Corporation's net profit subject to tax	$ 15,000

$15,000 is "extracted" from the professional's highest marginal tax bracket and is taxed instead at lower corporate rates.

In addition, if one can justify a salary payable to members of the family, there is a tax *saving* equal to the difference between the professional's marginal rate and that of the other family members. Whether earnings are retained corporately or paid out as salaries depends primarily on the living requirements of the professional and his or her family. A management company can also be used as a vehicle to invest surplus funds not required for living expenses.

Professional Corporations Versus Management Companies

Using the management company concept in your business planning may not be quite as advantageous as having a professional corporation. This is because only a relatively small amount of profits can be transferred out of the professional's hands and into a corporation. The management company does, however, permit one specific form of income splitting that is not available through the professional corporation. The management company may pay dividends out of after-tax profits to members of the professional's family—as long as these family members own shares in the company. This is not permitted in the case of a professional corporation, since only the professional is permitted to be a shareholder. Nevertheless, the ability to incorporate one's *total* earnings and the opportunity to maintain only one set of records favours the professional corporation. I expect that several of the other provinces will eventually join Alberta in passing enabling legislation. Certainly, it would be worthwhile for professionals across the country to lobby for these privileges. This is especially true as a result of the government's most recent decision to remove the tax biases against professionals, which are discussed in the next few pages.

Federal Legislation Governing the Use of Service Companies: 1979 to the Present

In order to understand whether or not benefits can be achieved through incorporation of a service company, it is necessary to learn how the rules have been amended over the past five years or so. You will see that we have come "full circle" in just this short span of time.

First, in 1979, Parliament enacted important legislation relevant to service companies, in order to more closely regulate the types of activity that would qualify for the very low small-business tax rate and to curtail abuses of the rate.

As of 1980, corporations used by doctors, dentists, lawyers, accountants, chiropractors, and veterinarians were no longer able to use the small-business tax rate. The tax rate for them was boosted to approximately $33\frac{1}{3}\%$. This was a compromise rate between the low rate previously available and the 50% corporate tax rate that applies in other cases.

While some professionals (through their governing bodies) voiced displeasure with these rules, the after-tax results were still much more favourable than would be the case where an individual practitioner was unincorporated. It was rare that one would encounter an established professional earning income insufficient to put him or her into a 50% bracket. Thus, where the individual was earning more than what he or she needed to live, it was certainly preferable to pay a tax rate of $33\frac{1}{3}\%$ than to pay 50%. The obvious tax advantage was the ability to reinvest

16^{2}/$_{3}$% of earnings not required for living expenses. This did not even take into account the other advantages of incorporation, such as profit sharing with members of one's family, as well as the opportunity to use the corporation as a vehicle for the investment of retained earnings.

In a sense, this legislation was a blessing in disguise. In the past, professionals worried that Revenue Canada would not recognize a valid tax status for their corporations. Senior officials had threatened that they would disallow the existence of these corporations and attribute all income back to the professionals. Alternatively, Revenue Canada had considered deeming these corporations (even if valid as separate entities) as not earning active business income, and as such not qualifying for the preferred low rate. Certainly, if a 50% tax were imposed on the income of a professional's corporation, most of the advantage of incorporating would be lost.

In the April 1980 Budget, a proposal was made that was subsequently adopted, curtailing the use of even the 33^{1}/$_{3}$% rate for corporate professional *partnerships*. Basically, this rule required all corporations acting in partnership to share between them one annual business limit of $200,000, which would qualify for the 33^{1}/$_{3}$% rate. Thus, in the case of a large partnership, the advantages of incorporation on a per-person basis became much less significant. In spite of the changes in tax rates described below, this "sharing" concept has been retained within the tax system.

I therefore recommend that wherever possible, corporate partnerships be dissolved. Instead, the organization should be structured as independent practices sharing common overheads. In other words, wherever possible, each individual company should do its own billings to patients, customers, or clients and a formula should be evolved for prorating *overheads only*. Each corporation would therefore be a completely separate entity. This is probably feasible for many medical and dental practices. In addition, this idea may have merit for certain law practices as well. The larger accounting firms may have more difficulty in implementing such an approach since it may not be practical. In the case of accounting firms, different accountants often do work for the same client during a given year and it would be difficult to split the billings.

The February 1984 Budget

In a surprising reversal of policy, the government decided to eliminate the special tax rates pertaining to incorporated professionals. As part of the small-business simplification proposals, the budget of February 15, 1984, proposed that incorporated accountants, lawyers, doctors, dentists, veterinarians, and chiropractors be treated for tax purposes in the same manner as any other business. In other words, the small-business tax rates would apply on the first $200,000 of annual business profits, although incorporated groups would still have to share one annual limit.

The relevant legislation was enacted in 1985, and it now becomes more attractive than ever before for professionals to incorporate their activities. Again, since the federal government now appears to be recognizing that a professional practice is basically the same as any other business, I strongly suggest that professionals in provinces outside Alberta begin to lobby for the right to incorporate their entire operations.

The Future of Service Corporations

With respect to entertainers, commissioned salespersons, and consultants, the 1984 tax changes provide that, beginning in 1985, the small-business tax rate will apply *as long as the corporation is in fact carrying on a business*. If, on the other hand, the corporation is nothing more than an "incorporated employee," Revenue Canada will be justified in disallowing any low corporate tax rate entirely. The question of "what is a business" is more than ever the key question within the framework of tax planning. If a corporation has not got a business purpose and its only objective is to reduce taxes otherwise payable, the rules that I described in the section on incorporated employees will allow the Minister of National Revenue to look through the corporation and deem its owners to be earning personal employment income. The following sections examine the current status of specific types of service companies.

Athletes
It will be difficult for most incorporated football or hockey

players to consider their sporting activities as an active business. Since athletes clearly earn their incomes through *personal* service, a corporation will not provide any benefits. However, what about other income, such as from advertising or endorsements? If a corporation earns significant income from other activities of this kind, it is likely that the corporation can show that it has a valid business purpose. If that is the case, it appears that the corporation will be allowed to stand and that the low tax rate of around 25% will apply. This results in a substantial deferral when compared to a personal rate of 50%.

Entertainers

Canadian entertainers should be able to benefit nicely from the amended tax rules since, in most cases, they will have sufficient diversity of income to substantiate the fact that they are carrying on a business. To illustrate how arbitrary the rules are, however, consider the position of an entertainer who has a solo act and accepts a long-term contract to perform in one place. His company may become ineligible in that year for the small-business tax rate. However, where that same entertainer performs his nightclub act in several different locations during the year (even within the same city), his company would qualify for the small-business incentive.

Commissioned Salespeople and Other Consultants

For commissioned salespeople and other consultants, the service-corporation rules mean that special care must be taken in order to meet the required guidelines. Consider, for example, the case of two incorporated insurance agencies—one selling general insurance and the other selling life insurance. Assume that both have no outside employees. Because it sells insurance on behalf of several insurance companies, the general insurance agency would automatically qualify for a 25% tax rate. On the other hand, a life insurance agency typically sells insurance on behalf of one major insurance company. Since its commission revenue comes primarily from one entity, it may be classified as a business that will not qualify for the low rate. Notwithstanding the law, one can argue that this is unfair. This is because both companies are independent agents and have basically similar business activities. Unfortunately, fairness doesn't count in this case.

As a further illustration, a structural engineer whose corporation services one major client in a given year could find his or her company blocked from the low rate of tax for that year unless he or she can clearly prove independence. This may suggest a merger with other unrelated companies within the same field, and if the engineer is not willing to merge, he or she would have to take into account the cost of higher taxes as a penalty for accepting one major client or contract. (Even a merger may not be advisable, since the problem here would be the requirement that the low-rate base of $200,000 be shared among otherwise unrelated parties.)

Incorporated Executives—Revisited

For an executive's management company to qualify for the small-business rate, it is imperative that the individual remove all signs of employment. If the individual is a shareholder, he or she may continue to retain stock, but should resign any director-ship and cease to hold a position as a company officer. A bona fide attempt to achieve diversity of income is extremely important. In cases where a former employer requires the executive to carry out his or her activities solely for and on behalf of that company, the use of a personal-service corporation is no longer viable. Revenue Canada will just look through the company and tax its income at top rates of 50%.

While the legislation pertaining to incorporated employees has not yet been tested, I don't think that an executive will be able to "beat the system" by simply contracting services to several different subsidiaries of the same employer. This will probably not constitute diversity of income. Similarly, an executive will not be able to take advantage of the tax rules by taking a few employees onto his or her payroll who were previously employed by the ex-employer. Revenue Canada will deem this arrangement to be a sham.

If, however, the executive truly does have "outside" consulting income, a corporation may still be viable. The executive would be required to report his or her major income sources as personal employment income, but could still shelter miscellaneous fees through a corporation. In practice, a decision will probably depend on the dollars involved. Only the individual can judge if the tax deferral is worthwhile.

Organizing the Personal-Service Company

For most people, the question of whether or not to set up a personal-service company cannot be resolved without the assistance of professional advisers. Your accountant and lawyer should be able to explain your tax position to you, and also *quantify the benefits* that you may derive. Since each individual's income, expenses, family situation, and living requirements are different, you cannot simply rely on what your friends are doing when it comes to making your own business decisions.

Assuming that such a company is advisable, how is one set up? The steps would include the following:

- You must decide whether or not the company is to be exclusively concerned with one type of activity only, or whether it will undertake many different kinds of projects.
- You must then incorporate a company with the appropriate objectives and share capital—including the right to reinvest accumulated income in diversified investments.
- The shares must then be issued to the intended shareholders. (At this stage, estate-planning considerations should be taken into account by having, in some cases, the incorporator's spouse and/or children subscribe for shares in the corporation.)
- You must arrange for a management agreement between you, as the incorporator, and the company to be prepared in writing. The agreement should set out in detail the services to be provided by the corporation and the fees to be charged for such services.
- In the case of a professional practice, the present employees (other than those who are required to be employed directly by the professional) should become employees of the corporation. The change of employers should not be overlooked when preparing annual T-4 slips.
- The corporation should then proceed to do everything necessary to enable it to operate. These activities would include opening bank accounts, obtaining a telephone listing, ordering stationery with an appropriate letterhead, arranging with Revenue Canada to make required payroll deductions, and generally carrying out all steps necessary to perform its management contract.

Each step must be carried out in a proper and specific sequence in order to avoid problems at a later date. For example, the corporation should not begin to render services until after its charter has been obtained and the management and employment contracts have been duly and properly signed. In addition, if one is setting up a personal-service company *following* the severing of one's relationship with an employer, all signs of the previous employment relationship should be removed. For example:

- The individual should no longer be allowed to sign letters or contracts on behalf of the former employer—especially using the former employer's letterhead.
- The former employee should be removed from the former employer's group insurance and pension plans.
- If possible, the service company should operate out of different premises from those in which the former employer carries on its business.
- A company-owned or company-leased car should be surrendered and/or transferred by the past employer to the new service company.
- The executive's corporation must be permitted to carry on outside work as long as it is not in direct conflict with the contractual arrangements with the former employer. Again, if the former employer is unwilling to completely sever the employer-employee relationship, the corporation should probably not be formed in the first place.

CHAPTER TWELVE

Tax Planning for New Business Ventures

New businesses can make use of a number of strategies that maximize their returns and minimize the risks if the business turns out to be unsuccessful. There are different strategies for unincorporated and incorporated business ventures, so one of your major objectives should be to decide whether you should or should not incorporate.

How to Show You Are in Business

In many instances, a new business will produce a loss in its initial phases. Business losses are deductible against income, but only provided that *the business had at least an expectation of profit*.

Income-tax assessors are very strict about differentiating between a viable business on the one hand and a hobby on the other. There are certain steps that you can take from the very start to show that you are actually going to be carrying on a bona fide business. First, you should choose a name for your venture that is descriptive of the goods, services, or activities that you will be providing. Even if you don't incorporate, your business name should be registered. This is a relatively simple procedure but you would be well advised to seek some assistance in this area from your lawyer. Then, once your name has been accepted, a bank account should be opened in the name of that business. All income received from the business should be deposited to that bank account. Any expenses pertaining to your business should be paid out of that same account by cheque.

One of the biggest mistakes that beginners often make is to intermingle their business records with their personal records. Not only does this show that you don't really have confidence in the viability of your business but it also makes the record keeping for tax purposes at the end of the year that much more difficult to sort through.

Perhaps most important is that you must keep reasonable books and records of your activities. If your business is just starting out, you certainly don't need a sophisticated system. Basically, all that's required is a ledger in which you keep track of your receipts and disbursements. Even if you have no book-keeping training whatsoever, a half-hour spent with a qualified accountant should be enough to show you how to keep these simple records. You will be able to total your figures on a monthly basis and balance your records against your bank statements. Then, at the end of the year, if you have no desire to learn accounting, you can get your accountant to make the necessary summaries and prepare your annual financial statements.

From the very outset, I believe that it is worth your while to invest a few dollars in order to print proper stationery, invoices, and any other forms that you require. If you don't want to go through the expense of printing, at least have some rubber stamps made showing your business's name, address, and telephone number.

While on the subject of telephone numbers, one of the key criteria to convincing Revenue Canada that you are involved in a viable business activity is a separate telephone line with a listing in your business's name, especially if you are going to operate out of your house.

Finally, I believe it's extremely important from the very outset (even before you commit yourself to any other expenditures) to prepare a budget for your first year of operations. This budget should show your anticipated revenues and also the types and amounts of expenses that you expect to incur. Then, you yourself will be able to determine whether or not your business does in fact have a reasonable expectation of profit. If you are counting on your business to provide a livelihood for yourself and your family, you should budget for a regular draw from that business to meet your personal and living expenses. Your budget should also take into account all capital expenditures that you may require, such as furniture, fixtures, equipment, special vehicles, and so on.

In most cases, a new business requires external financing from a lending institution. If you can convince your banker that you have a reasonable expectation of profit, that should also help you if you ever run into problems with Revenue authorities.

One important word of caution. There are all kinds of potential business operations in which you can get involved. These range from wholesaling to retailing, manufacturing, construction, farming, and so on.

One very popular business activity is to become a consultant and earn your income by rendering services either on a commission or fee basis. Generally, a business tends to get much more favourable tax deductions than does employment income. In addition, as I'll explain later in this chapter, if the business is profitable and you incorporate, you may be able to take advantage of corporate tax rates that are significantly lower than personal rates on equivalent amounts of income.

Because businesses do enjoy favourable tax treatment, there has been an inclination over the last ten years or so for many people to incorporate service companies even in situations where they can be more readily considered to be earning employment income. One good example is the individual who is perhaps a middle-income executive with a large company. The executive resigns his or her position of employment and forms a personal consulting company through which he or she renders services back to the former employer. Another example is the commissioned salesperson who devotes perhaps all of his or her time and effort towards selling the products produced by one company only.

In the last couple of years, the Revenue authorities have begun to crack down on people who are really employees of another entity but who try to erect the façade of self-employment. If you are contemplating a service venture, you must be sure that you will truly be an independent contractor, regardless of whether you will be receiving fees or commissions. If your relationship with the entity that pays for your services can reasonably be considered employer-employee, then any attempt to take tax advantages from business expenses or from incorporating will be negated under the law. If you are in doubt as to your status, read Chapter Eleven carefully. You are also well advised to spend an hour or so reviewing your situation with your own tax adviser.

Do I Start a Business or Buy One?

Leaving aside the subject of service businesses, I suppose I can generalize and suggest that there are two ways of starting a business. Either you begin one by yourself or you buy the assets of somebody else's business. If you are buying a going concern, you must make sure that your contract specifies exactly what you are buying. This is extremely important for tax purposes since the tax rules are quite different, depending on whether you are purchasing inventory, depreciable assets, customer lists, or what have you. In most jurisdictions, the purchase of property other than inventory will be subject to provincial sales tax considerations. Make sure that you acquire the necessary licences in order to claim sales tax exemption in the proper circumstances. For example, if you are buying property for resale, you are usually, if not always, exempt from provincial sales tax on your purchases.

If you buy someone else's business and pay more than the value of all tangible assets acquired, the difference is usually allocated to goodwill. This is because, if you are buying a going concern, you will be able to capitalize on the time and effort that were put in by someone else to help get that particular business established.

For tax purposes, half of the cost of goodwill can be deducted at the rate of 10% a year on a declining-balance basis. In other words, if you spend $20,000 for goodwill, your first year's tax write-off is 10% of $10,000. In the second year, you may claim 10% of $9,000, and in the third year, 10% of $8,100. This is illustrated in Figure 12-1.

Figure 12-1 **Tax Consequences of Purchasing Business Goodwill**

Cost of goodwill—$20,000
Portion subject to amortization for
   tax purposes (50%) $10,000
First year's tax write-off   1,000 (10% × $10,000)
                                9,000
Second year's tax write-off   900 (10% × $ 9,000)
                                8,100
Third year's tax write-off   810 (10% × $ 8,100)
                           $ 7,290

The opportunity to write off only half the cost of goodwill over a period of time is not particularly attractive. If, on the other hand, part of your purchase cost can be reasonably allocated to the value of a lease, or a franchise that runs for a specific length of time, then the tax rules will permit you to deduct your *full* cost over the time remaining before the lease or franchise expires. It is certainly worth your while to take that little bit of extra time to negotiate with the seller of the business to have part of your purchase price allocated to properties for which you can claim a full depreciation instead of a write-off based on only half your cost.

What If I Incur Losses?

One of your most important tasks is to try to estimate whether or not your business will be profitable from the outset. If it is likely that your business will generate a loss for tax purposes, my general advice, subject to the comments I will make in the next few pages, is *don't incorporate*. Under the Canadian tax system, business losses can be carried back three years as an offset against prior years' income or forward up to seven years.

Let's assume that you have decided to go into business for yourself after many years of having been employed by someone else. If your business generates a loss, you can offset that loss against your other income for that same year and, if the loss exceeds your other income, you have, as I just mentioned, the option to carry back up to three years. If you take this option, what effectively happens is that you can recover prior years' taxes payable against your salary income.

If, on the other hand, you were to incorporate, the loss carry-over rules would be the same—except for one thing. A corporation is a separate legal entity and, as such, *the losses of that corporation cannot be used to recover personal taxes that you yourself have paid*. In other words, the corporation would have no choice but to carry its loss forward against future income—if and when profits are eventually made. In order to maximize your tax savings from a business loss, the object of the game is always to try to use that loss as quickly as possible. Thus, incorporating a new business can present a substantial disadvantage.

On the other hand, you must always keep in mind one of the greatest advantages of incorporation—that is, limited liability. If the business is unsuccessful, the unsecured creditors, such as your suppliers, cannot generally come back against you personally for amounts owing. The only time there is personal recourse is in cases where you have given a personal guarantee. So, to summarize, what you really have to do in a situation where a business loss is anticipated is weigh the two alternatives: the tax advantages of offsetting losses against personal income compared to the danger that might exist if your business venture is totally unsuccessful and, in the final analysis, the business becomes insolvent.

Generally, the major creditor of any venture, new or old, is the business's lender. Today, it is very rare for any lending institution to provide financing without the personal guarantee of the principals. So, if your business is financed, for example, with a $50,000 bank loan and only owes, say, an average of $10,000 at any given time to other creditors, the corporate advantage of limited liability is not that substantial. After all, if the business turns sour, it doesn't make much difference whether you end up owing $50,000 under your guarantee or $60,000 to both your lender and your other creditors.

In any event, once you understand the principles involved, I suggest that you spend a few minutes with your own advisers before you decide whether or not to incorporate.

Husband-Wife Partnerships

One further option that you might consider, even if you don't incorporate, is having your business structured as a partnership between you and your spouse. One of the major advantages of such an arrangement is the opportunity to split income in order to take advantage of lower personal tax brackets. This is an important concept that is quite unique to Canada and I have provided a detailed discussion of income splitting within the family business in Chapter Thirteen.

Setting up a husband/wife partnership has another major benefit beyond the splitting of income. There could also be an advantage if your business incurs losses in the initial stages. For example, let's assume your situation is such that both you and your spouse have full-time jobs. However, you've hit upon what you think is a good business idea and initially you believe you can operate that business on evenings and weekends. You expect, however, that in the first year or so, the business will generate losses for income-tax purposes. If both you and your spouse are in relatively equal tax brackets, you might be better off splitting the loss through a partnership arrangement rather than having the loss incurred by one person only. This would mean that the taxes recovered would be from the higher end of the scale. A partnership might then be very much to your advantage.

If you do set up a husband/wife business partnership, I make the strong suggestion that you prepare proper documentation—in other words, a *written* partnership agreement. If your arrangement is audited, the tax department will take the relevant documentation into account as well as the question of whether both parties are at risk of losing capital. For example, if you take a mortgage against your home, which is jointly owned, in order to provide funds for your business, this will show that both you and your spouse are sharing the risk.

Another important factor is the time and effort that is spent in administering the operations. If both spouses contribute equal amounts of capital and equal portions of time and effort, you would expect that profits should be divided 50/50. On the other hand, if one spouse operates the business exclusively while both spouses contribute equally to the required capital, perhaps a 75/25 or 60/40 split might be more appropriate. Again, these are matters that you might discuss with your own advisers. The profit-sharing ratio should also apply to losses as well.

Selecting a Year End

After deciding how your business is going to be structured, whether as a proprietorship, partnership, or corporation, your next step is to select your business's year end. Now, what are the various criteria for selecting a year end? First of all, as you probably already know, an individual is deemed to have a calendar year end for Canadian tax purposes. However, a business can pick any year-end date that it desires as long as there is consistency after the first year. The only other rule is that no business can have a fiscal cycle that is longer than twelve months in total.

For the first reporting period for tax purposes, it is permissible to select a year end less than twelve months after commencement of business operations. In theory, for example, if you start your business on March 30 of a given year, you can even take March 31 as your first year end. In other words, you could conceivably have as little as a one-day business year the first time around. However, after that first year end, you are committed to a March 31 year end each year subsequently. The only exception is if you apply in writing for a change of year end to your local District Office of Revenue Canada and permission for a year-end change is granted. Normally, you would require a good business reason for such a change to be accepted, such as a drastic shift in the nature of your products or services.

What I would like to do now is review some of the criteria for selecting your new business's year end. First of all, let's assume your business starts off as an unincorporated venture. You begin to carry on operations in mid-March 1986, on a part-time basis, while you continue to earn income from employment. If you select a year end any time in the 1986 calendar year, and your business is profitable, the income from that business would be added to your other income for the 1986 year. You would then have to pay your taxes on all this income no later than the end of April 1987. Conversely, if the business incurs a loss, as I indicated previously, you could offset that loss against your 1986 income.

On the other hand, what if you pick a year end in either January or February 1987? Even though your business will have operated for a period in excess of nine months in 1986, the business profits will only be reported when you file your 1987 income-tax return. In other words, you won't have to report your business profit until April 1988.

In simple terms, selecting a year end in the next calendar year gives you an initial tax deferral in cases where your business is profitable. Moreover, the tax deferral is an ongoing benefit. If, for example, you choose a January or February year end, your profits for the twelve months ended January or February 1988 will only be reported when you file your 1988 personal-income-tax return in April 1989. All of this is illustrated in Figure 12-2. On the other hand, if your business is going to sustain a loss in the first few months of operations, you may want a short initial year end sometime in 1986 in order to crystallize that loss so that you can offset it against your other income.

Figure 12-2 **Selecting a Year End for Your Business**

Individual is employed but also carries on a part-time business beginning mid-March 1986.

One alternative: Initial year end December 31, 1986
Income for 1986 (tax return due April 30, 1987)

Employment income	January–December 1986	12 months
Business income	March–December 1986	10 months

Income for 1987 (tax return due April 30, 1988)

Employment income	January–December 1987	12 months
	January–December 1987	12 months

Another alternative: Initial year end February 28, 1987
Income for 1986 (tax return due April 30, 1987)

Employment income	January–December 1986	12 months
Business income		Nil

Income for 1987 (tax return due April 30, 1988)

Employment income	January–December 1987	12 months
Business income	March 1986–February 1987	12 months

Business income taxable in 1988 (tax return due April 30, 1989)

Period from	March 1987–February 1988

So, the first criterion in selecting a year end is the question of whether or not you want a tax deferral. Again, a few minutes with your accountant can help you make this very crucial decision.

In many cases, the year end of a business is selected on the basis of seasonal considerations. For example, let's assume that you will be in a lumber-supply business. You will supply wood products to the building trades and to people who are doing renovations to their homes. Assume that you intend to stock a substantial inventory of wood products at an outdoor location. In most places in Canada, you wouldn't want to pick a year end in the heart of winter. After all, how could you count your inventory if it's covered in snow?

Often, businesses pick their year ends at a time when their inventory is lowest. This is because often the biggest difficulty in preparing financial statements is physically taking inventory. As I'll soon explain, however, you may want to pick a year end when your inventory is *highest* as long as you're dealing in "big-ticket items," which don't require too much effort to count.

A retail business will sometimes adopt a flexible year end,

such as the last Saturday in January. This way, it can count its stock each year on the day following the year end—a Sunday—when the business is generally closed to trade and it becomes relatively easy to manoeuvre around the store. Always pay attention to your own circumstances before making a choice of a year end.

The 3% Inventory Deduction

Before selecting your year end, however, there are two further items that should be considered. The first is the 3% inventory deduction. Back in 1977, the government of Canada introduced a special tax concession for businesses. In arriving at profits, any business is permitted to deduct 3% of its opening inventory of goods held for resale, whether these goods are finished goods, raw materials, or even work in progress. In other words, if you have a $100,000 inventory at the beginning of your business year, your profits for tax purposes are automatically $3,000 less than your accounting profits before considering other differences.

If your business year is less than twelve months long, however, the inventory deduction must be prorated. Since the inventory deduction is based on opening inventory, a new business will not ordinarily get any benefit in its first fiscal period. There is, however, a way to beat the system. If you are buying substantial inventory just at the time you start your business, you can establish your first year end immediately after your buying is completed. For that particular period, your business will have, at best, a break-even position and it is unlikely that you will have any income taxes payable. However, in your first full year of operations you will be able to claim an inventory deduction based on what then becomes an opening inventory.

There are other ways that the inventory deduction can be maximized as well. For example, you might consider establishing the year end of your business to coincide with the month in which your inventory level is generally the highest. As I suggested before, this would make sense if your business sells big-ticket items. Another opportunity is to arrange with your suppliers to provide you with inventory at the tail end of your business year on an extended credit plan. You don't even have to

212

take delivery. If you place an order and it is invoiced to you by your supplier before your year end, you can still include the purchased items as part of your inventory. Your supplier would warehouse your purchases but they would be part of your inventory for tax purposes.

In some instances, if you sell items such as cars or fur coats, you may be able to defer your sales for the last day or two. This way your closing inventory would be that much higher and that amount becomes your opening inventory for the next period. In addition, the profit on sale is deferred until the following tax year, as well. So, consider your inventory position before selecting a year end.

Capital Cost Allowances

Another point to consider is capital cost allowance or depreciation for tax purposes. Capital cost allowance under Canadian tax law is an optional deduction. You don't have to claim depreciation on machinery, equipment, buildings, or other assets owned by your business unless you want to. Most of the time, however, a profitable business claims the maximum capital cost allowance that it can in order to reduce income for tax purposes. In 1981, however, the government brought down legislation under which depreciation in the year any particular property is acquired is limited to one-half the tax write-off otherwise allowable. For example, while the ordinary depreciation rate on furniture and fixtures is 20% a year on a declining balance basis, in the year of acquisition you may only claim 10% of the cost of the property purchased.

What if your business is going to acquire substantial depreciable property right from the outset? Again, you might consider selecting your first year end right after your major fixed-asset acquisitions are completed. You don't have to claim capital cost allowance unless you want to, but the point is that in your first complete twelve months of operations that follow, you will then get a *full* capital-cost-allowance claim, instead of only one-half. If you do choose to claim capital cost allowance, you should be aware that you would have to prorate even the reduced amount (i.e., one-half the normal rate) over the number of days in that first fiscal period as a percentage of 365.

Employing Family Members

Earlier in this chapter, I discussed setting up your new business as a partnership between husband and wife. Even if you don't choose to use that format, keep in mind that your spouse can qualify as a legitimate employee of your business, whether it is an unincorporated proprietorship or a limited-liability company. Not only can your spouse be an employee, but you are permitted to pay tax-deductible wages to any of your children who are active in your business.

The opportunity to split income by paying salaries and wages to a spouse and other family members is one of the major attractions of any business. It is such an important concept that it merits a much more complete discussion in the next chapter.

Incorporation

From the outset, it is important that you note that any business can be incorporated except (generally) the professional practice of an accountant, lawyer, doctor, or dentist. Alberta is the only province in which professionals in these particular fields can incorporate all of their activities.

It really doesn't matter for income-tax purposes whether you incorporate your business to begin with or whether you incorporate perhaps several, or even many, years after your business is formed. There is a provision under Section 85 of the Income Tax Act that will permit an unincorporated business proprietorship or partnership to be transferred to a Canadian corporation without triggering income taxes in the hands of the transferor. Basically, the corporation assumes the assets and liabilities of the transferor and continues operating from that time on.

I don't wish to imply, however, that the rules of application of Section 85 are necessarily simple. The concept of what is commonly called a "tax-free rollover" is easy to understand. After all, if you simply move a business from your left hand to your right—in other words, you retain beneficial ownership of that business both before and after incorporation—you can see the logic of why you should be able to reorganize without triggering income for tax purposes.

However, the actual application of Section 85 is fairly complex and, if you do choose to incorporate a business that has already been operating, you must make sure to seek professional legal and accounting advice before moving ahead.

Let me, however, highlight some of the major points that you should consider. First, the opportunity to transfer business assets to a corporation without triggering taxes only applies if the corporation is a Canadian corporation. In other words, if you live in Canada but your business venture is in the United States, you may not transfer your business to a U.S. corporation on a rollover basis for Canadian tax purposes.

Generally, most business assets are eligible for the rollover. The one exception is real estate inventory. If you are in the business of buying and selling real estate, you may not transfer your holdings to a corporation without doing so at fair market value.

Perhaps the most important consideration, though, is family involvement. Even if you were previously operating your business as a proprietorship, you can, if you so desire, incorporate the business and allow your family members to become shareholders in the corporation. In this manner, they may participate in the future growth and income generated by that business. However, you must be very careful in structuring your transfer under Section 85 so as not to convey any retroactive benefits to related family members. Your accountant and lawyer can help you so that you do not run afoul of the rules.

Advantages of Incorporation

One of the major advantages of incorporation from a tax point of view is that it allows you the opportunity to use a corporation as a vehicle to split income among family members. As I explained earlier, if you wish to have salaries paid to members of your family, these people must be active in the day-to-day business operations. However, if the business is incorporated and your family members hold shares, the company can be structured to pay dividends out of profits in the ratio of the shareholdings. In this way, it is possible to split income among the family, even in cases where family members do not take active roles. Moreover, if the business is ever sold, having involved the family in the ownership sets the stage for capital-gains splitting as well.

In most cases, unless your children are actively involved or unless you as parents are very wealthy, it is unusual for a business, especially a new business, to be incorporated in such a manner that the children are shareholders. However, even if you choose not to involve your children as owners, bear in mind the advantages of splitting the shares with your spouse for the reasons mentioned in the previous paragraph.

There is one additional benefit of incorporation. Under existing Canadian tax rules, if shares of an active business company are passed on to children or grandchildren, a transferor is permitted to defer up to $200,000 in capital gains. This concept is referred to in the Income Tax Act as the Cumulative Small Business Gains Account. If a husband and wife are both shareholders, the $200,000 benefit is potentially doubled. The $200,000 amount applies on a per-transferor basis, irrespective of how many businesses one has and irrespective of how many children. You can take advantage of the opportunity to pass on shares in a private business without triggering capital-gains taxes *either* in your lifetime *or* on death. Of course, to double the advantage means that both husband and wife must be involved in the shareholdings.

You should note that the $200,000 cumulative small business gains account is due to be phased out in 1988 when the new general capital-gains tax exemption reaches $200,000. By 1990, the new exemption will be, as mentioned several times already in this book, $500,000. Again, splitting an ownership interest with a spouse means a potential escape from taxes on a family limit of $1,000,000 in capital gains. Over the next couple of years, it may be possible to "piggy-back" the old and new capital-gains tax relief provisions together on transfers of shares in family businesses from parents to children. At the time of writing, it is unclear whether the eventual legislation following the Spring 1985 Budget will block individuals from doing this. If the concept of "piggy-backing" appeals to you, I suggest that you contact your own professional advisers.

Possibly the most important advantage of incorporating a small business, however, arises in cases where a business earns more than what the owners require on an annual basis to meet their living expenses. The schedule in Figure 12-3 gives you an outline of what the 1985 tax rates are in various income brackets.

You can see that once you reach a taxable income of around $23,000, the government will begin to take almost forty cents out of each additional dollar that you earn. By way of contrast, a

216

Figure 12-3 **Approximate Marginal Tax Rates for Individuals—1985**

Taxable Income	Tax + Marginal Tax Bracket
$23,000	$ 6,000 + 37% on next $13,000
36,000	10,800 + 44% on next $24,000
60,000	21,400 + 50% on the remainder

Canadian-controlled private corporation that earns active business income pays taxes of around 25% on the first $200,000 of business profits. (The actual rate varies from province to province.) Thus, the theory behind proper tax planning should be quite evident. On excess profits not required by an owner-manager to meet living expenses, there is the opportunity to reinvest through the corporation seventy-five cents on the dollar, which is a lot better than reinvesting only sixty, fifty-five, or fifty cents on the dollar after the payment of personal income taxes.

You should note that the very generous small-business tax rate is designed to encourage and facilitate business expansion. However, after-tax profits can also be used to build up investment capital. A corporation can make whatever investments you might otherwise want to make personally. For example, a corporation can buy term deposits, invest in the stock market, or acquire real estate or even precious metals such as gold and silver.

If your business is involved in manufacturing or processing, there is an even better tax break, since the corporate tax rate is 5% less than the rate that applies to other small businesses. Thus, in total, your profits would only be subject to tax rates of approximately 20%, depending on the province in which you operate. This is discussed in more detail in Chapter Fourteen.

One of the most underrated aspects of a corporation that qualifies for small-business tax rates is the ability it has to repay business financing liabilities with cheaper after-tax dollars. Almost any business requires at least a certain amount of funding in order to get started. Whenever money is borrowed for business or investment purposes, the interest is, of course, tax-deductible but repaying the debt itself requires after-tax money. Thus, incorporation does provide you with the opportunity to use cheaply taxed funds for that purpose, instead of income that is first subjected to much higher personal-income-tax rates.

In these turbulent economic times, as I indicated previously, we must be concerned, unfortunately, not only with business profits but with losses as well. If a corporation is used for business purposes, "allowable business investment losses" become deductible from a shareholder's or noteholder's total income. This type of loss arises when a share or debt investment is made in a Canadian-controlled private corporation and the investment subsequently loses its value or, in fact, becomes completely worthless. In the year such a loss is realized, one-half of the loss, instead of being treated as an ordinary capital loss, becomes deductible from the shareholder's or noteholder's total income, irrespective of whether or not he or she has capital gains. By way of contrast, advances made to a proprietorship or partnership, either by way of loan or capital, are not given this treatment. They are treated as ordinary capital losses and may essentially only be deducted against capital gains from other sources.

Using a corporation to carry on business can also set the stage for using death-benefit programs in tax planning. In the event that a shareholder-manager dies, a death benefit received by his or her spouse, or perhaps even by other heirs, will be either partially or totally tax-free. The death-benefit concept is not available to the spouse of a proprietor or partner since the tax-free element is tied in to salaries previously paid. This was covered in Chapter Four.

Finally, by using a corporation, you may also introduce a retiring-allowance program (also dealt with in Chapter Four) and group life and health insurance plans, where these benefits are also tied in to salaries paid. These are matters that you should discuss with your own advisers once your business becomes profitable or if you are planning to retire within a short time.

Disadvantages of Incorporation

Of course, incorporation does have some disadvantages. I have already discussed some of these, such as the inability to use a corporate business loss as an offset against personal income. Another important disadvantage for a new business is the fact that a corporation carries with it the necessity of additional annual reporting requirements, including corporate tax returns. While this may not be a disadvantage from the standpoint of your lawyer or accountant, the cost is certainly a factor if you are an owner of a business.

Finally, recognize that incorporation is very much a one-way street. While, as I explained earlier, you can use Section 85 to transfer properties *into* a Canadian corporation, there is no rollover back to an individual shareholder on winding up the company. If assets are distributed in kind, the corporation will first be deemed to have disposed of its property at fair market value and this will trigger income. In addition, any distribution to the shareholders over and above the paid-up capital of the shares will be treated as a dividend. So, be careful. Don't transfer property into a company unless you want that company to keep that property until it is sold to third parties.

CHAPTER THIRTEEN

Tax Planning for the Private Canadian Business When the Small-Business Rate Applies

Before 1972, the calculation of corporate income taxes was quite simple. The first $35,000 of annual taxable income was taxed at approximately only 21%. Any taxable income in excess of $35,000 was taxed at around 50%. These were combined federal and provincial rates and, although the actual percentages varied slightly from province to province, the concept was clear: a low rate of tax applied initially, followed by a high rate thereafter.

Prior to 1972, no attempt was made to differentiate between large and small companies, and no significant attempt was made to distinguish between business and investment income. In the case of a small company, it was usually advantageous to declare bonuses to the owners in order to keep annual corporate taxable income below $35,000. Beyond that, very little tax planning could be done. Actually, since personal brackets at that time reached as high as 80%, one would not normally recommend large bonuses to avoid the corporate high rate. There was no advantage in "saving" taxes at 50%, when the "penalty" was payment of 80% at the personal level.

In trying to refine the corporate tax system, the legislators involved in tax reform came to two conclusions: (1) big companies do not need a low rate of tax to facilitate business expansion, and (2) a corporation should not be available as a vehicle for wealthy taxpayers to shelter investment income from what would otherwise be high rates of (personal) tax.

Under the current system, only Canadian-controlled private corporations are allowed to pay taxes at a low rate. The low rate is also restricted to "active business income." Investment income earned by a private company is initially taxed at 50%, but is subject to the refundable-tax rules, which were reviewed in

Chapter Nine. We have already seen how the tax system for investment income can effectively be beaten through family involvement. In this chapter and the next, we will examine the methods available to optimize after-tax profits from business operations.

The Canadian-Controlled Private Corporation

The "Canadian-controlled private corporation" is the only kind of company that still has low-rate privileges. By definition, a Canadian-controlled private corporation (CCPC) is a company that is *not controlled* by one or more non-residents *nor* by a combination of non-residents and Canadian public corporations. Because this definition is phrased in the negative, a corporation will qualify for CCPC status even where non-residents or public companies own exactly 50% of the voting shares.

It is not uncommon to find joint-venture arrangements in Canada between Canadian individuals and either public corporations or non-residents. If the joint venture is carried on through a separate corporation, which is owned exactly 50% by each, this corporation will qualify for favourable tax rates. It would often pay the non-residents or public companies to relinquish control for the benefit of the lower rates of tax that would then apply to the joint-venture corporation, since the lower the tax rate on earnings, the greater the ability to pay dividends.

Starting in 1982, the first $200,000 of active business income earned by a CCPC has been taxed at between 15% and 25% each year. The actual tax depends on the relevant provincial rate. At the present time, newly-formed CCPCs carrying on business in Ontario pay as little as 15% (10% if they are involved in manufacturing), since the Ontario government has given new small businesses a temporary provincial-tax holiday. Small businesses in Quebec pay tax at 18%, while those in Alberta pay 20%. In the other provinces, the combined federal and provincial tax rate is approximately 25%. Before 1985, the low rate only applied until $1 million of pre-tax profits had been earned on a cumulative basis for years after 1971. The optimum utilization of the low rate occurred if a company earned $200,000 each year for five years. If a corporation had the "misfortune," on the other hand, to earn the full $1 million in its first year of operations, the low rate of tax was only available in that one year. In subsequent years, having reached the maximum cumulative figure, the low rate did not apply. Before 1982, if dividends were paid out, the company could again become entitled to the low rate of tax. This is because personal taxes would then have become payable on dividends received by the shareholders. Between 1982 and 1984 the opportunity to reinstate entitlement to the small-business tax rate by paying dividends was no longer available—in spite of the fact that such dividends were (and are) still taxable.

Small-Business Simplification—The February 1984 Budget

In his Spring 1984 Budget, former Finance Minister Marc Lalonde proposed the elimination of the $1 million limit on the cumulative business income of a CCPC eligible for the small-business tax rate. This proposal was passed into law, and is effective for 1985 and subsequent years. Accordingly, Canadian private businesses no longer have to maintain a "cumulative-deduction account," the measurement of which was perceived as one of the most complex areas within the small-business tax system. (The cumulative-deduction account measured how much of the total business limit had been used up.) However, the annual business limit of $200,000 that qualifies for low tax rates remains unchanged.

The removal of the total business limit concept has the following impact:

1. The small-business tax rules have been substantially simplified and shortened and a good deal of tax reporting and year-to-year record keeping has been eliminated;
2. Corporations do not need sophisticated tax planning as they approach the $1 million limit. Corporations that were previously ineligible to take advantage of small-business tax rates because of excess cumulative earnings now find their eligibility for low-rate taxation restored. Thus, medium-sized businesses gain an increased opportunity to defer taxes on retained profits;
3. The corporate tax form has also been substantially shortened.

The government intends to maintain the concept of associated corporations, which is discussed in detail at the very end of this chapter. For the time being, however, you should note that if two or more corporations are under common control, they must share one allotment of the annual $200,000 limit. As mentioned in Chapter Eleven, corporate partnerships are also required to continue to share one small-business deduction, as well.

When a corporation has a taxation year less than twelve months in length, the annual business limit of $200,000 must be prorated, based on the number of days in the particular year as a percentage of 365. Before, corporations with short years were able to obtain full benefits from the small-business tax rates.

You should note that the removal of the $1 million total business limit should have a dramatic effect on future business acquisitions. Generally, business in Canada is carried on in corporate form. If someone wishes to acquire an existing business, there is usually the choice of either buying the shares of the corporation or the underlying assets. In the past, one of the reasons that many purchasers chose to acquire assets as opposed to shares was the reluctance to inherit the vendor's cumulative deduction account. For example, if an existing business had already used up, say, $700,000 out of its total business limit, a purchaser would be reluctant to acquire the corporation's shares, recognizing that under the new ownership only $300,000 of total future earnings would be eligible for favourable tax rates. This problem ceases to be relevant now that the new rules have been implemented. Even under new ownership, the corporation continues to qualify for low tax rates on $200,000 of annual business profits. The subject of business acquisitions is covered in Chapter Fifteen.

Definition of "Active Business Income"

Until a few years ago, the Income Tax Act did not contain any definition of the term "active business income." Accordingly, by diversifying their activities, taxpayers were able to arrange their affairs so that interest income on mortgage portfolios and rental income on properties could be deemed to be from active businesses. In addition, many individuals took advantage of the generous low rates to incorporate service companies. In late 1979, however, Parliament finally got around to passing legislation that tightened these loopholes.

The definition of active business income, which applies for

1980 and subsequent years, includes manufacturing operations, natural resource activities, construction, logging, farming, fishing, wholesaling and retailing, and transportation. In addition, certain service corporation revenues will qualify, while rental and interest income may be deemed to be from an active business in some cases.

Before 1985, rental and interest income only qualified as active business income of a CCPC when the company had a minimum of six full-time employees throughout the year—*each of whom owned not more than 10% of the shares of the company and all of whom dealt at arm's length with the majority shareholders*. Thus, unless a corporation had six or seven rental buildings with full-time janitors, it was unlikely that the income would qualify. It was also unlikely that small mortgage or money-lending companies could qualify by meeting the above requirement.

As a further concession in order to simplify small-business tax rates, the government decided in its February 1984 Budget to remove the requirement that employees of investment businesses must be at arm's length in order for income to qualify for low tax rates. This basically means that major shareholders and their family members *actually employed* in an investment business now begin to count as qualified employees.

It is unlikely, however, that interest income will be eligible for small-business tax rates. This is because a portfolio of many millions of dollars of interest-bearing securities can be managed with fewer than six full-time employees. Nevertheless, in some cases, Canadian-controlled private corporations earning rental income will qualify for small-business tax incentives now that the new rules are implemented. It will probably still require as many as four or five rental buildings if not the six or seven that are necessary today. Again, I must stress that family members will only be counted if they are actually employed and are paid for rendering services.

In passing, it should be noted that interest income will qualify for small-business tax rates if it is "incidental" to an active business. This would include interest received by a business on overdue trade receivables or interest on term deposits when surplus funds are held *temporarily* during a *portion* of the business cycle.

Where rental and interest income do not qualify, corporate

taxes of approximately 50% will be levied, subject to the refundable tax rules that I explained in Chapter Nine. Where a private corporation earns substantially more than $200,000 of profits from rental activities (or interest) after operating expenses, it in fact pays that corporation to try to carry on with fewer than six employees. After all, given the refundable tax rules, dividend payments of 66²/₃% of earnings are potentially possible. Where the high rate of 50% applies on "active business income" and there is no refundable tax, dividend payments cannot exceed the remaining 50% of after-tax profits.

For service corporations, as I discussed in Chapter Eleven, a low rate of tax will only apply if the corporation is carrying on a bona fide business. An employee really will find no tax advantages in incorporating himself or herself and may, in fact, be penalized.

In this chapter and the one that follows, we will deal specifically with income that qualifies for the small-business tax rate, such as that derived from wholesaling, retailing, construction or manufacturing, and bona fide service companies.

Tax Planning for Public and Foreign-Controlled Corporations

Before examining CCPCs in detail, however, let's explore the question of whether one can tax plan for *public* companies. For example, what if a public company shows a pre-tax profit on its draft financial statements of $10 million?

Since the low rate of tax does not apply to public corporations, one could anticipate taxes of approximately $5 million. Can these taxes be avoided? Perhaps. Consider, for example, the declaration of a bonus to the chairman of the board, the president, and five key directors in the full amount of $10 million. Naturally, these bonuses would become an expense of the corporation and would reduce the pre-tax profit to nil. This would have the effect of reducing taxes by the $5 million payable in the first place.

Of course, such a scheme would not be feasible. A public corporation is one that traditionally has an ownership that is separate and apart from management. Consequently, the shareholders would be rather upset with any plan along the lines described above. They would certainly rather have $5 million of after-tax profits for themselves than have no profit at all. The purpose of this somewhat ridiculous example is, however, to indicate that tax planning is rather limited for public companies. You can never do anything for the benefit of management that is detrimental to owners, and vice versa.

What about the case of a *foreign-controlled* private corporation? Its owner is an American citizen who lives in Florida and never sets foot in Canada. Assume, as well, that the profit of the Canadian company is $100,000. Without any tax planning, it is obvious that taxes payable at 50% (since no small-business deduction is available) would amount to $50,000. In this case, could a bonus of the full $100,000 be paid to the non-resident to avoid all Canadian taxes? There would be no complaints from other shareholders because there aren't any. In addition, creditors would not complain as long as their claims are satisfied on time.

The only problem, however, lies with Revenue Canada. There is a nasty little provision in the Income Tax Act that prohibits the deduction of any outlay or expense that is "unreasonable in the circumstances." Faced with the possible loss of $50,000 in tax revenues, the authorities may just try to deem a good part of that $100,000 bonus as unreasonable. Assume that the full bonus were disallowed as an expense. This would result in Canadian taxes of $50,000—the same amount that one tried to avoid in the first place.

The problem does not, however, end here. In the meantime, for U.S. tax purposes, an American citizen would have received a salary payment of $100,000. This would have to be included in his or her U.S. income. Assuming U.S. taxes payable of $50,000 on this salary, what would be the result? Out of the original $100,000, there would be Canadian taxes of $50,000 on a disallowed expense and U.S. taxes of $50,000 on a salary. *The net after-tax retention would be zero.*

This scenario is not nearly as ridiculous as the first example involving the public company. The possibility of double taxation is quite real. In fact, the problem could not even be alleviated through an application for foreign tax credits. To obtain a foreign tax credit, one always must be dealing with the *same taxpayer* who is subject to tax under two different jurisdictions. In this case, $50,000 of tax would apply to a Canadian corporation on a disallowed expense, with the other $50,000 being levied against a U.S. individual. When dealing with separate taxpayers, no relief is possible. It is for this reason that accountants and lawyers should be extremely careful in advising their non-resident clients with respect to salary policies. You must be cautious in order to avoid the possibility of severe double taxation.

Tax Planning for Canadian-Controlled Private Corporations

What about the Canadian-controlled private corporation? Are there similar restrictions with respect to salary or bonus payments? Fortunately, the situation here is flexible. The corporate high rate of tax does not "cut in" until a CCPC has earned over $200,000 of profits. Where a company earns in excess of this amount, the chances are that the owner-manager is already drawing more than, say, $60,000 per annum. The reason for this is simply a function of the owner's standard of living. What good is it to earn a lot of money if you cannot live comfortably?

Assuming, then, corporate profits in excess of $200,000 (and a desire to avoid the high rate of corporate tax), and also assuming that the shareholder-manager is already drawing at least a $60,000 salary (which is deducted in arriving at corporate profits in the first place), I suggest that there is tremendous flexibility. Why should Revenue care about losing the 50% corporate tax as long as it is going to get the same dollars as additional personal taxes? In fact, there have been no reported tax cases on the subject of excessive remuneration of an owner-manager of a Canadian private company.

Remuneration of Spouses

The only time that Revenue Canada raises the question of excessive remuneration is when the owner-manager attempts (in an unreasonable manner) to split income with members of his or her family. In such circumstances, there are two possibilities. Either the excess remuneration will be disallowed, or it will be tacked on to the income of the person who really earned it. In practice, the authorities would take the approach that yields the greater tax recovery.

When it comes to dealings with a spouse, you must be careful not to allow your corporation to overpay his or her salary.

227

Revenue assessors often question the degree of activity of the spouse within the owner-managed business and, based on industry norms, they are often in a position to assess at least a range of values. This range may, of course, be quite broad and, within reason, payments at the top end of the scale should be acceptable. For example, if a husband runs a manufacturing concern and his wife is the office manager, who is to say whether she is "worth" $12,000 or $20,000 per annum? Of course, you may even argue that, in some cases, controllers earn over $50,000 a year.

However, accountants and lawyers have evolved a rather interesting method of dealing with such an issue. The concept is called the "chicken threshold." In a layperson's language, this simply means the point beyond which one is afraid to plan aggressively because one is "chicken." While a slight overpayment of salaries may be tolerable, sooner or later everyone reaches his or her "chicken threshold"—and that is when you should stop. The hard thing to do is to balance your chicken threshold with Revenue Canada's assessment threshold! (The meaning of this latter term should not require any explanation.)

In dealing with spousal remuneration, there are always special circumstances. If, for example, a corporation manufactures dresses and Mrs. Shareholder is an expert in choosing designs, it may be that she works only the equivalent of three or four weeks a year. Perhaps Mrs. Shareholder is the one who visits London, Paris, and New York in order to decide on the styles to be manufactured each season. Clearly, if her choices are good, the company will prosper. Design services of this nature could be worth many thousands of dollars and may not be subject to the normal remuneration criterion of time spent on the work. Here, the key is the value provided, which is certainly not time-related. Each case is, of course, different and I strongly recommend that the business owner discuss these matters with his or her own advisers.

Before planning too aggressively, however, there is one particular case that is worth mentioning. In this situation, a corporation controlled by the husband paid a salary to the "owner's" wife. The Minister of National Revenue deemed the salary excessive and unreasonable and added it back to the husband's income. The husband objected and the case wound up in court. At that time, the lawyer representing the Minister put the wife on the stand and asked one question: What is the address of your husband's business? She didn't know. Guess who won the case? The moral to be drawn from that situation concerning business involvement is quite evident.

Loan-Guarantee Fees

As a result of losses incurred during the recent recession, lending institutions have become much more cautious in granting credit. In dealing with small businesses, a lending institution will now often require a personal guarantee not only from the owner-manager but also from the owner-manager's spouse. Of course, whenever possible, the owner-manager should do what he or she can to avoid the spouse furnishing a guarantee to the lender. After all, even if an owner-manager has absolute confidence that the business will be successful, there are always unforeseen circumstances. No one wants to be in a position in which virtually all family assets are seized in order to meet the obligation of the business to its financiers.

Despite the advantages of avoiding spousal guarantees, these nevertheless tend to be a fact of life. The question then arises: why not pay the spouse a reasonable *fee* for providing this guarantee?

What is reasonable is, of course, a matter of conjecture. In my opinion, a fee in the vicinity of, say, 5% or 6% of the credit line would not be unreasonable. Thus, for example, if the average loan is, say, $200,000, a guarantee fee of $10,000 or $12,000 might be realistic. After all, if *you* were asked to guarantee a business loan for a friend or relative, what would you charge in order to justify the risk factor?

If a guarantee fee is then paid by the corporation it appears that the corporation itself should have no trouble claiming it as a tax-deductible expense to borrow money. The recipient of that fee would not treat it as a salary but as business income. (Even if the fee is a "one-shot deal" each year, the income would still be deemed business income under the wording of the Income Tax Act, as profit from an "adventure in the nature of trade.")

Thus, even in cases where a spouse (or other guarantor) is not active in the day-to-day operations of the business, it is certainly feasible to remunerate that person. It is also interesting that, as business income, the guarantee fee would qualify for tax sheltering within the normal limits of a Registered Retirement Savings Plan. It further appears that participation in such a program would make the guarantor eligible to contribute into the Canada/Quebec Pension Plan as well.

Again, I stress that you should not ever voluntarily offer to guarantee a corporate business loan. However, if a guarantee is required, why not make the best of the situation and take a tax advantage?

Remuneration Guidelines for One's Children

There is also a good deal of flexibility with respect to the role of your children within the CCPC. If the children are actively involved in the business, reasonable salaries can be paid. Once again, what is reasonable is a matter for conjecture. For example, if my son had just started working for my shoe-manufacturing business and I wanted him to learn the operation from the "bottom up," could I get the company to pay him $50,000 a year for sweeping the floors in the plant? This would not be reasonable. On the other hand, what if my son's title were Vice-President, Maintenance, and Director of Sanitary Engineering?

Over the years, I have not noticed Revenue taking too vigilant an approach in auditing remuneration paid to children who are active in their parents' business on a full-time basis. However, a business owner might not wish to overpay in any event because of *non-tax* reasons. Many times, the owner would prefer to avoid "too much too soon" and would rather pay higher taxes than overpay his or her children.

One ploy that is definitely not recommended is the payment of salaries to children when Father intends to take back the paycheques and deposit them into his own account. There was, for example, an interesting tax case, which was heard a few years ago. In this situation, an Alberta farmer paid each of his ten children $1,000 for work allegedly done in that year on the farm. The Minister deemed the payments unreasonable and added them back to the farmer's income. The taxpayer objected and the case wound up in court.

In rendering a decision, the judge found that he had no difficulty accepting the idea that each of the children would have done enough work on the farm to warrant the payment of $1,000 apiece. However, the facts showed that the farmer paid each of the children a single lump sum and, on the next day, took the dollars back again into his own bank account. These transactions were alleged to be by way of loans, although no documentation was prepared. In addition, some of the children were minors and could not legally lend money to their father in any event. The judge therefore sided with the Minister and the taxpayer lost. The moral is quite clear. If you pay children, the payments should be bona fide and for services that are actually rendered.

Where many people fail to take advantage of income-tax opportunities is in the area of remuneration to "dependent" children. In 1985, for example, a child eighteen or over qualifies for a dependency exemption of $1,420, as long as that child's net income (after tuition fees, if any) does not exceed $2,720. Almost any dependent child has to cost his or her parents at least $2,720 a year for support. If you look at the owner-managed business as the "golden goose" from which all the golden eggs pass, it becomes evident that if Father is in a 50% bracket, he would personally have to draw $5,440 of *additional* pre-tax remuneration to net $2,720 for the support of a child.

However, if the child were employed in the business, he or she need only draw a salary of $2,720 to net the same amount. There is a potential saving, therefore, of $2,720 of "earning power." Also, the salary of $2,720 would not even affect Father's personal exemption for that child. Similar provisions also apply with respect to children under the age of eighteen (as long as they make a satisfactory contribution to the business). Thus, there is an opportunity for income splitting and effective tax reduction. Whenever possible, dependent children should become employees of the family business.

The opportunity to save taxes is actually even greater because of recent changes regarding the employment-expense deduction. The maximum $500 tax write-off now applies against employment incomes of $2,500 or higher. Thus, a child eighteen years of age or older can really earn up to $3,220 (plus an amount equal to his or her tuition fees) before a parent begins to lose the dependency deduction.

The remuneration package should not, however, provide for an annual salary paid as a single amount on the night before Christmas. Rather, the payments should be made throughout the year commensurate with the services rendered by the child. In all cases, the child should actually work for his or her remuneration. I would be very unhappy, for example, about trying to defend a taxpayer who has paid salaries to a child when the child cannot describe in his or her own words exactly what was done to earn the income. It would also be somewhat difficult to explain away circumstances where payments are made and the parents then take back the money. All salaries paid should, in fact, be deposited in the children's bank accounts and expenditures for their benefit should be paid from these accounts.

Of course, if you are blessed with four teen-age children, you may not have enough clerical, office, or maintenance work in the business to gainfully employ all four. However, in many circumstances, you can easily justify salaries to one or two children. From an educational perspective, let alone from a tax-saving standpoint, employment of the children can be most advantageous.

Directors' Fees

There is a common misconception that you can remunerate family members by simply making them directors of the company. Excessive directors' fees are, however, far more vulnerable to reassessment than excessive salaries. This is because there is an established market in Canada for the remuneration of a corporate director.

If a director of a *public* corporation receives between $3,000 and $10,000 for his or her efforts, how can the average Canadian *private* company pay similar amounts on a tax-deductible basis? A director of a public company must attend meetings, sit on committees, and is exposed to potential negligence suits. In the case of a private corporation, the meetings are very often a matter of formality only and may not, in fact, really take place.

Remuneration Guidelines for the Owner-Manager Where the Company Qualifies for the Small-Business Deduction

Having dealt with salaries to spouses and other members of the family, is it possible to evolve distinct guidelines for the purpose of determining the "best" remuneration package for the owner-manager himself or herself? Actually, such guidelines *can* be established by using simple arithmetic.

232

In the examples that follow, it is assumed that a shareholder-manager of a Canadian private corporation generally operates the business *primarily* in order to satisfy his or her personal or living requirements. This means that the first dollars earned by the corporation (after paying all other company expenses) must be drawn out one way or another (by salaries, bonuses, or dividends) for the shareholder-manager and family to live on from day to day. Thus, only dollars *over and above* personal living requirements can be devoted towards savings, and it is these *excess* dollars around which tax planning revolves.

For purposes of illustration, let us look at $100 of corporate profits from active business that remains after all operating expenses have been paid for out of revenues and *after* the remuneration needed for living expenses by the shareholder-manager has already been taken. The amount of $100 is very easy to work with, and we can easily convert from dollars to percentages where our base is 100; however, the *most* important point is that whatever holds true for $100 of business profits of a Canadian-controlled private corporation also holds true for *any* profits for which the small-business tax rate applies. In other words, the profit of $100 is representative of a range—all the way from the first dollar of earnings up to the annual business limit of $200,000.

In order to simplify the examples in this chapter and the next, the individual's personal exemptions and other deductions have been ignored in most cases. If you wish, you can assume that the shareholder-manager has other income which offsets these additional amounts.

The first possibility is that a shareholder-manager could draw the entire $100 profit by way of salary or bonus, even though he or she has already satisfied all personal living requirements. As such, depending on how much the individual has already drawn, we can estimate the taxes payable on an additional draw of $100 as follows:

Amount previously drawn as salary	$25,000	$35,000	$60,000
Combined marginal tax brackets (approximate)	*40%*	*45%*	*50%*
Taxes payable on an additional bonus of $100	$40	$45	$50
After-tax retention on bonus	$60	$55	$50

As an alternative, however, the corporation can retain this profit after paying corporate taxes. Where the small-business deduction applies, the corporate tax payable will only be 15%–25% ($15–$25), leaving after-tax retained earnings of $75–$85. Thus, *our first conclusion is that a corporation that is subject to the small-business deduction offers its shareholder-managers the opportunity for a significant tax deferral.* In other words, the company can reinvest significantly more after-tax dollars than the amount otherwise available to the owners themselves.

It is evident from the comparison shown in Figure 13-1 that the minimum tax deferral is 15% based on the underlying income of $100 that was earned in the first place. It is generally unrealistic to assume owner-managers in tax brackets less than 40%. This is because if you anticipate earning below $25,000 per annum for an extended period of time, you would be better off working for someone else. The opportunities for tax deferral do, however, extend to a possible 35% when the owner-manager is in the top tax bracket of 50% and has a CCPC in Ontario carrying on a newly formed but profitable business.

Figure 13-1 **A Comparison of Corporate and Individual After-Tax Earnings**

			(New Business)
Corporation	*N.S.*	*Alta.*	*Ont.*
Earnings	$100	$100	$100
Corporate tax	25	20	15
Retention	$ 75	$ 80	$ 85
Individual			
Income level	$25,000	$35,000	$60,000
Tax bracket	*40%*	*45%*	*50%*
Salary	$100	$100	$100
Personal tax	40	45	50
Retention	$ 60	$ 55	$ 50

Note: $100 is representative of a range between $1 and $200,000 each year as long as the company is a CCPC earning business income.

Meaning of Tax Deferral

In the previous discussion, I have consciously stayed away from referring to the term "tax saving." Actually, there are three possibilities if you opt to allow a corporation to pay tax instead of the owner-manager.

First, where the corporate tax rate is only 15%–25% and the company has $75–$85 out of $100, it is certainly much easier to subsidize business expansion. Corporate retention would provide many more dollars than if the shareholders were to take out the funds personally and then lend back their after-tax proceeds.

Second, it is important to realize that the accounting concept of a private corporation being separate and apart from its owners is a pure fiction. You can never tax plan properly for a private company unless you look at the owners *and* the company as if they were, in effect, one entity. If, for example, a corporation does not need after-tax profits for business expansion, these same dollars could be used for a build-up of investment capital. The corporation could purchase term deposits, dividend-bearing securities, real estate, gold, silver, or, for that matter, any other kind of investment. All investment decisions would, of course, be those of the owner-managers. Thus, the corporation is simply an extension of its owners. The corporate low rate provides more funds for investment purposes than would otherwise be available to the owners themselves.

A third possibility is if the owner wants the after-tax profits for personal luxury items. This is the one area where, in a sense, the idea of a corporation being just an extension of its owners breaks down. Soon after a corporation takes its profits and uses them for the personal benefit of its owner-managers, individual taxes must be paid. (See Chapter Two for a discussion of loans to shareholders.) Thus, we do not refer to corporate retention of profits as providing a tax *saving*. It is just a *deferral*. The advantage of corporate retention lies in *reinvestment* of profits only.

The tax-deferral benefits are indefinite as long as the shareholder-manager can afford to leave the dollars inside the company without drawing on them for personal or living expenses. What happens, however, if a shareholder-manager does decide, in some future year, to draw out funds, which have been accumulated by the corporation, for personal or living expenses?

Special Tax on Corporate Distributions
Recent federal budgets introduced a brand-new "dividend-

distributions tax." The new tax applies to dividends paid out of earnings that qualify for the small-business tax rate in tax years following 1982. The rate of this new tax is 12.5%. Later on in this chapter, we will explore some opportunities for tax planning to postpone the impact of this new tax. The following examples will, however, assume that the tax must eventually be paid. Its effect, as illustrated in the table in Figure 13-2, is to limit maximum dividend payments to $66.67 for each $100 earned by a corporation in the first place—assuming an initial corporate tax of 25%. For newly incorporated small businesses in Ontario, it is still possible to pay dividends of as much as $75.55 for each $100 of earnings. Special planning for these Ontario corporations and their shareholders is discussed on pages 240–41.

Figure 13-2   **Impact of the 12.5% Corporate-Distributions Tax**

	Most Provinces	*(New Business) Ontario*
Corporate income	$100.00	$100.00
Less: Corporate tax	25.00	15.00
After-tax income	75.00	85.00
Less: 12.5% tax on dividends		
(12.5% × $66.67; 12.5% × $75.55)	8.33	9.45
Dividend to be distributed	$ 66.67	$ 75.55

Salaries Versus Dividends
You must never try to compare a $100 salary to a $100 dividend. A salary is paid from pre-tax profits, while a dividend comes out of after-tax corporate earnings. Where the small-business deduction applies, you now always compare a $100 salary to a dividend of between $66.67 and $75.55.

The example in Figure 13-3 illustrates what happens when dividends of $66.67 are paid out to shareholder-managers. As discussed in Chapter Nine, a Canadian dividend is grossed up by 50%. This factor applied to a dividend of $66.67 always produces (for each of the taxpayers in the example) an income for tax purposes of $100. This income is then subjected to tax in the respective marginal brackets as indicated in the example. However, the tax otherwise payable is then reduced by a dividend tax credit.

The operation of the dividend tax credit is the key point to an understanding of how corporate taxes and personal taxes interact when dividends pass to shareholders.

The Dividend Tax Credit
The federal dividend tax credit is 22.67% of the grossed-up dividend. Thus, in the example in Figure 13-3, the federal dividend tax credit on a cash dividend of $66.67 (grossed up to $100) is 22.67% of $100, or $22.67. However, when the example refers to marginal tax brackets, this means not only federal taxes but provincial income taxes as well.

In all provinces (other than Quebec, which has its own tax credit system), provincial taxes are levied as a flat-rate percentage of the federal tax otherwise payable. This percentage of provincial taxes is levied *after* the federal income tax has already been reduced by the federal dividend tax credit. Thus, in the

Figure 13-3 **Tax Treatment of Dividends out of Small-Business Profits to Shareholder-Managers**

	$25,000	$35,000	$60,000
Income level			
Marginal tax brackets	*40%*	*45%*	*50%*
Retention on $100 bonus	$ 60.00	$ 55.00	$ 50.00
Dividend in cash:			
Corporate retained earnings	$ 75.00	$ 75.00	$ 75.00
Less: New 12.5% tax on dividend			
(12.5% × $66.67)	8.33	8.33	8.33
Cash dividend	$ 66.67	$ 66.67	$ 66.67
Cash dividend	$ 66.67	$ 66.67	$ 66.67
50% gross-up	33.33	33.33	33.33
Income for tax purposes	$100.00	$100.00	$100.00
Federal and provincial tax in marginal bracket	$ 40.00	$ 45.00	$ 50.00
Dividend tax credit (combined)	33.33	33.33	33.33
Net tax	$ 6.67	$ 11.67	$ 16.67
Cash flow (cash dividend of $66.67 – net tax)	$ 60.00	$ 55.00	$ 50.00
Cash flow on $100 salary	$ 60.00	$ 55.00	$ 50.00

following example, if the federal tax otherwise payable is reduced by $22.67, the provincial tax is also reduced by the provincial percentage multiplied by $22.67.

Assume that a particular province levies income taxes at 47% of the federal tax. (Provincial rates outside Quebec currently vary between 43.5% and 60% of the federal tax.) A resident of that province who receives a cash dividend of $66.67 and who therefore reduces his federal tax by $22.67 will then reduce the provincial tax by a further 47% × $22.67 or $10.66. The total dividend tax credit (on a combined basis) is therefore $33.33. *In all provinces, the combined effective dividend tax credit is approximately equal to the dividend gross-up.*

Returning to the example in Figure 13-3, it is evident that the net retention on a $66.67 dividend is exactly equal to the net cash retention otherwise possible on a $100 bonus. The effect of the dividend gross-up is to bring the individual shareholder-manager into a position where he is subject to tax on the *underlying income that was earned by the corporation in the first place.*

The result of the dividend tax credit is then to give that same shareholder-manager an effective credit for the corporate tax that has already been paid on this income. Therefore, the individual shareholder-manager is only responsible for the difference between his personal marginal rate of tax and the corporate rate. His after-tax cash flow on a dividend is the *same amount* that he would have received had he taken a bonus or salary of $100 in the first place. This is called an "integrated tax system."

To summarize, the use of a corporation to retain active business income not required by a shareholder-manager for living expenses produces a substantial, indefinite tax deferral as long as the small-business deduction applies. The deferral provides excess funds for reinvestment until such time as the shareholder-manager decides to take out dividends. At that point, however, the total tax cost still does not exceed that which would have been paid had the deferral not been chosen.

Between 1978 and the end of 1982, the special 12.5% corporate-distributions tax did not exist. In the "good old days" it was possible for any Canadian small business to pay dividends of $75 (instead of $66.67) out of each $100 of earnings. This produced an "overintegration" of between $5 and $12 for each $100 that was earned in the first place. The intention, then, was to encourage business expansion and to stimulate investment activity. The new 12.5% tax removes this incentive, to the detriment of most Canadian entrepreneurs and small-business owners. Only in Ontario can shareholders of new business corporations still receive dividends of $75 for each $100 of pre-tax earnings. Essentially, the temporary provincial corporate-tax holiday offsets the impact of the federal 12.5% distributions tax. The owner-manager of a newly formed Canadian small business in Ontario is therefore, at least for the time being, in a better tax position than his or her counterparts in other provinces.

Additional Implications of the Gross-Up and Credit System

The gross-up and credit system has another far more significant effect. As explained in Chapter Nine, when a Canadian resident has no other income and receives a $36,000 dividend from a Canadian corporation, he or she will pay *no personal income taxes at all*. (See Figure 9-3.)

Although there is no personal tax payable on dividends of up to $36,000 received by an individual, you should note that in most provinces a business would still have to earn $54,000 in order to be capable of paying a $36,000 dividend (after corporate tax.)

Corporate earnings	$54,000
Less: Income tax at 25%	13,500
	40,500
Less: 12.5% corporate-distributions tax	
(12.5% × $36,000)	4,500
	$36,000

As an alternative to the $36,000 dividend, the corporation could pay a salary of $54,000, thereby saving the $18,000 of corporate taxes otherwise payable. The individual's tax position would be as follows:

Salary	$54,000
Less: Personal exemptions and	
other deductions (estimated)	4,000
Taxable income	$50,000

However, the combined federal and provincial income tax payable on a taxable income of $50,000 is approximately $18,000. The retention on a salary of $54,000 is therefore the *same* $36,000 as if corporate taxes were first paid and a dividend was then distributed.

Tax Planning for a Proper Salary-Dividend Mix

From the foregoing examples, it would appear that it really doesn't matter whether a salary of $54,000 or a dividend of $36,000 is paid—at least when a CCPC is eligible for the low rate of corporate tax. However, whenever you tax plan, you must take into account different segments of the legislation contained throughout the Income Tax Act. In this case, specifically, tax planning should include provision for the registered retirement savings plan (RRSP), which was discussed in Chapter Five.

Figure 13-4 **Some Earned Income Is Required for Effective Tax Planning**

Alternative 1: The corporation pays income taxes on the first $27,500 of 1985 profits (before shareholder-manager remuneration) and distributes the balance (after a further tax of 12.5%) as a dividend. The shareholder then retains $5,500 for investment purposes (to provide ultimately for his or her retirement).

	(New Business) Ontario	(Any Business) Most Provinces
Income earned by corporation	$27,500	$27,500
Corporate income tax at 15%; 25%	4,125	6,875
	23,375	20,625
Less: 12.5% corporate-distributions tax (12.5% × dividend paid)	2,599	2,291
Dividend paid*	$20,776	$18,334

*No personal taxes are payable on the dividend since it is less than $36,000.

Cash flow:		
After-tax disposable income	$15,276	$12,834
Invested for retirement (income yield will be taxable)	5,500	5,500
Corporate taxes paid (income + distributions)	6,724	9,166
	$27,500	$27,500

Alternative 2: A salary of $27,500 is paid for 1985, and an RRSP is purchased (to provide ultimately for the shareholder's retirement).

Salary	$27,500
Less: RRSP	5,500
Net income	22,000
Estimated personal exemptions	4,000
Taxable income	$18,000
Federal and provincial taxes on $15,500	$ 4,050
Tax on $ 2,500 at 34% (combined marginal rate)	850
	$ 4,900

Cash flow:

After-tax retention of salary – RRSP – tax	
$27,500 – ($5,500 + $4,900)	$17,100
Invested for retirement (income earned on RRSP funds will be tax sheltered)	5,500
Corporate taxes paid (since salary is deductible)	Nil
Personal taxes paid	4,900
	$27,500

Advantage of salary (i.e., extra disposable income):

Most provinces	
$17,100 - $12,834 =	$ 4,266
Ontario (new business)	
$17,100 – $15,276 =	$ 1,824

For a taxpayer to make use of an RRSP or even to benefit from the Canada/Quebec Pension Plan, he or she requires "earned income." Thus, if a shareholder-manager ceases to draw any salary, he or she would have to forgo all benefits from these programs. The alternatives of choosing dividends or salaries in 1985 are compared in Figure 13-4.

The reason a salary is preferable is that a corporation pays a tax rate of 25% to 33⅓% (including the corporate-distributions tax) on *all* profits (from the first dollar) before dividends can be paid out, while an individual does not reach as high an effective rate of tax on his or her income after RRSP contributions and personal exemptions are deducted. The tax saving of a salary over a dividend is, as illustrated, between $1,824 and $4,266 annually.

Even though taxes will eventually have to be paid on a withdrawal from an RRSP, these taxes cannot, under the present personal tax-rate system, amount to more than 50% on $5,500 or $2,750. This is far less than the *original* saving of $4,266 for residents of most provinces. Even Ontario residents will find that the benefits of investing their savings of $1,824 for just a few years will outweigh the future tax on RRSP withdrawals.

Note that the example does not take into account the other advantages of receiving salary, which include eligibility for the annual $500 employment-expense deduction and participation in the Canada/Quebec Pension Plan.

Since the corporate tax rate on *retained* income is between 15% and 25%, and since the shareholder-manager will now be in approximately a 34% bracket (after his or her salary), *no additional remuneration* should be paid *unless* the shareholder-manager requires such additional payments for personal or living expenses.

If the owner-manager does require additional remuneration in 1985, all additional payments could be made either by way of salary or dividend depending on individual circumstances.

Another advantage of a salary-oriented remuneration package involving RRSP contributions is the fact that RRSP funds will earn income that compounds on a tax-deferred basis. This is preferable to income earned on investment capital, which is fully taxed when earned.

Summary

The guidelines for what I consider the best remuneration package for a shareholder-manager of a Canadian-controlled private corporation can thus be outlined as follows where the small-business tax rate applies:

1. Draw as little income from the corporation as possible and make use of the tax-deferral aspects of the small-business rate structure.
2. In 1985, the first $28,000 of gross remuneration (and not just $27,500) should be taken by a shareholder-manager as a salary. This will make him or her eligible for the $500 employment-expense deduction and the Canada/Quebec Pension Plan. $5,500 should then be invested in an RRSP.
3. Since the shareholder-manager is in a 34% tax bracket

(after Step 2) while the corporation pays taxes at only 25%, no additional remuneration should be taken out, if possible. This assumes that the shareholder-manager can meet all personal or living expenses on an after-tax retention of approximately $17,500.

4. If additional remuneration is required for personal spending, either salary or dividends may be extracted.
5. Pay dividends to family members if salaries are unreasonable.

Of course, these are general guidelines, and it should be noted that extenuating circumstances may, in certain cases, warrant a deviation from the suggested pattern. When RRSP maximum limits are adjusted upwards starting in 1986 (as explained in Chapter Five), additional salaries may then become more advantageous. This is something you should discuss with your advisers in that year.

Tax Planning for the Family

Logically, if a tax plan is advantageous for one owner-manager, it can provide twice the benefit in the case of two owner-managers. For example, if husband and wife are both active in the business, salaries of $28,000 should be paid to each of them for 1985 as long as this amount is reasonable. Each would then contribute $5,500 to RRSPs. The cash flow and tax effect of this is illustrated in Figure 13-5.

If the illustrated arrangement is feasible, the family's disposable income would be approximately $35,000 and the effective tax cost only about 18%. *Any time taxes on earnings of $56,000 can be kept at this level, tax planning has been effective.*

Figure 13-5 **Tax Planning in 1985 for Husbands and Wives (Earned Income)**

	Earnings	RRSP Deferrals	Taxes	Net Cash
Salary to husband	$28,000	$ 5,500	$ 5,000	$17,500
Salary to wife	28,000	5,500	5,000	17,500
	$56,000	$11,000	$10,000	$35,000

$$\text{Effective tax cost} \frac{\text{Taxes}}{\text{Earnings}} = \frac{\$10,000}{\$56,000} = 17.9\%$$

What happens if husbands and wives do not contribute to a business equally—at least to the point where a 1985 salary of $28,000 can be justified for each? Consider, for example, the situation in which the husband is active while the wife is at home working hard to bring up children (without receiving any remuneration for this position). They might try this approach to tax planning:

- The husband should still draw $28,000 in 1985 by way of salary and contribute to an RRSP.
- The next $54,000 of pre-tax profits should then be taxed at the corporate level. This would create an opportunity to pay dividends of $36,000 (after all corporate taxes).
- $36,000 could then be paid out as a dividend to the wife. The example in Figure 13-6 shows how this would work.

In this case, the family's disposable income becomes $53,500 and the entire tax bite is only 28% on a total income of $82,000. This too is quite inexpensive. Note that the $18,000 tax on the dividend to the wife is *not* really a tax payable by *her* but is the corporate tax payable initially in order to free up $36,000 of dividends on which no further taxes need be paid.

Figure 13-6 **An Alternative Tax Plan for Husbands and Wives in 1985**

	Earnings	RRSP Deferrals	Taxes	Net Cash
Salary to husband	$28,000	$ 5,500	$ 5,000	$17,500
Dividend to wife	54,000		18,000*	36,000
	$82,000	$ 5,500	$23,000	$53,500

Effective tax cost	Taxes	= $23,000	=	28.0%
	Earnings	$82,000		

*Corporate tax at 33⅓%, including the 12.5% corporate-distributions tax.

Separate Classes of Shares
At this point, you might question how one can pay dividends to a wife without also paying dividends to a husband who is (presumably) also a shareholder.

For several years, it was fashionable to set up the share structure of private businesses in such a way that different family members held different classes of shares. In many instances, the classes were identical in all respects, except that the board of directors was given the opportunity to declare dividends on one class without necessarily declaring dividends on another. Thus, if a husband owned Class A shares and his wife owned Class B shares, and the husband was active while the wife was not, the custom was to pay a salary to the husband and dividends to the wife.

Unfortunately, in several recent tax cases, Revenue Canada successfully attacked such programs. The courts found that any arrangement in which dividends are paid on one class but not on another and where the shares are effectively the same is an indirect transfer of rights to income. As a result of these decisions, it may be wise to change existing arrangements that would give rise to such a problem. Specifically, it might be best for the husband in our example to own voting preferred shares only, which are redeemable, retractable, and even convertible, but do not necessarily bear dividends. These shares could also participate in the future growth of the business. Retractable means that these shares can be redeemed at the option of the holder, as well as at the option of the company. Then, if the wife holds all the common shares, dividends can be paid to her alone.

An arrangement to exchange the husband's capital stock for shares of another class can be structured using Section 86 of the Income Tax Act. I regret that a detailed analysis of Section 86 is beyond the scope of this book. However, suffice it to say that with qualified legal and accounting advice, a suitable share structure can be arranged that would accomplish income-splitting objectives.

Tax Planning for the Corporate-Distributions Tax

Before we leave the topic of dividend payments, it would be worthwhile exploring some of the opportunities of postponing the new corporate-distributions tax. Originally, this tax was to apply against dividend payments after 1981. As well, the tax was to be imposed on all corporate retained earnings that had received the benefit of the small-business tax rate over the prior ten years. However, on October 27, 1982, former Finance Minister Marc Lalonde made significant modifications to the proposed rules. Specifically, the corporate-distributions tax now only applies to corporate small-business income earned in taxation years starting *after* the end of 1982. It appears that dividends will be first deemed to come from current income. Dividends in excess of post-1982 earnings may *then* be paid without triggering the new tax.

With proper planning, it may be possible to circumvent Mr. Lalonde's proposals and extract pre-1983 earnings before profits made after 1982. I recommend that the shareholders of Canadian-controlled private corporations with substantial retained earnings from before 1983 consider the possibility of moving their business operations into new companies. If this is done, the old operating companies can remain in existence and from time to time can pay dividends out of pre-1983 earnings, while the new companies would pay salaries on an ongoing basis instead.

For some organizations, it may be a good idea to have the new companies pay salaries of up to $28,000 to each owner-manager and have the old company pay dividends out of pre-1983 earnings to supplement the owners' living requirements. This would make sense in cases where an organization is not in any imminent danger of losing the small-business tax rate (that is, where annual earnings are considerably less than $200,000). In any event, these are matters to be discussed with your own professional advisers since the actual implementation of reorganizations in this area can be rather complex.

Associated Companies

While on the subject of corporate groups, without special rules it would be quite simple to "beat" the system that allows a Canadian-controlled private company to earn $200,000 a year at favourable tax rates. All one would have to do is incorporate a second company and arrange to have excess profits above this limit channelled into that other corporation. This type of planning is so obvious that special provisions are needed by the government to cope with it. The Income Tax Act therefore contains rules pertaining to "associated corporations": two or more corporations that are controlled by the same person or group of persons must share one small-business limit. Control, for tax purposes, always means ownership of more than 50% of the voting shares. Thus, for example, if Mr. Taxpayer has a controlling interest in two or more companies, only one low-rate tax-base applies. This is the case even if the two companies are engaged in entirely different businesses.

However, what is the situation if there are two corporations, one of which is owned 100% by Mr. Taxpayer and the second is owned 100% by his wife? Are these corporations associated? In many cases, rules requiring these two companies to share one small-business tax rate would be unfair. For example, what if the husband's company is involved in manufacturing furniture while the wife's corporation operates a book store? It is clear that one spouse should not be penalized for the other's business activities.

On the other hand, what if the husband's corporation were set up for the purpose of providing income-tax consulting services and the wife's company was involved in bookkeeping? What if by strange coincidence, the clients of both firms were the same? In this case, it would appear that the separate existence of the two companies might be primarily for the purpose of reducing taxes otherwise payable.

In order to accommodate different types of business circumstances, the rules in the Income Tax Act are therefore flexible. There is actually no automatic association of a husband's company with that of his wife. This is provided that the husband does not have an interest of 10% or more in his wife's company and that the wife does not have a similar cross-holding in her husband's firm. However, the tax rules go on to say that, if the Minister of National Revenue is of the opinion that the separate existence of the two companies is not primarily for the effective conduct of business, but rather has as one of its prime objectives the reduction or avoidance of taxes otherwise payable, the two corporations can be *deemed* to be associated. This would require them to share the small-business tax rate.

In reality, situations are rarely black or white. In many cases, the separate existence of two companies, one owned by the husband and the other by the wife, can be justified for business purposes other than tax reductions. Under those circumstances, each company may utilize the small-business tax rate to its full extent. While a strict interpretation of the law would allow either husband or wife to have a small interest (up to 10%) in the other's corporation, the taxpayer is better off if there is no cross-holding whatsoever.

Planning for a Multiple Use of Corporations
In the most usual situation, a family unit of husband and wife starts out with one business. In most cases, it is advantageous for

the shares of that corporation to be owned by both in relatively equal proportions. There are several advantages:

- Even if one of the two spouses is not *active* in the administration of the business, that spouse can receive remuneration by way of dividends.
- If the shares of the business are ever sold, the capital gain can be apportioned between the spouses. The new lifetime capital-gains tax exemption can also be doubled as it is phased in over the next few years.
- Having both husband and wife involved in the ownership of the business will allow for a doubling of the "cumulative small-business gains account" for sales of shares to children before 1988. This concept, as explained more fully in Chapters Twelve and Sixteen, permits shares of active businesses to pass, on a tax-deferred basis, between parents and children either by way of gift or on death. (This "rollover" will soon be replaced by the more generous and more general $500,000 lifetime capital-gains tax exemption.)

However, what if the family decides to start up a second business? Even if this new business is entirely different from the first, there will be an automatic association of the companies if the shares of the second company are owned by both husband and wife (even in different proportions).

Fortunately, however, there is an alternative. The alternative would require one of the two spouses to sell his or her interest in the first business to the second spouse *before* the second business is incorporated. Subsequently, whoever sells his or her interest in the first business would become the sole shareholder of the second. Then, as long as there is a good business reason for the separate existence of the two corporations, the family could enjoy a second small-business tax rate.

You should note that the sale of the shares in the first business can be made literally for "$1 and other valuable consideration" without necessarily requiring a price to be determined or a payment to be made. This is because, as described in Chapter Seven, transactions between a husband and wife are generally deemed to take place at cost in any event. This means that the fair market value becomes irrelevant. It is true that if the shares that are transferred bear dividends or are ever sold, the income will revert back to the transferor. However, a sale of shares in the first business does pave the way for the formation of a second corporation in order to take advantage of a second small-business tax rate.

In fact, as an additional planning mechanism, each and every corporation owned by a husband and wife should be set up in the first place with separate classes of shares. Not only does this provide the opportunity to pay dividends on one class without paying on the other, but also, if a husband's shares are ever transferred to his wife (or vice versa), one could then arrange *not* to pay dividends on that class in the future. This would avoid the income-attribution rules.

It is extremely important that the timing be arranged properly. If a husband and wife together own the shares of a first company, and then subscribe to the shares in a second, the corporations will automatically become associated. If share transfers are made later so that the husband disposes of all his shares in one company while the wife disposes of her shares in the other, the Minister, on audit, will recognize that this was done for tax purposes only. An ideal opportunity to avoid questions would arise in circumstances where the vendor of the shares of the first company sells out to a spouse in order to devote his or her entire attention to the operations of the new second company.

As a further extension of the foregoing, you should also note that it may be possible to get a *third* use of the small-business rate. This is when the children eventually grow up and (perhaps with financing from their parents) start their own business. As long as the parents have no share interests in the children's company and vice versa, *another* small-business tax rate may become available. Again, there must be a good business reason for this new company beyond just a reduction in taxes. Eventually, the children would presumably inherit the shares of their parents' companies. From that time on, the corporations would become associated and would no longer enjoy multiple small-business benefits, but there is no tax to recapture prior years' benefits.

The subject of associated corporations has been dealt with in many court cases and, in practice, is one of the most complex areas within the small-business sections of the Income Tax Act. You are therefore strongly advised to consult with your own accountants and lawyers before setting up multiple business ventures.

CHAPTER FOURTEEN

Maximizing Profits From All Private Canadian Businesses

Taxation Guidelines for Business Income That Does Not Qualify for the Small-Business Tax Rate

A Canadian-controlled private corporation that earns more than $200,000 of active business income in a given year will not qualify for the small-business tax rate on its profits over this limit. Let us again use an example of $100 of active business income; this time, $100 will represent all amounts that do *not* qualify for the small-business deduction. The range, in this case, is therefore any business profits from $200,001 (in a given year) and up. Again, whatever holds true for $100 will also hold true for all active business income that does not qualify for the low rate. (The exception for manufacturing and processing profits is dealt with later on in this chapter.)

Salary Versus Dividends

The shareholder-manager has the alternative of either taking a salary or bonus currently, or retaining the income in the corporation and later declaring a dividend for his or her class of shares.

Figure 14-1 **Tax Prepayment at Corporate High Rate**

Alternative 1: A bonus of $100 is paid, representing active business income that does not qualify for the small-business deduction.

Income level	$25,000	$35,000	$60,000
Tax bracket	*40%*	*45%*	*50%*
After-tax retention on $100 bonus	$60	$55	$50

Alternative 2: The corporation pays tax on its "profit" of $100

Income of corporation	$100		
Corporate tax (high rate applies)	50		
Retained earnings	$50		

Tax prepayment where corporation pays the tax	$10	$ 5	Nil

Figure 14-1 illustrates an important point. If the shareholder-manager is in a tax bracket *below* 50%, allowing a corporation to pay taxes on profits at the high rate results in a tax *prepayment*. A taxpayer should therefore never put himself or herself into a tax bracket below that of the corporation.

In fact, there is not only a prepayment in cases where a corporation pays tax at rates higher than personal levels, but there are also severe penalties at the time dividends are later paid out, as we will see.

When a shareholder-manager reaches the 50% bracket, the choice between paying a bonus and letting the corporation retain the funds appears to be equal. However, to assess the situation completely, we must chart what happens when a shareholder-manager decides to extract dividends at some point in the future. Here, the dividend will be $50 out of each underlying $100 of income and not $66.67 as is the case for a company that qualifies for the small-business rate. (There is no 12.5% corporate-distributions tax on profits that are not eligible for the small-business deduction.)

Once again, we must take care never to attempt to compare a $100 bonus to a $100 dividend. Where the small-business rate does not apply, the correct comparison is a bonus of $100 against a potential dividend (after corporate taxes) of only $50. The tax consequences when such a dividend is paid are shown in Figure 14-2.

The example indicates that there is a substantial tax penalty for individuals in *all* marginal tax brackets for having first allowed active business income to be taxed at high corporate tax rates before dividends are paid out.

Specific guidelines for tax planning can also be derived from this example. A shareholder in a 40% or 45% bracket should automatically draw a salary. This is because of the initial prepayment of $5 to $10 per $100, as well as the penalty of 14%–15% that arises upon the payment of dividends.

Where shareholders are in 50% brackets, the original choice between personal and corporate tax was equal. However, at the time of a dividend, there is a penalty of $12 on each underlying $100 that had been earned initially. *Therefore, even an individual in the 50% bracket is better off receiving bonuses in the first place to reduce the amount of corporate tax otherwise payable.*

Income level	$25,000	$35,000	$60,000
Tax bracket	*40%*	*45%*	*50%*
Retention on $100 bonus	$60	$55	$50
Dividend in cash = Corporate retained earnings	$50	$50	$50
50% gross-up	25	25	25
Taxable income	$75	$75	$75
Federal and provincial tax payable	$30	$34	$37
Dividend tax credit (combined)	25	25	25
Net tax payable	$ 5	$ 9	$12
Cash flow:			
Dividend	$50	$50	$50
Net tax	5	9	12
Retention on $50 dividend	$45	$41	$38
Tax penalty	$15	$14	$12

Effect of Recent Tax Changes

Now that personal income-tax brackets above 50% have been eliminated, it is never worthwhile to pay corporate taxes of 50% on active business income. There is no longer any opportunity to defer taxes through corporate retention. In fact, the opposite now applies. There is a substantial penalty if corporate profits are taxed at 50% and are then paid out as dividends.

All profits from active (non-manufacturing) business income that do not qualify for the small-business deduction should now be paid out as salaries. The owner should pay personal taxes after sheltering as much as possible through an RRSP. If the owner's after-tax retention exceeds his or her living requirements, excess funds can either be loaned back to the corporation for reinvestment into the business or can be channelled into an investment company as described in Chapter Nine.

A Canadian corporation should *never* pay taxes of 50% on active business income followed by *immediate* dividends to shareholder-managers, since there is an automatic 12% penalty.

Planning for Public Corporations

There is now a brand-new planning technique for senior managers of public corporations that normally pay dividends. This strategy will be of use to the senior manager who is *also* a significant stockholder.

If possible, the senior manager should *waive his or her rights* to dividends in exchange for bonuses. A bonus of one dollar is certainly better than a dividend of fifty cents, and from the employer's standpoint the choice between (pre-tax) salaries and (after-tax) dividends is the same.

Income from Manufacturing and Processing

Since 1973, a special incentive provision has had the effect of reducing the *basic* corporate tax rate on manufacturing and processing profits to 40%, with a parallel reduction to 20% where the small-business deduction is also applicable.

Although the phrase "manufacturing and processing" is not defined in the Income Tax Act, there are several industries, such as farming, fishing, logging, on-site job construction, and certain exploration activities, which are specifically *excluded* from the incentives. In addition, the rules require that at least 10% of a corporation's gross revenue for the year from all active businesses be from the sale or lease of goods that are manufactured or processed by that corporation in Canada.

Because there is no specific definition as to what is included, you are free to take a very liberal interpretation of the term "manufacturing and processing." For example, the activities of a restaurant should be eligible for this incentive since a restaurant processes food. Similarly, a newspaper or magazine processes paper, and even though the major revenue is derived from advertising, it can be said that publishing still qualifies.

Any time a business purchases goods in bulk and repackages them for sale in smaller quantities, it would appear advantageous to at least try to claim the reduced tax rate. Again, the "no-worse-off" principle would apply. I had one particular client that was able to save $36,000 in taxes in 1979 simply by mixing with water certain chemicals that had originally been purchased for resale to customers.

Calculating Manufacturing and Processing Profits
Once it is determined that a corporation is engaged in manufacturing or processing, there is a formula to determine what percentage of active business income is deemed to be from these activities. The formula may be expressed as follows:

$$\begin{array}{l}\text{Manufacturing} \\ \text{and Processing} \\ \text{Profits}\end{array} = \begin{array}{l}\text{Active} \\ \text{Business} \\ \text{Income}\end{array} \times \dfrac{\dfrac{100}{75} \times \begin{array}{l}\text{Manufacturing} \\ \text{Labour}\end{array} + \dfrac{100}{85} \times \begin{array}{l}\text{Manufacturing} \\ \text{Capital}\end{array}}{\text{Total Labour} + \text{Total Capital}}$$

This formula ties in manufacturing and processing profits as a percentage of active business income, based on a composite of both labour and capital (fixed assets) employed. The first part of the formula takes into account manufacturing labour and total labour for the year. The formula recognizes that even "pure" manufacturing companies require a certain amount of non-qualifying "support" labour. For example, every business must have salespeople, an office staff, and executive personnel. The fraction "100/75" allows for a 25% support factor. As long as not more than 25% of the total labour is devoted to non-qualified activities, the gross-up of 100/75 will produce no erosion in the amount of active business income that qualifies for the credit.

"Capital," as used in the formula, includes both fixed assets owned and fixed assets leased (other than land). The fraction "100/85" means that a corporation can have some non-qualified fixed assets without eroding its manufacturing and processing base—as long as these assets do not exceed 15% of the total. Thus, a capital investment in office and showroom furniture or automobiles will not necessarily reduce the availability of the special rate.

Tax Planning for the Manufacturing and Processing Incentive
Because of the arbitrary nature of the above formula, there are some excellent tax-planning ideas that can be adopted. For example, take the situation of a corporation engaged in both manufacturing and non-manufacturing activities. If the corporation's manufacturing profits are high while the non-manufacturing branch operates at just above the break-even level, you should consider splitting the business into two separate companies. You would transfer as much as possible of the non-manufacturing labour, fixed assets (such as office equip-

ment) and overheads to the non-manufacturing company, and keep the manufacturing operations as "pure" as possible. Thus, the non-manufacturing activities would not diminish the use of the special deduction, as could be the case if the two types of operations were combined under one corporate roof.

Conversely, if manufacturing and non-manufacturing activities are carried on by two separate but related corporations, and the manufacturing business is marginally successful while non-manufacturing is very profitable, you should consider amalgamating the two corporations. Because of the arbitrary percentages in the formula, a portion of the non-manufacturing profits may end up qualifying for the deduction.

Small manufacturing companies with annual profits below $200,000, whose businesses consist primarily of manufacturing and processing, do not have to use the somewhat complicated formula described in the previous section. Such corporations may claim the manufacturing tax rate on *all* business income.

It is important to note that the manufacturing incentives apply to *all* corporations, even if public or non-Canadian-controlled. There is ample opportunity in many instances to obtain substantial tax savings.

Tax Planning for Owner-Managed Manufacturing and Processing Operations—Salaries Versus Dividends

In order to complete our examination of the remuneration guidelines for corporations and their shareholders, we should now review the integration concepts as they apply to corporate tax rates ranging from 20% to 40%.

Logically, if a 25% corporate tax results in deferrals, you would expect to find slightly better results when the initial corporate rate is only 20%. In addition, when dividends are then paid out, there is a small overintegration effect, in spite of the new special 12.5% corporate-distributions tax.

Where the corporate tax rate is 40%, you would expect to find some tax deferrals, but nevertheless an ultimate tax penalty on payment of dividends. Depending on the tax bracket of the shareholder and the length of time of the deferral, it may pay to forgo the small-business deduction and allow the corporation to pay 40% without worrying too much about double taxation. These points are illustrated by the next two examples.

The first example (Figure 14-3) deals with income of $100 that qualifies for both the small-business deduction and the manufacturing and processing incentives. An effective federal and provincial tax rate of 20% is assumed. Even though the corporation can initially retain eighty cents on the dollar, the new 12.5% corporate-distributions tax means that only 71% of the profits are available for dividend payments. For the reasons given in Chapter Thirteen, in 1985 the first $28,000 of shareholder-manager remuneration should still be by way of salary. This would enable the shareholder-manager to take advantage of an RRSP, the Canada Pension Plan, and the $500 employment-expense deduction. Any additional remuneration beyond this base salary could be by way of dividends. At this point, a 3%-4% advantage sets in, over the corresponding alternative of additional salaries. (For new manufacturing businesses in Ontario, the advantage is much higher, since the initial corporate tax rate is only 10%.)

In manufacturing businesses eligible for the low rate of tax, profits not required for personal living expenses should be retained corporately to provide business and investment capital.

The example in Figure 14-4 covers the taxation of manufacturing income that does not qualify for the small-business deduction. This would apply in the case of a Canadian-controlled private corporation on annual profits in excess of $200,000 from manufacturing. From the example, it can be seen that only a taxpayer in a bracket below 40% would not get a deferral advantage by allowing the corporation to pay the tax. Of course, it is very unlikely that the owner-manager would be in a bracket below 50%, considering that we are dealing with income from an active business in excess of $200,000 per annum.

When the shareholder is in a 45% or 50% bracket, corporate retention provides a potential tax deferral of 5%-10%. On future payment of dividends, the tax penalty is quite small. An investment of the dollars deferred within the corporation for a few years will generally override the adverse effects of the penalty.

As a general guideline, therefore, when business income qualifies for the manufacturing incentives, but is substantially in excess of that which is eligible for the small-business deduction, the loss of the small-business credit is not of serious conse-

Figure 14-3 **Dividends Versus Salary Where a 20% Corporate Tax Rate Applies**

		$25,000	$35,000	$60,000
Income level				
Tax bracket		*40%*	*45%*	*50%*
Alternative 1:				
After-tax retention on				
$100 bonus		$ 60	$ 55	$ 50

Alternative 2: The corporation pays tax on profit of $100

Income of corporation	$100			
Corporate tax (after small-				
business deduction and				
manufacturing and processing				
tax credit)	20			
Retained earnings	$ 80			
Tax deferral where corporation				
pays the tax		$ 20	$ 25	$ 30
Payment of dividend:				
Retained earnings	$ 80			
Less:				
New 12.5% tax on dividend	9			
Cash dividend	$ 71			
Cash dividend		$ 71	$ 71	$ 71
50% gross-up		35	35	35
Income for tax purposes		$106	$106	$106
Federal and provincial tax				
in marginal bracket		$ 42	$ 48	$ 53
Dividend tax credit (combined)		35	35	35
Net tax		$ 7	$ 13	$ 18
Cash flow				
(cash dividend of $71 – net				
tax)		$ 64	$ 58	$ 53
Cash flow on $100 bonus		$ 60	$ 55	$ 50
Advantage of dividend of $71 over				
salary of $100 (overintegration)		$ 4	$ 3	$ 3

Figure 14-4 Dividend Versus Salary Where a 40% Corporate Tax Rate Applies

	$25,000	$35,000	$60,000
Income level			
Tax bracket	40%	45%	50%

Alternative 1:

	$25,000	$35,000	$60,000
After-tax retention on $100 bonus	$ 60	$ 55	$ 50

Alternative 2: The corporation pays tax on profit of $100

Income of corporation	$100	
Corporate tax (after manufacturing and processing tax credit only)	40	
Retained earnings	$ 60	

	$25,000	$35,000	$60,000
Tax deferral where corporation pays the tax	Nil	$ 5	$ 10
Payment of dividend:			
Cash dividend	$ 60	$ 60	$ 60
50% gross-up	30	30	30
Income for tax purposes	$ 90	$ 90	$ 90
Federal and provincial tax in marginal bracket	$ 36	$ 40	$ 45
Dividend tax credit (combined)	30	30	30
Net tax	$ 6	$ 10	$ 15
Cash flow (cash dividend of $60 − net tax)	$ 54	$ 50	$ 45
Cash flow on $100 bonus	$ 60	$ 55	$ 50
Penalty for not having taken bonus of $100	$ 6	$ 5	$ 5

quence. The owner-manager (and members of his or her family to the extent that this is reasonable) should draw salaries needed to meet living requirements. Maximum contributions should be made to RRSPs. Over the long run, if a shareholder-manager does not need to draw large sums of money out of his or her corporation immediately upon (or soon after) earning it, the tax-deferral advantages will more than outweigh the negative impact of double taxation. Again, you should never pay corporate taxes in excess of 33⅓% followed by an *immediate* dividend.

The Inventory Deduction

A discussion of business income would not be complete without further reference to the special 3% inventory deduction, which was introduced into the Income Tax Act a few years ago and which I discussed briefly in Chapter Twelve. For years, business owners have complained that profits for tax purposes have been overstated as a result of inflation. Assume, for example, that a business sells a product at $20 per unit. If the cost per unit is $16, each item sold gives rise to a profit of $4. Also assume, however, that the selling price is relatively fixed because of competition, but to replace a unit of inventory now costs $18. In such circumstances, the company may have to use its entire profit just for inventory replacement and the "real" pre-tax gain on the first sale should therefore be only $2. If the entire $4 profit were taxable (at full corporate rates), the business would not really be earning anything.

	First Unit	Second Unit
Selling price (fixed)	$20	$20
Cost	16 ⟶	18
Profit for tax purposes	4	
Taxes thereon (50%)	(2)	
	2	
Less: Additional cost of second unit	(2)	
"Real" profit	Nil	

In order to alleviate this problem, Parliament passed a 3% inventory deduction in 1977. The inventory deduction applies to the opening inventory of tangible property held for resale by any business. The only excluded businesses are those that are engaged in property ownership and development. (This is because real estate has generally tended to appreciate with inflation.)

The inventory deduction applies not only to finished goods but also to raw materials and work in progress. It is a permanent difference between accounting profits and profits for income-tax purposes. Thus, if a corporation has a $100,000 profit for accounting purposes while its opening inventory was, say, $600,000, the inventory deduction of $18,000 would reduce income for tax purposes to only $82,000.

The deduction is also not recapturable. It never has to be brought back into income whether or not, in fact, inflation causes an overstatement of profits for tax. Certainly, the 3% factor is somewhat arbitrary and the rules tend to benefit those businesses with low inventory turnovers. A meat packing company that turns over its inventory daily may not get much benefit from this deduction, while a jewellery store, which might be capable of raising its prices weekly, can get an extra advantage.

Planning to Maximize the Inventory Deduction
The arbitrary nature of the inventory deduction lends itself to extensive tax planning. Traditionally, businesses have always chosen year ends when inventory levels are lowest. This is to facilitate the preparation of financial statements where the most difficult task is usually the job of counting stock. Because of the 3% deduction, however, thought should be given to changing year ends (or establishing them in the first place) at the point when inventory is *highest*. Of course, if the costs of stock taking exceed the tax savings, this is not feasible. However, as I explained in Chapter Twelve, such a change in policy is definitely recommended for businesses that sell "big-ticket" items. Good examples would include dealers in cars or appliances, and jewellery and fur distributors.

For example, a car dealer is likely to have a constant inventory of parts throughout the year. (The dealer never has in stock the parts you need, but that is an entirely different question.) However, in November, he might only have twenty new cars on the lot, while at the end of May, he might have eighty units. How much longer does it take to count an additional sixty cars? Yet, the effect on the value of inventory and the 3% deduction becomes extremely significant. The same would hold true for a store selling television sets, where inventory would generally be lowest at the end of January after the post-Christmas sales and highest at the end of November.

If it is not feasible for a business to change its year end, it may still be possible to accelerate purchases so that more goods are held at the end of the fiscal year. This is especially feasible if extended credit terms can be obtained from suppliers. If this "excess" inventory is stockpiled and not even unpacked, you would simply add the dollar value of purchases to both inventory and accounts payable and there would be no effect on either profitability or the cost of stock taking. Consistent use of this method would produce a higher inventory from year to year, with the closing inventory of each year forming the basis of the *following* year's 3% deduction.

In the year that you change inventory policies, your company's banker must be informed. Otherwise, anyone reviewing the financial statements from a lender's standpoint would see a dramatic increase in inventory and would be somewhat concerned about the liquidity position of the business.

To maximize inventory, it is not even necessary to take delivery of goods. The courts have held that goods belong to an entity as long as legal title passes, even if they are held by someone else. If you have a supplier who is willing to hold goods but still transfer ownership before the purchaser's year end, the inventory deduction benefits flow. Of course, if the supplier has the same year end as the customer, he or she should be unwilling to make such an accommodation. This is because increasing the customer's inventory has the effect of decreasing the supplier's.

Finally, as I also explained in Chapter Twelve, in some cases it may be possible to defer the last day's sales. If a furrier sells a coat on the last day of the year, it is usually possible to arrange to postpone delivery and have the sale dated the following day. After all, in almost all cases, there would be some alterations that would need to be done. In this way, the furrier could get a double-edged advantage. The closing inventory would be that much higher and recognition of the profit could also be postponed until the following fiscal year.

These are all legitimate methods of maximizing the 3% inventory deduction. Other (not so legitimate) methods come to mind, such as purchasing goods just before the year end and then returning them for a credit note shortly thereafter. You might even consider going so far as to obtain an invoice from a "friendly" supplier for goods that were, in fact, never shipped. A credit note would follow in due course.

These last few methods are certainly not recommended since they *at least* border on being fraudulent. Also, the Income Tax Act prohibits artificial schemes conceived to extend the benefits of the inventory deduction. This, of course, does not negate some very real opportunities for effective tax planning, as long as the methods chosen are reasonable.

CHAPTER FIFTEEN

The Art of Buying a Business and the Use of Holding Companies

Introduction

From the point of view of taxation, one of the worst traps that you can possibly fall into is buying shares of a private business in your own name. Proper tax planning almost always involves the use of a holding company for business acquisitions. If you take the easy way out and transact directly, you could end up paying more taxes as a result of this one error than from all your other mistakes combined.

Holding companies have many other uses beyond being the ideal vehicle for business acquisitions. In fact, they are the key to "empire building." However, before we can fully appreciate the use of holding companies and their role in the tax system, a short review of some preceding material is in order. As described in the last two chapters, the Income Tax Act is designed so that corporate taxes are levied on business income at one of several different effective rates:

- Income that is from manufacturing and that qualifies for the small-business deduction is taxed at approximately 20%.
- Income that qualifies for the small-business deduction but is not from manufacturing is taxed at approximately 25%.
- Income that is from manufacturing but does not qualify for the small-business deduction is taxed at 40%.
- Income that neither qualifies for the small-business deduction nor is related to manufacturing is taxed at 50%.

When a dividend is received by an individual from an "operating company" (Op Co), the system of gross-up and credit at least partially compensates for the fact that the dividend is a distribution out of profits that have already been taxed once. The shareholder is credited for at least part of the corporate taxes previously paid.

Figure 15-1 **Dividend Flow From Operating Company Through Holding Company to Individual**

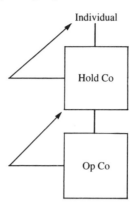

Individual

Hold Co

Op Co

It is, however, possible that an individual shareholder might not own a controlling interest in Op Co directly but through a "holding company" (Hold Co). In such circumstances, dividends would pass from Op Co to Hold Co before the individual could receive any funds personally. (See Figure 15-1.)

The Taxation of Intercorporate Canadian Dividends out of Business Income

If dividends were taxed as they passed from one corporation to another (out of business income), in a *chain* of corporations, there would be less and less ultimately available for the person at the "top" of the chain. If that were the case, the individual would suffer double and triple taxation, depending on how many corporations stood between the individual and the source of income in the first place. This is illustrated in the example in Figure 15-2, which assumes that intercorporate dividends out of business income not eligible for the small-business deduction were subject to *even one dollar* of tax.

To avoid double taxation, the system was designed in 1972 so that only the corporation that earns business income (i.e., Op Co) pays tax on that amount and type of profit. If there is any further tax to be paid, the rules were also designed so that this additional tax is not extracted until the *individual* (or individuals) who control the holding company ultimately receive dividends. Thus, dividends out of business income have traditionally passed

Figure 15-2 **If Intercorporate Dividends out of Business Income Were Taxed**

tax-free between a parent corporation and a controlled subsidiary. There is, however, one special rule, which applies starting in 1983. If the income earned by an operating company qualifies for the small-business tax rate, the special 12.5% dividend-distributions tax must be paid *before* a holding company can receive any cash. Thus, assuming an initial small-business tax rate of 25%, holding companies can only retain 66⅔% of the underlying profits. This is illustrated in Figure 15-3.

You should note that a holding company *itself* pays no tax as long as it owns more than 10% of the paid-up capital and the voting powers of the corporation that paid the dividend. If a top tax-bracket individual were to receive a dividend *personally*, he or she would only retain 50% of the underlying profits.

Where a holding company owns an interest of "10% or less," this is referred to as a "portfolio investment." Portfolio dividends are also subject to a special 25% flat-rate (refundable) tax, dealt with in Chapter Nine, which is repaid to the holding company at the time dividends are, in turn, distributed to the shareholders.

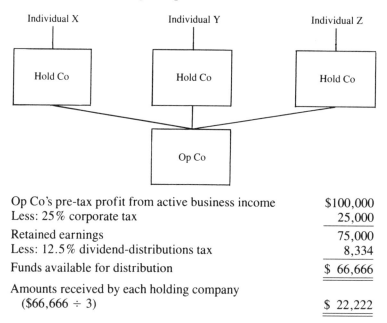

Figure 15-3 **The Flow of Dividends out of Small-Business Profits to Holding Companies**

Individual X   Individual Y   Individual Z

Hold Co   Hold Co   Hold Co

Op Co

Op Co's pre-tax profit from active business income	$100,000
Less: 25% corporate tax	25,000
Retained earnings	75,000
Less: 12.5% dividend-distributions tax	8,334
Funds available for distribution	$ 66,666
Amounts received by each holding company ($66,666 ÷ 3)	$ 22,222

Tax-Planning Opportunities

If control of an operating business is acquired, the purchase should be structured through a holding company so that the acquired corporation can end up *paying for itself* by flowing dividends through to its new parent. The following example illustrates the advantages of using a holding company to make an acquisition of an operating business.

Assume that an individual, X, is an investor in the 50% bracket. X would like to acquire more than a 10% interest in Op Co. He negotiates with the prospective vendor, and the purchase price is settled at $100,000. Assume, as well, that X does not have the necessary cash to make the purchase. He does, however, know of a lending institution that is willing to finance the acquisition.

Effectively, the transaction can be structured in one of two ways: either X can make the acquisition personally, or he can use a holding company to do so on his behalf.

Figure 15-4 **Individual Purchases Business**

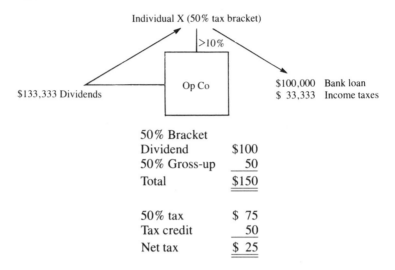

Individual X (50% tax bracket)

>10%

Op Co

$133,333 Dividends

$100,000   Bank loan
$ 33,333   Income taxes

50% Bracket	
Dividend	$100
50% Gross-up	50
Total	$150

50% tax	$ 75
Tax credit	50
Net tax	$ 25

Effective tax on dividends is 25%
Let D = Gross dividends needed to pay off bank
.75 D = $100,000
    D = $133,333

Figure 15-5 **Holding Company Is Used to Purchase Business**

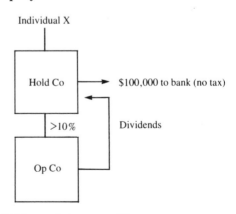

Individual X

Hold Co

$100,000 to bank (no tax)

>10%   Dividends

Op Co

Only $100,000 is needed to pay off loan
Op Co "saves" $33,333 of dividends

266

Presumably, X would not make an investment in Op Co unless he felt sure that the investment would ultimately pay for itself. In other words, he would expect that dividends from the newly acquired company would subsidize its cost. If X makes the purchase in his own name, he would have to draw dividends over a period of time so that his after-tax retention is sufficient to pay off the financing of $100,000. As described in the examples in Chapter Nine, an individual in the 50% tax bracket pays an effective tax of 25% on Canadian dividend income—after the gross-up and credit. Thus, X would need $133,333 of *gross* dividends to retain a net amount of $100,000 for purposes of discharging his bank indebtedness.

In contrast, if a holding company is used to structure the purchase, Op Co will only have to generate $100,000 of dividends to its new "parent." As long as the parent holds more than 10% of the shares of the subsidiary, the dividend will be received tax-free and can then be paid over *directly* to the lending institution. To summarize, with proper planning, *it is possible for X to save as much as $33,333 for every $100,000 of purchase cost.*

Carrying this example one step further, if an extra $33,333 is not needed to pay taxes at the personal level, Op Co "saves" not only the dividend itself, but an even greater amount of "earning power." If Op Co is extremely profitable and pays taxes at the high corporate rate, the fact that $33,333 is not needed translates to an earning power of $66,666. This is illustrated in Figure 15-6.

Figure 15-6 **Op Co "Saves" $66,666 of Earning Power**

Earnings	$66,666
50% tax	33,333
Dividend (not needed)	$33,333

From the foregoing, it becomes evident that you *must* use a holding company as a vehicle to acquire shares of other companies, at least where the share interest is greater than 10%. *To do otherwise would result in unnecessary personal taxes that could be easily avoided with proper planning*!

Although the example assumes that the purchase price is borrowed from a lending institution, the same planning would hold true even if X acted as his own banker. He would want to be able to recoup his investment on a tax-free basis, without the necessity of extracting dividends subject to personal taxes. This can be achieved by lending his own capital to the holding company, which would in turn acquire Op Co. Dividends could then be paid from Op Co to the holding company and the funds could be used to repay X's own advances.

Is there a catch? You might ask why the government has been so magnanimous in permitting such a wonderful opportunity to structure business acquisitions. Fortunately, there is no oversight in the law and the use of holding companies for such purposes is by no means a sham nor does it constitute undue tax avoidance.

The reason the government has beneficial rules on the flow of intercorporate dividends is that for every acquisition there is a corresponding sale. So far, we have only examined the position of the purchaser. For every purchaser there is a vendor who will (at least in theory) be paying a "capital-gains tax" as a result of having sold his or her interest in Op Co. If the government gets its capital-gains tax "up front" from the vendor, it may as well make it easier for the purchaser to buy.

You might also wonder whether the government is sacrificing substantial revenue by permitting a purchaser to structure his or her affairs to avoid taxes on dividends. Actually there is no loss from the treasury's standpoint, as we will see in the next section.

The Relationship Between Dividends and Capital Gains

Most of us have to reorient our thinking if we wish to use the tax system effectively. Before 1972, everyone preferred capital gains to any other type of income because it was not subject to tax. Since that time, only one-half of capital gains is taxable subject to the new $500,000 exemption. However, the 50% gross-up and credit that took effect in 1978 changes the relationship between dividends and capital gains. As strange as it may seem, almost all Canadians should now prefer receiving dividends to capital gains (if their lifetime capital-gains exemption has been used up)—even though dividends are fully taxable. This can be shown with the aid of the simple example opposite:

	40%	45%	50%
Effective tax on $100 dividend (after gross-up and credit)	$10	$17	$25
Effective tax on $100 capital gain (taxable gain is $50)	$20	$22	$25

As discussed in Chapter Nine, the effective tax on dividends is only 10% to someone who is in the 40% bracket. Thus, taxpayers in 40% brackets or lower will pay significantly less tax on dividends than they would on capital gains. Even where an individual is in the 50% bracket, the choice between receiving a dividend and a capital gain is equal. Thus, the government has obviously decided that it really doesn't matter whether a tax on capital gains is paid by a vendor or whether a tax on dividends is charged to a purchaser!

Of course, no attempt is made by the government to publicize the advantages of using holding companies for business acquisitions. Presumably, Revenue officials would not be too upset about receiving tax dollars *twice*—once from a vendor when he or she pays tax on capital gains arising from the sale, and again from the purchaser who struggles to pay for an acquisition that has been made personally.

As you might expect, the new lifetime capital-gains tax exemption may have a dramatic effect on a vendor's tax position. Barring any rule changes, it may be possible for a vendor to sell his or her shares and effectively escape taxes, especially if the share ownership has been split among family members and the total capital gain per person is under $500,000. On the other hand, a purchaser, by using a holding company, can complete his or her acquisition without paying personal income taxes. Remember, however, that it will take until 1990 for the new capital-gains tax exemption to be completely phased in.

Corporate Reorganizations

The use of holding companies also has advantages when it comes to reorganizing existing business situations. Assume, for illustration, that A, B, and C are unrelated individuals, each of whom owns one-third of the issued shares of an operating company. The operating company, for purposes of this example, has $75,000 in surplus cash that has been generated from prior operations in which $100,000 had been earned and taxed at 25%. While A, B, and C get along quite well when it comes to administering the daily affairs of their company, they do not necessarily see eye to eye when it comes to investments. A is a big spender and would like to draw his share of the surplus funds as a dividend in order to meet his living requirements; B, on the other hand, wishes to invest his share of the money in term deposits; while C would like to acquire real estate. Under the existing structure of the company, illustrated in Figure 15-7, a problem exists, because the diverse objectives could not be realized without paying out taxable dividends.

Figure 15-7 **Before Reorganization**

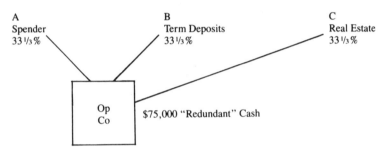

Figure 15-8 **Holding Companies Can Be Used to Meet Shareholders' Diverse Requirements**

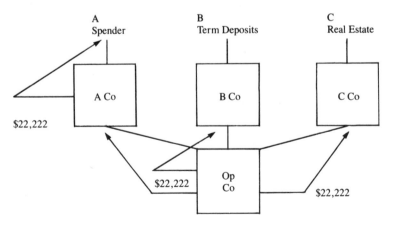

270

If, however, the shareholders each had personal holding companies, the problem could be solved. Using special provisions of the Income Tax Act, A, B, and C could each transfer their shares to their own holding companies (on a tax-free basis) in exchange for shares of the holding company. After the 12.5% corporate-distributions tax, Op Co could then pay three dividends of $22,222 to each of the "new" shareholders. A could draw his portion as a further dividend and use the after-tax proceeds for living expenses, while B and C could cause their holding companies to invest in term deposits and real estate respectively.

A could obtain a further advantage by dividing the ownership of A Co among his family. If the Op Co dividend of $22,222 were split between the family members, it is possible that the tax bite could be eliminated completely.

Another advantage of the holding-company structure just described is that each of A, B, and C would be free to involve their families in the ownership of their personal holding companies without necessarily consulting the other "partners." In cases where the shares of Op Co are held directly, B might (for example) object to A's spouse being a shareholder. No similar objections could be voiced by B with respect to A Co's share structure.

In summary, holding companies can be very effective in segregating the diversified spending or investment desires of business owners from their common operating objectives. There are also other advantages. By keeping Op Co free from excess or "redundant" assets, if business every turns sour, there is less for the creditors to seize—although this does not mean that a corporation can pay large dividends when bankruptcy is already imminent. In addition, Op Co becomes far more saleable if it does not own assets that a prospective purchaser would not be interested in acquiring. Investments out of excess profits could be made by the holding companies just as easily, and there is no need for any prior payment of personal taxes.

While holding companies have their advantages as a vehicle to reorganize business situations, the complexities of rearranging one's affairs should not be understated. For example, specific tax rules must be followed in order to transfer shares in a business to a holding company without attracting tax. In addition, if A, B, and C had owned their shares in Op Co before

1972, certain other tax problems could arise with respect to capital-gains considerations. These complexities would have to be handled by qualified legal and accounting professionals.

Finally, I must stress that the use of holding companies is primarily for the benefit of flexibility. The fact that A Co is owned only by A, and B Co by B, etc., will *not* provide for a multiple use of the small-business deduction. For all practical purposes, the entire group of companies will only be permitted to earn $200,000 annually at low corporate rates. (An exception would be where one or more of the holding companies are *independently* involved in operating an active business.)

Certainly, the use of holding companies for the purpose of reorganizing existing structures is worth exploring, and they should almost always be used for business acquisitions.

Bringing Buyers and Sellers Together

A comparison of the net tax costs of dividends and capital gains for taxpayers in various marginal brackets lends itself to some excellent planning opportunities when buyers and sellers are being brought together. An adviser working with both parties and without any personal involvement can help greatly to facilitate business acquisitions.

For example, if a prospective vendor of a business is in a low tax bracket and has already used up his or her capital-gains tax exemption, it would be advantageous for that individual to take a dividend *before* selling his or her shares. Of course, if he or she takes a dividend, this would reduce the tangible net worth of the company and would result in a corresponding decrease in the purchase price. If the purchase price is reduced by the same amount as the dividend, the vendor's capital gain would become that much smaller and the tax thereon is decreased as well. Thus, a vendor in the 40% bracket could pay ten cents on the dollar on a dividend, instead of twenty cents on the dollar on capital gains.

Very often, good timing can help a deal progress much more smoothly. If a business sale is being negotiated towards the end of the year, it may be advantageous for the vendor to take a dividend before December 31. He or she would then sell the shares (for a smaller price) on January 2, and in this manner, the dividend and the capital gain would be reported in different years.

The Ideal Corporate Structure

As indicated in the diagram of the "ideal" corporate structure (Figure 15-9), X should own his shares in Op Co through a holding company. It doesn't really matter whether the holding company has been used to acquire Op Co from someone else, or whether the business of Op Co was *started* by X in the first place.

As long as Op Co earns active business income that qualifies for the small-business deduction, it should float its after-tax profits up to Hold Co by way of dividends. Whether or not X's spouse is involved in the ownership of Op Co (indirectly through the holding company) is optional. If the family only has one business, it is generally advantageous for both X and X's spouse to participate in the ownership. If there is a second business operation *unrelated to the first*, it would usually be more advantageous for X to own all of the shares of the first corporation and for X's spouse to be involved only in the second business. In this manner, it may be possible to obtain two low

Figure 15-9 **The "Ideal" Corporate Structure**

273

rate tax bases instead of one. (See Chapter Thirteen, pages 246–48.)

As Hold Co receives dividends (tax-free) from the business income of Op Co (after the 12.5% corporate-distributions tax), the dollars that are not needed for business expansion should be transferred across as investment capital to a separate investment company (Invest Co). The investment company would be controlled by X through voting preferred shares, while the family members would own the common shares either directly or through a trust. The income of the investment company would be taxed initially at 50% (as discussed in Chapter Nine), but is subject to refundable taxes. Dividends could then be paid to the family and the funds would then be loaned back to the investment company.

The capital of Invest Co would increase each year from a combination of Op Co's profits (to the extent that these are not needed for business expansion) and the reinvestment of dividends paid out to the family. No personal taxes need be paid by X on any dollars other than those needed for living expenses, while X's spouse and the children can each receive dividends of up to $36,000 a year from Invest Co tax-free. Of course, if X's spouse is active in the business of Op Co, she might receive a salary and participate in an RRSP program. In these circumstances, she might not share in dividend distributions from Invest Co.

Expanding the Business Empire

As an offshoot to the "ideal" corporate structure, there is also the opportunity to use the profits of Op Co as capital to invest in further business acquisitions as shown in Figure 15-10. If X (the indirect owner of Op Co 1) becomes interested in a new venture, the holding-company structure would enable him to acquire the new business without any personal tax penalty. Again, the source of the funds would be Op Co 1, which would first pay dividends to Hold Co. The holding company would then reinvest these funds to acquire Op Co 2. The shareholders of Op Co 2 can actually be any combination of family members. Wherever possible, you would consider creating a structure under which the two businesses are not associated for tax purposes.

The advantage of having the businesses of Op Co 1 and Op Co 2 in separate corporations goes beyond the potential of

Figure 15-10 **Structure for Further Business Acquisitions**

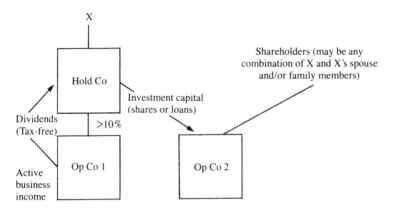

doubling up on the small-business tax rate. This structure also facilitates a sale of *either* business and the retention of the other. If separate businesses are under one "corporate roof," a sale becomes much more difficult. In addition, X may consider involving key employees in the ownership of one business without necessarily having them participate in the growth of the other.

From Figure 15-10, you should also be able to visualize the benefits when Op Co 2 happens to be a company whose only asset is real estate used by Op Co 1 as business premises. Keeping the real estate in a separate corporation generally facilitates business arrangements. It may be possible to sell the real estate without disposing of the operating business and vice versa. In addition, you can involve key employees in the business activities without also making them equity holders in the real estate.

The Era of the Holding Company

We are now well into the era of the holding company in Canada. There are many who feel that a multitude of companies tends to be somewhat cumbersome and may diminish the effectiveness of business operations. This could be true. You must always weigh the business advantages and disadvantages of two alternative approaches before making *any* decision. Prior to incorporation, you must determine in each case whether or not the dollars to be saved warrant the existence of a new company.

If the owners of Op Co are not looking to expand and all profits are needed for their personal living requirements, a holding company may not be useful. On the other hand, for substantial share acquisitions, a holding company is mandatory. In practice, decisions can only be made on the basis of specific facts and with the aid of your professional advisers. Of course, an understanding of the tax system helps.

CHAPTER SIXTEEN

A Common-Sense Approach to Estate Planning

Your major concern in estate planning should be to ensure that your assets eventually pass on to your designated heirs— preferably without Revenue Canada taking too large a share. The first step in minimizing taxes is to know what you are up against. The post-1971 system is designed so that wealth is taxed as and when it is accumulated. Subject to the new lifetime capital-gains exemption, each time you realize a capital gain, one-half of your profit is taxed on a pay-as-you-go basis. This is the opposite of the rules prior to 1972, under which capital growth accumulated during an individual's lifetime and was not taxed until death. At that time, the old Estate Tax Act applied, with calculations based on a person's net worth.

Under the present system, since capital gains are only taxed when realized, you can always postpone the necessity of sharing profits by not selling your property. In Chapter Seven, for example, we explored the idea of borrowing against increases in values, especially over the next few years until the full $500,000 exemption is phased in.

Can capital gains be avoided completely? In the absence of specific tax rules, there are only three ways that come to mind: giving property, becoming a non-resident, and death. Provisions have, however, been designed to prevent an easy escape. We have seen, for example, that a gift of property to anyone other than a husband or wife is a deemed disposition at fair market value. A gift will thus trigger accumulated capital gains, al-though future growth will pass to the benefit of the recipient.

Rules have also been designed to prevent anyone from avoiding taxes by becoming a non-resident. At the time of departure from Canada, the Income Tax Act deems a disposition at fair market value on many kinds of capital property, such as publicly traded securities. The deemed disposition forces a taxpayer who is giving up Canadian residence to include in his or her income one-half of the difference between the cost and the fair market value of property at the time of departure. Taxpayers are permitted to request a postponement until an actual sale is made—provided they furnish adequate security to the tax collector.

Deemed Dispositions on Death

Even if there were tax advantages, not everyone wishes to leave Canada or give away property. Eventually, therefore, everyone encounters the "ultimate" of the deemed dispositions—that which takes place upon death. The tax rules are summarized in Figure 16-1.

Figure 16-1   **Deemed Dispositions Upon Death of a Taxpayer**

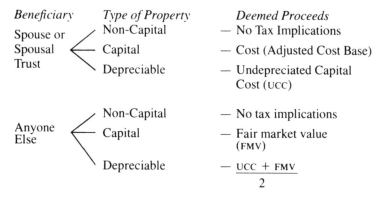

Beneficiary	*Type of Property*	*Deemed Proceeds*
Spouse or Spousal Trust	Non-Capital	— No Tax Implications
	Capital	— Cost (Adjusted Cost Base)
	Depreciable	— Undepreciated Capital Cost (UCC)
Anyone Else	Non-Capital	— No tax implications
	Capital	— Fair market value (FMV)
	Depreciable	— $\dfrac{\text{UCC} + \text{FMV}}{2}$

Non-Capital — Cash, Government of Canada Savings Bonds, term deposits, life insurance proceeds
Capital — Most corporate bonds, land, personal effects (jewellery, art, etc.), shares in public and private corporations
Depreciable — Buildings

From the schedule, it is evident that the consequences of death depend on two factors: to whom the property is bequeathed and the kind of property the deceased had. For non-capital property such as cash, Canada Savings Bonds, and life insurance benefits, there are no income-tax implications whatsoever—no matter who the individual's beneficiary happens to be. This is because cash, Canada Savings Bonds, and other non-growth assets represent income on which taxes have

278

already been paid. In the case of life insurance, the proceeds are not taxable since policy premiums are not deductible.

With respect to all other property, husband and wife are considered as the equivalent of one person. No tax need be paid until the last of the two dies. Thus, whenever capital property is bequeathed to a spouse, there is a (tax-deferred) transfer at cost. No gain is recognized until the recipient spouse either sells the property or, in turn, dies and passes it on to someone else. Similarly, depreciable property passes at undepreciated capital cost (cost minus accumulated depreciation for tax purposes).

If capital property is passed to heirs other than a spouse, there is a deemed disposition immediately before death at fair market value. This will trigger all accrued capital gains on the deceased's last tax return. To the extent that the deceased still had all or part of the lifetime capital-gains exemption yet available, no taxes will become payable.

Whenever *depreciable property* passes to other heirs (upon the death of either or both husband and wife), there is a deemed disposition halfway between undepreciated capital cost and fair market value. The "halfway" rule will result in the recognition of less income than would otherwise be the case on a disposition deemed to take place at fair market value. This is illustrated in the example in Figure 16-2.

Figure 16-2 **Deemed Disposition of Depreciable Property (Building) to Heirs Other Than a Spouse**

Fair market value *(A)*	$120,000	$140,000	$200,000
Cost	100,000	100,000	100,000
Undepreciated capital cost *(B)*	60,000	60,000	60,000
Deemed disposition = $\frac{A + B}{2}$	$ 90,000	$100,000	$130,000
Recaptured depreciation	$ 30,000	$ 40,000	$ 40,000
Taxable capital gain	Nil	Nil	15,000
Total "deemed" income	$ 30,000	$ 40,000	$ 55,000
If sold before death:			
Recaptured depreciation	$ 40,000	$ 40,000	$ 40,000
Taxable capital gain	10,000	20,000	50,000
Total income if sold	$ 50,000	$ 60,000	$ 90,000

The reason for having special rules for depreciable property seems to be that this kind of property is less liquid than other growth assets and, as well, is less susceptible to being sold in part. For example, if you die leaving 10,000 shares of a public company, 2,000 shares can always be sold if necessary in order to pay taxes. It is not quite as easy to dispose of a 20% interest in a building.

Although the deceased escapes full taxation, the rules go on to provide that the heirs will become liable to recognize the remaining income at the time they actually dispose of the property. Thus, there is no forgiveness of tax, only a deferral.

The Use of Spousal Trusts

The concept of the husband-wife unit is perhaps the most important factor when it comes to estate planning. To repeat, there is complete "rollover" (that is, a tax-deferred transfer) when property passes from either spouse to the other. The rollover applies not only to outright bequests, but, as well, whenever property is left to a *trust* for the benefit of the surviving spouse.

A "spousal trust" may have two advantages. The first pertains to situations in which an individual feels that his or her spouse is either not interested in administering property or does not have the necessary expertise. Instead of leaving property directly to the spouse, the person drawing up his or her will can create a trust. This gives the "testator" (the person making up his or her will) the opportunity to appoint outside executors and trustees. In this manner, the responsibility for investment and business decisions can either be taken away entirely from the other spouse or the burden can be shared with the spouse. The second advantage of a spousal trust is even more important. Leaving property in trust, instead of outright, gives the testator the opportunity to control the *ultimate* disposition of his or her property—even after death.

If, for example, I were preparing my will today, I would start by estimating my current net worth in the event of death. Let us assume, for purposes of illustration, that this amounts to $500,000. Now, before you assume that I am wealthier than you are, note that most business owners, professionals, and executives are worth much more dead than alive because of life insurance. Estates ranging from a half a million dollars and up are therefore not uncommon. Returning to my situation, I have one wife and four children. My objectives, like yours, are, first, to protect my wife and, second, to provide for the children. If I were to leave all my property directly to my wife, she could then do whatever she wanted with the assets. She could remarry and give all the property to her new husband. She could spend all the money, lose all the assets in the stock market, gamble away everything in Las Vegas, have children with a new husband and disinherit our children, or conversely take the capital and triple it.

The point is, I don't know what would happen. Thus, by leaving my property in trust, I could control the ultimate disposition. I would have the opportunity to appoint trustees and executors so that my wife could not act alone. If I followed standard practices, I would nominate three trustees or a trust company. If individual trustees were appointed, the power to make all decisions would usually be left to the majority.

If I made these arrangements, the trustees would have a dual responsibility after my death—to my wife and to the children. My will would provide for the assets to be maintained for my wife's benefit with the residual amount to be divided among the children upon her death.

I would instruct the trustees to pay out capital amounts (in addition to income) upon reasonable request only. For example, if my widow remarried and proceeded to ask the trustees for $200,000 out of the estate to finance her new husband's business, the request would presumably be refused. After all, the trustees could not agree to anything that might jeopardize the position of the children.

On the other hand, if my wife were to approach the trustees after my death for $5,000 towards the purchase of a new car, the trustees would probably sanction such a withdrawal of capital. After all, one of the objectives of building an estate is to ensure that a spouse can maintain a certain lifestyle.

The trust-will therefore allows for the fulfillment of two basic objectives: protecting a surviving spouse and also (ultimately) providing capital for your children.

In many cases, a trust-will is *not* necessary—especially if the holdings of an estate are not complex. However, such an arrangement becomes almost mandatory where a husband and wife have children by previous marriages. *A trust arrangement is the only way to guarantee that the children of the deceased eventually inherit their parent's assets.*

Income-Tax Requirements for Spousal Trusts

For assets to pass into a spousal trust on a tax-deferred basis, the trust must meet two specific conditions:

- The surviving spouse must get all the income earned by the trust in her or his lifetime.
- No one other than the surviving spouse may encroach upon the capital of the trust before she or he dies.

The first rule requires the surviving spouse to receive all *income* earned *without any strings attached.* If you put a clause into a will prohibiting your spouse from deriving income from the trust if she or he remarries, or reducing the amount of income that she or he would be entitled to receive, this would negate the rollover benefits of the trust for tax purposes. You would still have a valid trust from a legal standpoint, but all assets passing into that trust would be received at fair market value. This would trigger the taxes on death that you are presumably trying to postpone.

The second rule contains another restriction and the difference is rather subtle. You can have a perfectly valid trust for tax purposes even if your spouse is *not* permitted to touch any of the *capital* (provided she or he receives all the income), as long as no one *else* can encroach on capital *either.*

Capital-Encroachment Powers

What is the advantage of a complete prohibition against capital encroachment? If you make up a will prohibiting your spouse from encroaching on capital, you can be quite certain that your children (or other heirs) will inherit at least the same amount of assets as went into the trust in the first place—even if your spouse spends or otherwise disposes of all the income received in her or his lifetime.

Returning to my $500,000 estate, I think it would be nice to be able to ultimately give $125,000 of assets to each of my four children. If I forbid my wife to encroach on capital, this "objective" is easily attainable. On the other hand, is a blanket prohibition against capital encroachment really wise? If I left my wife $500,000 of assets, today it is reasonable to project a conservative annual return of about 10%, or $50,000. While this might be more than adequate for her current needs, what about inflation? Of course, a lot depends on my wife's age, spending requirements, the ages of the children, and so on. To completely prohibit capital encroachment can be somewhat risky in the long run unless an estate is very large. The term "very large" is itself subjective and each person must evaluate the meaning of this independently. Yet to allow my wife an unlimited capital encroachment would negate the value of having a trust in the first place. I would therefore try for a flexible arrangement. The flexibility is achieved by appointing several trustees (generally including my spouse) and having each decision on capital encroachment left to the majority.

"Overprotecting" a Spouse
While providing adequately for a spouse is probably the prime objective of estate planning, I think that there is such a thing as "overprotection." In the classic case, a man dies leaving an estate of $5 million to a trust for his wife, with instructions that on her death, the assets are to pass to the children. At the time of the man's death, his wife is seventy years old. He, of course, has wrongly assumed that she will be dead within two or three years of his own death. He has forgotten that her life expectancy from age seventy is still *another fifteen years* (see Chapter Five). If the wife had her children when she was around the age of twenty-five, the children will then be in their sixties before their mother dies. In novels and movies, the children become disgruntled and help Mother along on her way to the pearly gates. In "real life," however, the family relationships often simply disintegrate.

When there are more than enough assets to go around, I think that it might be better social planning to divide these assets either during an individual's lifetime or at the time the first spouse dies. Even if taxes do become payable, the social benefits could outweigh the tax disadvantages. For instance, in March 1979, a friend of mine asked me to provide some tax and general investment counselling to his widowed mother. My friend's father had recently died, leaving a will under which all assets were to be held in trust for his wife until her death, at which time there would be a distribution between his two children (both were in their mid-thirties at the time). My friend gave me a list of the available assets to work with.

I determined that the value of the estate was approximately $450,000 and that the anticipated income yield was $45,000 a year. When I met with my friend and his mother, the first question I asked was how much she needed for living. She answered, "About $3,000." I made some quick calculations and suggested that if her living requirements were $36,000 per annum, and the investment yield was only $45,000, she had best invest rather conservatively. She interrupted, however, and told me that she meant $3,000 a year, not each month. When she saw the look on my face, she began to explain. She told me that her house is paid for, she never learned to drive a car, she doesn't have expensive tastes in clothing, never takes vacations, treats herself to a movie only once a week, and spends her other leisure time visiting her grandchildren. She assured me that $3,000 was more than adequate for her annual needs.

Under these circumstances, if my friend's mother does in fact live to be eighty-five years old, the $450,000 estate should be worth at least three times that amount. This is a good example of "overprotection." With all due respect to the deceased (whom I had never met), an estate of $450,000 is not large by today's standards. I really don't know whether I would have advised him to prepare his will any differently if I were in a position to do so. Perhaps if before his death he had had a frank discussion with his wife on the subject of her living requirements, he himself might have thought differently when making up his will. It might not have been such a bad idea to leave $50,000 directly to each of the two children so that each one could pay off his home mortgage. If this were done, "only" $350,000 would have passed to his wife.

The worst example of bad estate planning that I have ever seen involves the family of another friend. This friend has one brother and one sister and in each case, the family income is approximately $50,000 a year. All three are therefore comfortable but are by no means wealthy. My friend has a father in his early seventies who is a widower. This man is now retired, having made about $2 million in real estate transactions over the years. In fact, a good deal of his assets today consist of vacant land.

My friend's father has informed his children that under the terms of his will, the assets are to bypass them completely and will vest, on his death, in the grandchildren. His reasoning is that, although he cannot avoid capital gains on his own death, by passing the assets to his grandchildren, there will be no further deemed dispositions for the next sixty years. (After all, if the assets were only to pass to his *children*, the next deemed disposition could conceivably take place thirty years sooner!) Needless to say, my friend and his brother and sister are a little upset with their father's version of estate planning.

One might argue that a father does not owe his children anything once they are out on their own and that, if he wishes to pass his assets to the grandchildren instead, he has every right to do so. However, the motivation here is not that the grandfather does not get along with his own children, but rather a somewhat paranoid desire to reduce taxes otherwise payable. What upsets my friend most is not his own disinheritance, but the fact that his children stand to be considerably wealthier than *he* is within a few short years without having earned anything on their own. This is a clear case of the tax tail wagging the social and economic dog.

Sometimes, it may be necessary to pay more taxes than might otherwise be possible just to maintain good family relationships. Certainly "overprotection" and unnecessary tax avoidance should be considered when estate planning.

Appointment of Executors

One of the most difficult tasks that we all must face is choosing proper executors. It is more than just an honour to be an executor of an estate; it is a responsibility. Executors must be given broad powers and must have good administrative abilities. They must make sure that the deceased's wishes are carried out and that all assets are collected together and allocated properly. There are various "tax elections" that may be made in the year of death in the course of filing final tax returns, and they must be aware of all options. The executors must often deal with matters such as selling property and negotiating the best possible prices. Most of all, there is the responsibility of maintaining a balance between the relative rights of the various beneficiaries. Wherever possible, an attempt must be made to avoid potential conflicts of interest. Often, people appoint their accountants and lawyers as executors because of professional competence but without considering possible difficulties.

One of the most interesting cases that I ever worked on involved such a situation. I received a call one day from an accountant friend of mine who asked me to help him solve a conflict of interest. He had been appointed as an executor of an estate by one of his clients, who then died leaving behind a retarded son as his sole heir. The client also left a thriving business and it was his intention (although not specifically mentioned in the will) that certain key employees be given the opportunity to acquire this enterprise at a "fair price." The employees were more than happy to exercise their option and asked the same accountant to stay on as their auditor and adviser as well. The accountant thus found himself in an awkward position. He could not possibly allow himself to be in a position where, in negotiating a purchase price for the business, he would have to choose between his first client's son and the prospective clients.

In this case, the conflict was resolved rather nicely. The accountant asked me to act on behalf of the key employees and represent them in formulating a bid. He, in turn, represented the estate. The purchasers of the business understood the necessity of such an arrangement and co-operated fully. An agreement was reached within a short period of time as to the purchase price and method of payment and everybody wound up content. Unfortunately, this does not always happen.

Potential conflicts of interest are not the only problem with which you must contend in appointing executors. In another recent situation, I was asked to help a client reorganize his business holdings and to do some estate planning. The estate was rather complex and the work took several months to complete. By the time of our final meeting in the lawyer's office, the will had already been prepared and had been reviewed several times. All that was left was to fill in a few of the details and sign it. At one point, my client's lawyer asked him to name some executors in addition to his wife. The client thought for a moment and named his brother-in-law—who lived in Lima, Peru. The lawyer and I looked at each other in amazement and then explained to the client that the choice of a brother-in-law in a far-off country as an executor is just not feasible. Fortunately, the client saw the logic behind our arguments and appointed a more suitable substitute.

The most common problem, though, occurs when parents

appoint their children as executors. I have often been involved in cases where a client says to me: in the event my spouse predeceases me, I would like my oldest son, John, to be the executor.

The client usually thinks he knows what he is doing. He can give you all the right reasons. Not only is John the oldest child, but he is a university graduate, has a good "business head," and gets along well with his brothers and sisters. The problem, however, is that any time you appoint one of your children as an executor, if you don't take other steps with which I will deal shortly, you set the stage for a life-long enmity between that child and his or her brothers and sisters.

Let me explain with an example. Let's assume, as we did before, that my net worth is $500,000 at the time of my death and that I have four children. Assume that my wife predeceases me. I suggest that if my only asset were cash, I could almost get away with appointing a chimpanzee to act as the sole executor of my estate. One really doesn't need several college degrees to divide $500,000 by four and distribute $125,000 to each child.

And yet, no estate is that simple. There are always assets that are not divisable. Who, for example, will inherit my car? Who gets my wife's jewellery? What about the Group of Seven painting that hangs in our living room, or the gold pocket watch that I inherited from my grandfather?

As I mentioned before, executors must be given very broad powers. In fact, the clauses in a will prepared by most attorneys that deal with executors' rights and responsibilities tend to run perhaps three or four pages. This is more than just boiler-plate, designed to increase legal fees. Executors must be protected from lawsuits initiated by disgruntled beneficiaries. If an executor had to live in constant fear of getting sued, no one would ever accept such an appointment.

So the standard clause in the will states that an executor's decision is binding, and unless he or she has committed fraud, there is no recourse against his or her decision.

The problem basically is that anybody who picks one of his or her children as an executor must consider the types of properties that I just referred to which are not easily divisible and may have sentimental value to *several* of the children.

So, what can be done? There are really two choices. The first is to deal with all of these personal items specifically in the will. This is the textbook approach, but one which is frankly difficult to carry out in real life. This is because there may be literally hundreds of personal properties and a family's personal holdings tend to change from time to time.

What I recommend instead is that periodically you should have a family-council meeting with your children. For these purposes, the children do not all have to be adults. Children as young as eight or nine can understand this kind of subject as long as you use simple language. The idea is to sit down with your children and explain to them that, in the event that you and your spouse die, you have decided to appoint your son, John, as an executor. This means that he will have the job of distributing all your property. You can explain that the idea behind your will is to make the distributions equally, but that certain properties cannot be divided. Then, you can express your specific wishes. For example, John (being the only one old enough to drive) will inherit the family car. Mary, your only daughter, would receive Mother's jewellery, while Tom, who always liked the Group of Seven painting, would be able to keep that for himself. The gold pocket watch would then go to George.

If any of the children are unhappy with what you have decided, there are two possibilities. The first is that you can encourage the children to voice their opinions and, if expedient, to make trades between themselves. For example, what if Tom tells you that he really doesn't like the painting but he would rather have the gold pocket watch, while George prefers the painting instead of that watch? Having the children resolve their differences in your presence might be better for all concerned.

Alternatively, even if the kids walk away unhappy, the point is that they are angry with *you* and not with John who is the executor of the estate. After all, once you are dead, it really doesn't matter whether your children are slightly angry at something that you may have done. On the other hand, you must count on their living with their brothers and sisters for most of the rest of their lives.

To summarize, whenever possible, avoid conflicts of interest. Think about this problem before you finalize the appointment of your executors—especially in family situations, keep the lines of communication open.

Special Rules—The Family Farm

So far, this chapter has only dealt with the general rules pertaining to transfers of property on death. However, there are special rules that apply whenever a family farm is transferred from one generation to another. As long as the farm is located in Canada and is transferred to either children, grandchildren, or great-grandchildren, a transfer can take place with no capital gain being realized. (This is quite apart from the new general $500,000 capital-gains exemption.) These rules apply as long as the recipients of the farm are resident in Canada and the property had been used in farming by either the deceased, his or her spouse, or one or more children immediately before death. Vesting in the recipients must take place within thirty-six months.

In 1978, the Income Tax Act was amended to extend the family-farm "rollover" (which originally applied to only unincorporated farms) to interests in family-farm partnerships and shares in the capital stock of family-farm corporations. In most situations, it would now be advantageous to reorganize the structure of one's farm holdings to take advantage of the corporate tax rules for small businesses.

The Family Farm—Recent Changes

The Spring 1984 Federal Budget has brought in more significant changes with respect to family farms. First, on the death of an individual after 1983, it is now possible to elect to transfer farm property, including an interest in a family-farm partnership or shares in a family-farm corporation, to a child or children at any value between the cost amount of the property and its fair market value. Thus, if a farmer dies and has losses available for carry-forward at that time, or dies early in a given year and has little income otherwise taxable, it may now pay to trigger some capital gains. The advantage of an election at an amount in excess of the deceased's cost would be to provide a higher cost for tax purposes to the heir or heirs who receive the property.

For the purposes of the rollover rules, the definition of the word "child" has been expanded for transfers of farm property made after 1983 to include any person who, at any time before he or she attained the age of twenty-one years, was in law or in fact in the custody and control of the transferor and was wholly dependent on him for support. This would include, for example, foster children who were not legally adopted.

In addition, the farm rollover has also been extended to include property leased by an individual to his or her own family-farm corporation or to a family-farm corporation or partnership of the spouse or child. Such property will be deemed to be used by the owner in the business of farming for the purposes of providing a tax-deferred rollover. This new measure gives farmers far more flexibility in organizing the structure of their farm holdings.

In the past, much concern has been voiced about the situation in which farm property is transferred by a taxpayer to a child in the transferor's lifetime and the child subsequently dies. Under the prior income-tax rules, there was no provision for a rollover if the farm is then passed back to the parent who made the transfer in the first place. After 1983, this problem has been resolved. Thus, if a parent reacquires an interest in a family farm (incorporated or otherwise) upon the death of a child, there is now an election to deem the transfer back to take place at any value between the cost amount to the deceased child and the fair market value.

Finally, in cases where a family farm is sold to third parties, the entire $500,000 lifetime capital-gains exemption is available effective 1985, without reference to the phase-in rules which apply in other circumstances. As with any other small business, if interests are owned by several family members, the opportunity arises for multiple use of this new incentive.

Tax-Free Transfer of Small-Business Holdings

The concept of the family-farm rollover had also been extended, within the last few years, to shares of a "qualified small business" that are left to children or grandchildren. A qualified small business is any Canadian-controlled private corporation that earns active business income. Thus, qualified businesses include (among others) companies engaged in wholesaling, retailing, construction, manufacturing, natural resources and transportation, as well as certain service companies.

Under the special tax rules, every owner of shares of a qualified business has a (maximum) lifetime $200,000 exemption from capital gains. This exemption will be in force until

1988, at which time it is slated to be replaced by the new "blanket" capital-gains exemption. Because of the importance of these (temporary) rules over the next couple of years, I will now discuss them in detail.

The $200,000 limit applies irrespective of how many businesses an individual owns and/or how many children he or she has. An individual is free to allocate his or her $200,000 amount in any way that he or she desires, and the allocation can take place either during one's lifetime or upon one's death.

Assume, for example, that you have shares in a Canadian private business with a cost of $100,000 and a fair market value of $600,000. If you die before 1988 without having previously taken advantage of this special provision and leave these shares to one or more of your children, your deemed proceeds will only be $400,000 and your capital gain will be $300,000 (instead of $500,000).

Actually, it is not accurate to call the $200,000 difference an "exemption," for it is technically only a deferral. This is because if the child or children ever sell the shares and receive $600,000, they will be faced with a capital gain equal to the difference between their deemed cost of $400,000 and their selling price. This would not, however, result in any hardship for the children, since they would be receiving (cash) proceeds of disposition.

There are several opportunities for effective planning. First, you need not wait until death to take advantage of this $200,000 limit. If, for example, you wish to admit your children into your business, this special rule will help you greatly in meeting your objective. Using the above numbers, it is possible for a father or mother to literally give 40% of a business "tax-free" to one or more children. This would be especially advantageous when the children are already active in the business. The 40% factor just happens to be the percentage that would apply in this particular case:

Portion of business transferred to son/daughter		40%	
Fair market value	$600,000	$240,000	$200,000 gain is "exempt"
Cost for tax purposes	$100,000	$ 40,000	

291

As long as the difference between the cost of the interest sold and its fair market value is under $200,000, no gain need be recognized. In the preceding case, however, the child or children would pick up 40% of all future growth.

Effective tax planning also involves taking advantage of the potential to double up on the $200,000 "exemption" by *initially* involving both husband and wife in the ownership of a business. Traditional wills are often obsolete because they fail to incorporate the new small-business rollover provisions. Under the traditional approach, the husband usually leaves all his assets to his wife (either directly or in trust) and it is only on her death that the assets pass to her children. Where there is only one transmission of family-business shares to the children, only one $200,000 exemption is obtainable. Where the wife is a shareholder in the business, her will is usually identical to her husband's.

I suggest, instead, that the husband's will be redrafted so that on his death, some shares would pass immediately to the children in amounts sufficient to trigger $200,000 of capital gains (which would be exempt from tax in any event). The balance of his shares could continue to pass to his wife (directly or through a trust), so that she would have control over the business throughout the remainder of her lifetime. On her death, subsequently, the balance of the shares could then pass from her to the children and again the first $200,000 of gains would be exempt. Similarly, the wife's will should incorporate the same provisions, in the event that she dies first.

It is inappropriate to have the Canadian private business capitalized with only a few shares. To take an extreme position, what if a company were owned equally by a husband and wife, each of whom had only one share? The problem is that, no matter who dies first, the surviving spouse would not have control of the business if the deceased leaves his or her share to the children. Fortunately, this problem can easily be corrected by simply subdividing the shares (ten for one, or a hundred for one, etc.) as soon as possible. The splitting of shares would *not* attract any income taxes.

What is even more inappropriate is a case in which a company is owned 99% by husband and only 1% by wife. If the wife dies first, all she is capable of transmitting to the children is her 1%. Unless the company is worth somewhere in excess of

Figure 16-3 **Revising Wills to Double up on the Tax-Free Transfer of Small-Business Holdings**

TRADITIONAL

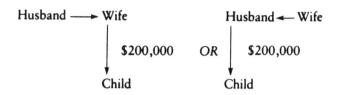

Only one "tax free" transfer is possible no matter who dies first.

ADVISABLE

INAPPROPRIATE

Survivor has no control no matter who dies first

If wife dies first, what is her interest worth?

$20 million, there is no possibility that her 1% could have appreciated by $200,000 since its acquisition.

A disproportionate ownership is also not well suited to splitting income by way of payment of dividends—even where separate classes of shares are held. I have dealt with this in previous chapters. The only time I would suggest that a company be owned completely by a husband (to the full exclusion of his wife) would be where separate businesses exist, each of which would qualify for the small-business tax rate. In these circumstances, if the husband owns 100% of the first company, his wife should own 100% of the second. If the family's intention is to own one business only, the ownership should be spread fairly equally.

If you are faced with a grossly disproportionate ownership among shareholders of a single family business, a reorganization of capital can be carried out. This is quite technical and requires professional assistance. The reorganization would allow the wife in the previous example to participate in *future* growth, which she could pass on to the children as part of her $200,000 exemption if she were to die first. These concepts are illustrated in Figure 16-3.

As mentioned previously, it may be possible over the next couple of years to "piggy-back" the existing $200,000 small-business capital-gains tax deferral together with the new blanket capital-gains exemption. Whether or not this will be possible will depend on the actual legislation following the Spring 1985 budget. At the time of writing, this legislation has not yet been formulated or released. If you plan on transferring shares in your business to one or more of your children in the next couple of years and your potential capital gain is in excess of $500,000 in total, I strongly suggest that you keep in close touch with your advisers. For some business owners, the opportunity to take advantage of both sets of rules may be the biggest tax-planning opportunity now available under the Income Tax Act.

Transfers of Small-Business Corporations—Recent Changes

The opportunities of transferring property on a tax-deferred basis to a foster child or from a deceased child back to his parents, recently provided for family farms, have also been extended to shares of other Canadian-controlled private corporations engaged in active business. However, the tax which may be deferred in conjunction with family-farm rollovers remains unlimited, while the maximum capital gains which may be deferred on the rollover of shares of other small-business ventures before 1988 remains $200,000.

Estate Planning and Life Insurance

The topic of estate planning couldn't possibly be covered without some reference to the role of life insurance as part of the overall picture. As a bare minimum, you should insure your life so that there need be no forced sale of assets at the time of death solely for the purpose of paying income taxes. For that purpose, some kind of permanent insurance is necessary and term insurance will not usually be sufficient. (A term policy will not help if it expires before your death.)

Basically, you should determine the tax consequences resulting from deemed dispositions on death for bequests to beneficiaries other than a spouse. Your accountant can assist you in putting together the figures. You would then apply combined federal and provincial marginal tax rates to the anticipated income. In order to be fairly conservative, you might assume taxes of about 50% on taxable gains after available exemptions have been used up.

Of course, the tax implications of death depend largely on the time of year in which you die. If you die early in a given year, the income arising from deemed dispositions might be taxed all by itself at favourable rates. However, if you die late in the year, the income from deemed dispositions is then added to all your other income of that year and the tax burden could be significant.

You should next calculate your available cash, Canada Savings Bonds, and "near cash," such as marketable securities. In addition, liquid assets realizable from the sale of a family business would be relevant if there is a buy-sell agreement between yourself and one or more partners. The minimum insurance you would then require would be that needed to discharge your tax liabilities after applying the liquid assets towards that purpose. Taxes arising from deemed dispositions may be spread over ten years, but each instalment would currently bear interest at 10%. This instalment interest is not tax-deductible and the financing therefore is expensive.

Of course, life insurance has additional uses beyond just paying taxes. Its role is also to provide a larger income to your heirs, especially for a spouse and dependent children. If your estate is tied up in either vacant land that yields very little income or growth stocks that do not pay dividends, your spouse may be in a rather embarrassing financial position without proceeds from life insurance with which to generate a future flow of income. If you own a part-interest in a private business, life insurance is almost mandatory to assist the surviving partners in buying out the estates of those who die first.

For individuals who maintain liquid estates and who require the bulk of their protection in the early years, perhaps term insurance would be advisable. When it comes to a business situation, however, many advisers would opt in favour of a more permanent type of coverage. This is because most term policies are calculated to expire at age seventy, whereas the average individual will probably not die until one or two years later. Term insurance therefore provides protection for your early needs while your children are young, but it is not adequate for long-range business planning and the preservation of property that is not liquid, such as real estate. When it comes to estate planning, a good insurance agent is just as important a member of the team as your accountant or lawyer.

The Time for Planning Is Now

Unfortunately, people tend to postpone estate planning, the preparation of their wills, and similar matters, because the contemplation of death tends to be a bit distasteful. However, ask yourself, what would happen to your family if you died today? If you spend a few minutes thinking about the consequences, tax and estate planning will become much more important. *The time for effective planning is now.*

CHAPTER SEVENTEEN

How to Deal With the Tax Collector

Reporting of Income

An individual is required to file a Form T1 for each year in which he or she owes tax before April 30 of the following year. An individual is also required to file this form within "a reasonable time" if a demand is made by the Minister. If an individual does not owe any taxes and does not receive a demand, he or she is not compelled to file. Effective 1985, if an individual realizes a capital gain or loss which affects the new $500,000 exemption, he or she must file a return even if no taxes are payable.

If you receive a substantial portion of your income from salary, and tax deductions at source are large enough so that you have a refund owing, it is, of course, in your interest to voluntarily file a return to get back your overpayment. In addition, a tax return is required if a claim is made for the child tax credit.

Although not all individuals are required to file, the law provides that *every* corporation must file an income-tax return (Form T2) in duplicate within six months after the end of each fiscal year. This return must show how income has been calculated as well as all taxes payable. In addition, if the company is exempt from tax, the return must indicate the reasons. A set of financial statements must accompany each copy of the return, together with schedules setting out such things as capital cost allowances, capital gains, and an explanation of differences between accounting income and income for tax purposes. All amounts owing should be paid on or before the due date for the filings to avoid (non-deductible) interest charges.

Contact With Revenue Canada

Your first contact with Revenue Canada is usually shortly after the required income-tax returns are filed. In most cases, you will receive a Notice of Assessment stating that the return has been assessed as filed and a statement indicating the balance of tax owing either by you or by the government. Additional correspondence with Revenue Canada can usually be avoided if all required receipts, vouchers, forms, and documents are filed with your return.

Aside from the usual mathematical errors, which are picked up by the computer, the most frequent cause of rejection or delay in processing a return is a form or voucher that is missing. You can never assume that Revenue Canada will know that you, in fact, have the missing document. For instance, assume that you were in full-time attendance at a Canadian university during the year and you submitted an official receipt for tuition fees for the fall session with your return. However, you also claimed the education deduction for the same four months without submitting Form T2202 or Form T2202A. In this case, Revenue Canada will allow only your tuition fees and disallow the education deduction.

Revenue Canada may contact you by telephone or letter, concerning your assessment or reassessment. Since anyone speaking on a telephone can state that they are from Revenue Canada, it is usually advisable to have all communication in writing. On the other hand, as long as a Revenue official has identified himself or herself to your satisfaction, you may wish to reply by telephone in cases where the information is not confidential or crucial. Nevertheless, in many cases, it is preferable to deal with a written query so that you may analyse the information requested and formulate a precise answer. Your reply to any queries from Revenue Canada is very important because they would not be asking for additional information or explanations if they were totally happy with the information that you had submitted in the first place.

Analyse the information that is being requested and determine why it is wanted. Something that may seem quite logical to you may, in fact, trigger a rejection by Revenue Canada because of a specific section of the Income Tax Act. Then again, there may be another section which overrides the restriction and it then becomes your responsibility to inform the officials. Remember that not all employees of Revenue Canada have the same knowledge, expertise or experience and you may be dealing with someone who has had only a few weeks of training and a very limited knowledge of the Income Tax Act. It is in your interest to be patient and courteous at all times.

Assessments and Reassessments

You should note that Revenue Canada does not have to accept any return as filed and may assess or reassess the taxes for the year within three (formerly four) years from the date of an original assessment, or at any time if the authorities can prove fraud or misrepresentation or if a waiver has been signed by the taxpayer for that particular year. The subject of waivers will be covered later on in this chapter.

A Revenue Canada Audit

Requests by Revenue Canada to examine your records, vouchers, receipts, cancelled cheques, deposit slips, bank statements, sales invoices, etc., are usually referred to as an audit. The audit may be restricted to only a few of your records or may encompass all of your records for one year or even several years. Some people take the attitude that something should always be left for the tax auditor to find. This is, however, a rather dangerous position because if the auditor finds one thing, he or she may continue looking until something else is found as well. Therefore, if your records are kept properly and only deductions that are permissible are taken, the audit should be of very short duration and no reassessment will be issued.

The auditor will complete the examination in as little time as possible if he or she is not unduly interrupted. The auditor may during the course of the examination make notes and if he or she cannot find certain answers while doing the examination, he or she will request explanations from you. Most audit queries can be satisfied by supplying a copy of a purchase invoice or a cancelled cheque or a receipt of some sort.

Don't be paranoid even though the tax auditor is usually there to try to extract more taxes than you would otherwise pay. Usually there is a specific reason for the audit. Possibly your entertainment and promotion expenses are too high. Sometimes Revenue Canada is simply investigating the particular industry that you are in or you have claimed a tax-shelter deduction and the validity of this is being questioned. In other cases, Revenue Canada may be looking at your records simply to see if payments you made are being reported by other people. On the other hand, they might also be checking to see if you have reported payments made by others who have already been audited.

It pays you to co-operate. Remember that the tax auditor has extensive powers. He or she can obtain any information to determine whether or not you are complying with the law. An auditor is also permitted to examine the records of a third party to substantiate a particular fact and if the auditor disagrees with your treatment, the onus is on you to prove that he or she is wrong.

How to Prepare for the Audit

The tax auditor will normally telephone in advance to arrange an appointment. If the time requested is inconvenient for you, you need simply ask for an extension. As long as you are reasonable, the tax auditor will co-operate. State your reasons for asking for an extension. For example, if you are in the midst of your busy season or plan to be out of town and would rather be available during the course of the audit, explain your position calmly.

Find out exactly what is being audited and prepare accordingly. Usually the tax auditor will look at two or three taxation years. If you know what he or she wants, this will save you the trouble of digging out records that are unnecessary. Remember that a tax auditor can only go back three years unless fraud is suspected.

Try to adopt a friendly manner. If you have the space, provide a clean desk and a good working environment. It is very important to discourage your staff from unnecessary contact with Revenue officials. Specific people should be delegated to discuss the different matters. If a business is being audited, it is usually necessary to have only three people talk to the assessor. You, as principal owner of the corporation, will want to be available to provide general information as to how the business operates. Your bookkeeper should be the one who explains how the records are kept, especially if there are any unique features to your particular business. And finally, your public accountant should be on hand to answer questions pertaining to the actual preparation of the financial statements or tax returns.

The fact that you should make yourself available does not mean that you have to babysit. In fact, if you hover around the auditor and keep him or her from doing the job, this will create unnecessary ill will. I recommend that you arrange with the auditor to have a daily question-and-answer period. Ask the auditor to write down all of his or her questions and set aside a half-hour to an hour each day so that you can deal with these matters. This is preferable to interrupting everybody's schedule several times a day as the auditor comes up with different questions.

Following the Audit

When the audit is finished, take the initiative to ask the auditor in a straightforward manner if he or she is going to make any adjustments. If changes are going to be made, obtain full and complete explanations of each and every proposed change. Tell the tax auditor you would like an opportunity to consider these changes and that you will get back to him or her within a reasonable period. Then, assess these changes very carefully. Make use of the government's own published tax information so that you can get a better idea of what the official Revenue Canada position is. Actually, this is not a difficult thing to do.

In 1970, Revenue Canada inaugurated a series of Information Circulars and Interpretation Bulletins. The Information Circulars are aimed at informing the general public about procedural matters relating to the Income Tax Act. The Interpretation Bulletins provide Revenue Canada's interpretations of the various sections of the law it administers. Both of these sets of information are available to the general public. There are now over five hundred Interpretation Bulletins. An Interpretation Bulletin does not have the force of law. It simply reflects Revenue Canada's opinion as to how specific matters in the Income Tax Act should be dealt with. From time to time, disputes are taken to the courtroom and if Revenue Canada loses its case, an Interpretation Bulletin may be retracted and re-issued. Nevertheless, it is important to know what Revenue Canada's opinion is. In general, Revenue assessors are bound by policy to follow the dictates of the official interpretations.

Once you know where you stand, go over each change with your public accountant and decide whether you are in agreement or whether you wish to challenge the change. Some changes might appear to be insignificant but you should realize that you may be setting a precedent for future years and there may be more serious consequences later on.

Waivers

In most cases, you will not be pressured by any time constraints as long as you are open and forthright with the Revenue officials with whom you are dealing. If it is taking you more time to assemble a defence for your position than you thought it would, try to set a reasonable deadline and you will find that the officials will co-operate.

Sometimes, however, you may encounter problems. Specifically, this is in cases where the actual audit and its aftermath take place as the normal "statute of limitations" approaches. As mentioned before, Revenue Canada cannot generally reassess after three years have passed following the date of a previous Notice of Assessment unless fraud or misrepresentation is alleged.

Sometimes if the three-year limit is rapidly approaching, the Revenue authorities may feel pressured into issuing an arbitrary assessment adjusting your taxes just to keep the particular year open. To avoid this, it is usually in your interest in these circumstances to file a voluntary waiver of the statute of limitations. In this manner, you will be able to defend your position on an informal basis without having to cope with an official assessment until all the facts are in. Generally your accountant can advise you on whether a voluntary waiver is in your interest.

Resolving Contentious Issues

It is always important to resolve as much as possible before an actual reassessment is issued. This is because interest claimed by the authorities accumulates until all liabilities have been settled. You should note that, if the amount of tax requested is large, you may find that it is feasible to furnish security to the Minister in lieu of an actual tax payment. Proper security would include an assignment of a term deposit, a bank guarantee, or perhaps, in some instances, a mortgage against real estate that you own.

Make sure that your public accountant meets with the Revenue Canada auditor and presents your position as clearly and as emphatically as possible. Then, if the auditor and your accountant cannot agree, arrange a meeting with the auditor's superior to try to convince Revenue Canada that your original treatment was correct. It is important for you to persist at the audit level. If you find (in rare cases) that the tax auditor is abusive or expects your entire business to stop while you hunt down a receipt, touch base with your accountant to decide whether or not you should request a change of auditor. Certainly you will have the right to appeal if an assessment is eventually issued, and this may turn out to be the only solution. However, it is far less expensive to settle the matter at the initial audit level and, sometimes, to effect a compromise.

Special Audits—The Net-Worth Assessment

A Revenue Canada audit may not be restricted to the mere verification of a few vouchers, cheques, deposits or sales. From time to time, the Department will proceed on what is called the "net-worth method." This type of procedure applies in instances where Revenue officials suspect that a taxpayer has unrecorded income.

Here is how a net-worth assessment works. First, a Revenue Canada assessor will attempt to determine your assets less liabilities at the beginning of a certain year. To that, he or she will add your income declared since that time and deduct a reasonable allowance for your cost of living. These cost-of-living expenses will include anything from a toothbrush to your monthly mortgage payments. The result will then be compared to your assets less liabilities at the end of a certain period.

If the balance obtained at the end is greater than your opening assets minus liabilities plus your reported income after deducting your living expenses, Revenue Canada will assume that you have earned other income and will tax you on that amount as if you, in fact, had earned it. It is then up to you to show that certain amounts were received during that period that increased your net worth but did not constitute income for tax purposes, such as an inheritance, a windfall, or the non-taxable portion of capital gains.

Dealing With a Notice of Assessment or Reassessment

If you receive a Notice of Assessment or Reassessment with which you disagree, your first step is to file a Notice of Objection which must be submitted within ninety days from the date of mailing of the Notice of Assessment or Reassessment.

You should note that late-filed Notices of Objection do not have to be accepted by the Minister and all taxes will then have to be paid without any further recourse.

The Notice of Objection must be prepared in duplicate, setting out all the relevant facts and reasons for the objection. It must be signed by the taxpayer or an authorized representative and sent by registered mail to the Deputy Minister of National Revenue for Taxation in Ottawa. A separate Notice of Objection should be filed for each taxation year under dispute.

When the Notice of Objection is received in Ottawa, one copy is sent to the local District Taxation Office of Revenue Canada for an independent review by the Appeals Section. Officials from that section will contact the taxpayer or an authorized agent, who may then make further representations concerning the objection. There is the opportunity to discuss the facts and possibly resolve the contentious issues. If successful negotiations can be concluded at the District Office level, this will save the costs of further appeals and court appearances.

If the dispute cannot be resolved at the District Office level, the Appeals Section must report to the Minister who is then obliged to inform the taxpayer by registered mail that the Assessment or Reassessment has been confirmed.

I strongly advise you to put a great deal of effort into dealing with the Appeals branch to avoid a costly courtroom battle. Produce proof to support your position and evidence to corroborate your facts. Be prepared to have your accountant quote specific sections of the Income Tax Act and Regulations or to refer to Information Circulars and Interpretation Bulletins. It is generally also advisable to see what jurisprudence is available to help you substantiate your position. In other words, make use of the expertise and knowledge that you can get from professional help. Although the objection stage is fairly informal, keep in mind that much of the information gathered will be useful if you choose to pursue the matter later on through the courts.

Appeals to the Courts

After the Minister replies to an objection and either confirms it or reassesses (but not to the complete satisfaction of the taxpayer), the taxpayer has the right to appeal to the Tax Court of Canada or to the Federal Court of Canada. Under the law, an appeal must be made within ninety days from the mailing date of the Minister's reply. If the Minister fails to reply to the Objection within ninety days, the taxpayer may take the initiative and appeal to the courts instead.

The sittings of the Tax Court of Canada are generally in the spring and fall in all larger cities. The different judges are not restricted to sitting in any particular area, so that the person who presides over the hearings in any particular location will vary from sitting to sitting.

When a case is set down for hearing in a particular location, solicitors in the employ of the legal branch of the Taxation Division will generally arrive a short time in advance of the date of the hearings in order to review the Crown's case with the officials of the District Office and to prepare the Crown's arguments.

During this period, which may be only a few days, it is common for discussions to take place between the Department's solicitors and the taxpayer's representatives, and often settlements of the points involved are made at this time. Consequently, it is not uncommon for the Court to have a lengthy list of cases to be heard, only to find that the docket has shrunk to as few as two or three cases when the hearings actually begin. Cases that have already been conceded or settled in one way or another are either withdrawn by one or other of the parties involved, or a consent to judgement is filed, allowing the appeal in part.

Several factors must be considered before appealing to the courts. First, you must decide whether instituting an appeal will be cost-effective. Are the additional dollars assessed worth the time, effort, and aggravation involved? What are the costs of presenting an appeal, including the prospects of being forced to absorb court costs if you go to the Federal Court and lose? What are the costs of obtaining professional legal assistance? Although proceedings in the Tax Court of Canada are less formal, the Federal Court operates under strict rules of presentation and process and any failure to properly prepare and present a position may result in a losing case.

Summary

These factors add up to a time-consuming and expensive undertaking. I therefore cannot stress enough the need to negotiate and compromise whenever feasible at each step along the way, beginning with the audit itself. To whatever extent possible, every available avenue of objection and appeal should be taken short of going to court.

Your main defences are good records, logical reasons for what you did, and competent tax planning. The best way to prepare for a tax audit is by sound thinking when your financial statements and tax returns are prepared in the first place.

Taking the "Ax" Out of Tax

If you have gotten this far without skipping too many chapters, you should now be quite familiar with just about every legitimate technique for effective tax reduction. Now it is time to apply these suggestions to your own situation. So, start again from the beginning. Open this book to the Table of Contents, and start making notes. Be brief. All you have to do is list some of the areas where you can take the "ax" out of your tax.

Begin with Chapter Two. List the fringe-benefit plans that you think are reasonable for you. The next time you are due for a raise, be ready for some serious negotiations. Remember, very often valuable benefits won't cost your employer a penny extra when compared to salary. If you earn your income from commissions, reread Chapter Three.

Are you ten years or less away from retirement? Is there any chance that you may be leaving the country soon? Are you thinking of selling your business? If the answer to any of these questions is yes, reread Chapter Four and make sure your boss (or accountant) buys a copy of this book and reads it too. If the answer to all these questions is no, go on to Chapter Five.

Do you have a Registered Retirement Savings Plan? If you do, continue to contribute. Keep in mind the advantages of spousal plans. If you still don't believe in RRSPs, reread this chapter—*slowly*. Study Chapter Ten and learn why you must plan carefully for your own retirement. You can count on government to help you, but not for your full support.

Do you have $1,000 a year of (tax-free) Canadian investment income? If not, start saving your pennies! Do you have more than $10,000 or $12,000 of capital and are you in a 50% bracket or higher? Do you have a son or daughter attending university? Remember, income splitting isn't difficult. A temporary loan will do the trick.

Are you separated or divorced or contemplating an end to your marriage? Protect yourself. If you don't look after your own interest, you will be the loser. Study Chapter Eight. Then seek professional advice geared towards your own circumstances.

Are you reading this book in the den of your Westmount or Forest Hill home or on a cruise ship bound for warmer weather or on the beach outside your Hawaii condominium? If your answer is yes, consider the benefits of an investment corporation. Dividends to the kids are an excellent way to get them to pay for their *own* vacations, cars, education, and so on.

Do you receive fees for services? Can you *diversify* your consulting activities so that you can be paid by several different customers or clients? If so, make an appointment with an accountant—even if it costs $100 or $150. After about an hour, he or she will be able to tell you if incorporation is feasible.

If you own your own business or are planning to start one, reread Chapters Twelve through Fourteen. I know they have lots of numbers and very few jokes and anecdotes. But they are worth the bother. Then, spend a morning with your accountant planning your strategy.

Are you about to buy or sell a business? See your advisers *before* you finalize a deal. Improper tax planning here can be the worst mistake you will ever make. Don't forget—this is the era of the holding company—don't fight progress. It's your money.

Don't ignore the inevitability of death. If you have a spouse, is she or he adequately protected? Is your spouse "overprotected"? Does your spouse know what you have and where it is? Communicate. Your lifestyles may depend on it.

Finally, if you are having problems with Revenue Canada, read Chapter Seventeen. Keep your cool and make sure you have a good case. Remember, Revenue auditors are just people trying to do their jobs.

Looking Ahead

Certainly, some of the incentives, loopholes, and other opportunities to reduce taxes have been eroded by recent federal budgets. As I indicated at the very beginning of this book, the current investment climate in this country is somewhat uncertain. If you are like most people, you are concerned with your investment picture. What should you buy? For the time being, perhaps nothing. A bad investment may be worse than no investment at all. Remember, however, that the investment market never stands still. The person who jumps in at the right time can do extremely well. There is an old Chinese curse which says "May you live in interesting times." These are definitely interesting times.

Glossary

Active Business Income Income from manufacturing, wholesaling, retailing, logging, farming, fishing, natural resource exploration and development, transportation, and in certain instances, services. This income qualifies for a low rate of corporate tax when earned by *Canadian-controlled private corporations*.

Adjusted Cost Base The cost of property for tax purposes. This may be either the cost to the taxpayer or the value as of December 31, 1971, subject to any adjustments required by the Income Tax Act.

Amortization The allocation of an expense or debt over a period of time.

Annuity A series of regular (and usually equal) payments consisting of interest and principal.

Arm's Length Where the parties to a transaction are unrelated by blood, marriage, or adoption.

Asset A property, which is owned and has value.

Attribution Rules A series of tax provisions whereby income generated from property transferred or loaned by one spouse to the other will be reallocated for tax purposes to the person who made the transfer. Similar provisions also apply for transfers to minors.

Beneficiary A person who receives or is named to receive money or property from an insurance policy or *will*. A person for whose benefit a *trust* exists.

Buy-Sell Agreement An undertaking among owners of a business whereby those that remain agree to acquire the interest in the business of an owner who dies, retires, or becomes disabled.

Canadian-Controlled Private Corporation (CCPC) A company incorporated in Canada where the majority of the shares are not held by non-residents or public companies or by any combination of non-residents and public companies.

Capital Cost Allowance A provision for depreciation as permitted under the Income Tax Act to recognize wear, tear, and obsolescence and to allocate the cost of an asset over the period for which it is useful in generating revenue.

Capital Gains The profit realized when certain assets such as real estate and shares of a public or private company are sold for proceeds in excess of cost. A taxpayer's capital gain is measured as the difference between the selling price of property and its *adjusted cost base*. Subject to the new $500,000 capital-gains tax exemption, one-half of a capital gain is taken into income when proceeds are received. This is called a taxable capital gain.

Classes of Assets For tax-depreciation (*capital-cost-allowance*) purposes, assets are divided into pools or groups. Each pool has its own depreciation rate, which is usually related to the useful life of the assets that it contains.

Collateral Stocks, bonds, or other property pledged as security for a loan. A lender has the right to sell collateral in the event of a borrower's default.

Combined Individual Tax Rates Rates (usually expressed in percentages) that take into account the effect of both federal and provincial taxes.

Controlling Shareholder Usually, a shareholder who owns more than 50% of the voting shares of a corporation.

Current Service Contribution A contribution made to an employer-sponsored pension plan by the employee and/or the employer in respect of the present year.

Deemed Disposition An event such as death, departure from Canada, or the making of a gift, where an individual is considered for tax purposes to have sold his property for consideration (generally) equal to its *fair market value*.

Deferred Annuity An *annuity* under which payments of principal and interest will only begin some time after the annuity is acquired.

Deferred Compensation An arrangement under which income is postponed until some future time, usually until retirement from employment.

Dividend A distribution out of after-tax earnings or profits, which a corporation pays to its shareholders.

Dividend Tax Credit A reduction from taxes otherwise payable by an individual who receives a dividend from a Canadian corporation. The tax credit takes into account the fact that a dividend is a distribution by a corporation out of previously taxed profits.

Earned Income The sum of incomes from employment, self-employment, pensions, and alimony minus losses from self-employment and/or rentals. For 1985, up to 20% of earned income qualifies for an annual investment into an individual's *Registered Retirement Savings Plan* (maximum $5,500).

310

Effective Taxes Combined federal and provincial taxes as a percentage of total income. (Compare *marginal rate of tax*.)

Equity Capital The funds in a business, which have been invested by the owners and not loaned by others.

Estate Freezing An exchange of assets whereby properties with growth potential are exchanged for properties whose value remains constant through time.

Estate Planning The orderly arrangement of one's financial affairs so that assets may be transferred on death to persons designated by the deceased, with a minimum loss of value due to taxes and forced liquidations.

Executor A person named in a *will* to carry out the provisions of that will.

Fair Market Value The price for property that a willing buyer would pay to a willing seller on the open market in circumstances where both parties deal at *arm's length* and neither is compelled to transact.

Front-End Load An administration charge for handling investment capital that is levied against the initial contribution(s) to a savings plan, such as an RRSP.

Grossed-Up Dividend When an individual resident in Canada receives a dividend from a Canadian corporation, the amount that is taxable is one and one-half times the actual payment received. The individual is then allowed a *dividend tax credit* approximately equal to the 50% gross-up.

Guaranteed Term A minimum term under which annuity payments are guaranteed. In the case of a life annuity with a guaranteed term, the payments will continue through the guarantee period even if the recipient of the annuity dies before the end of that period.

Income-Averaging Annuity A special type of annuity designed to spread the impact of Canadian taxation on certain (generally non-recurring) types of lump-sum receipts. The 1981 tax changes eliminated the use of such annuities for 1982 and subsequent years.

Investment Deduction A provision under which the first $1,000 of *arm's-length* interest and grossed-up dividends received by an individual from Canadian sources is deductible annually in arriving at taxable income.

Management Company A corporation set up by professionals such as doctors, dentists, lawyers, and accountants to provide administrative services to the professional business of the practitioner(s).

Marginal Rate of Tax The combined federal and provincial tax rate that would apply to the next dollar of taxable income earned by a taxpayer in a given year. Compare *effective taxes*.

Manufacturing and Processing Profits Deduction A special reduction from corporate income taxes otherwise payable, computed at either 5% or 6% of taxable income from manufacturing and processing activities.

Net Income Gross income from all sources less expenses to earn this income, but before personal exemptions and taxes.

Non-Resident Withholding Tax A flat rate of tax imposed on investment income such as interest, rents, dividends, and annuities paid to a non-resident recipient. In Canada, the rate of withholding tax is 25% unless reduced by a tax treaty with the country in which the nonresident lives.

Participating Shares Shares in a corporation, which participate in the growth of a business and its assets and on which (theoretically) unlimited dividends may be paid.

Past-Service Contribution A contribution made to an employersponsored pension plan by the employee and/or the employer in respect of prior years of employment.

Pension-Income Deduction A provision under which the first $1,000 of annual pension income (other than the Canada/Quebec Pension or the Old Age Pension) is deductible from an individual's income for tax purposes. The pension deduction applies to a pension received after retirement, while amounts received from an RRSP qualify if the recipient is at least sixty-five years of age.

Personal Exemptions An automatic deduction permitted to any individual in arriving at taxable income. For 1985, the basic personal exemption is $4,140. There are additional personal exemptions available to individuals who support other dependants, such as a spouse or children.

Personal-Service Corporation A corporation formed to earn fees for services or commissions where the income can be attributed to the personal efforts of one or a few individuals.

Principal Residence A housing unit ordinarily occupied by an individual during a given year and designated as being his (or her) principal residence. Only one such residence may be designated for each year. Where an accommodation that was a principal residence throughout the period of its ownership is subsequently sold, the *capital gain* thereon is exempt from tax. After 1981, a family unit of husband and wife can designate only one property at a time as a principal residence.

Registered Retirement Income Fund (RRIF) One of the settlement options available to taxpayers over age sixty who wish to draw an annuity from their Registered Retirement Savings Plans. Under this option, payments received increase annually until the recipient is age ninety.

Registered Retirement Savings Plan (RRSP) A government-approved program whereby individuals may make tax-deductible contributions with annual maximums as a savings towards retirement.

Recaptured Depreciation *Capital cost allowances* previously claimed, which are determined (in the year that depreciable property is sold) to be in excess of the actual amount by which the property in question has depreciated.

Refundable Tax A portion of corporate taxes previously paid by a private corporation on its investment income. Initially, the investment income is subject to a 50% tax rate, although an amount equal to $16^{2/3}\%$ of the investment income is refundable back to the corporation upon payment of dividends to shareholders. The net corporate tax on investment income is thus reduced to $33^{1/3}\%$.

Replacement Property In certain circumstances, gains on the disposition of property may be deferred for tax purposes if other property (i.e., replacement property) is acquired. The tax cost of the replacement property is reduced by an amount equal to the deferred gain.

Retiring Allowance A payment made by a former employer to an employee in recognition of long service or for loss of employment. In some cases, retiring allowances may be transferred to *Registered Retirement Savings Plans.*

Rollover A transfer of property from one person to another where the tax rules permit a deferral of gains at the time the transfer is made.

Small-Business Tax Rates A special incentive available to *Canadian-controlled private corporations* earning *active business income.* The first $200,000 of annual profits is taxed at approximately 25% (the rate varies from province to province).

Soft Costs Various specific components of a construction project that may be deducted for tax purposes during a construction period instead of being subject to a long-term write-off through depreciation (*capital cost allowance*). Soft costs include landscaping, interest on money borrowed during the construction period, and certain administrative expenditures. Only corporations whose principal business activities involve real estate may deduct soft costs for projects initiated after 1981.

313

Spousal RRSP An option available under a *Registered Retirement Savings Plan* whereby a taxpayer may earmark all or a portion of his or her annual contributions into a program for his or her spouse. This option is designed to ensure future *annuity* benefits for that spouse.

T-4 Slip A form prescribed by the Canadian government for employers to use in reporting salaries, wages, and benefits paid to employees.

Tax Credits A direct deduction against taxes otherwise payable. Among others, tax credits are available to individuals with respect to Canadian dividends received and to all taxpayers with respect to foreign taxes previously paid on foreign-source income.

Tax-Deductible Describes amounts which may be subtracted in arriving at one's income for tax purposes.

Tax Depreciation See *capital cost allowance*.

Tax Deferral A situation in which taxes on income or benefits are postponed until some future date.

Tax Loss Versus Tax Shelter A *tax loss* is a loss from business or property that is deductible when determining income for tax purposes. A tax loss becomes a *tax shelter* in circumstances where it is created by claiming *capital cost allowances* and does *not* involve an actual outflow of cash or a reduction in the value of one's investment. As a result of recent income-tax amendments, the use of tax shelters has been severely restricted.

Tax-Sheltered Describes income that is not taxable currently but will be taxed at some future time.

Taxable Benefit A benefit provided by an employer to an employee where the value is taxed in the hands of the employee as additional remuneration received.

Taxable Income Net income from all sources minus personal exemptions, the investment and pension deductions, a provision for medical expenses and donations, and miscellaneous other deductions. For Canadian corporations, taxable income is computed after deducting dividends received from other Canadian corporations. Taxable income is the base on which income taxes are levied.

Term Insurance Life insurance that only pays if death occurs within a specific time period. There is usually no cash value under such a policy. Compare with *whole life insurance*.

Testator A person who makes a *will*.

Tracking Earmarking the flow of borrowed funds to clearly indicate the purpose for which these funds have been used.

Transferee A person to whom a transfer of title, rights, or property is made.

Transferor A person who makes a transfer of title, rights, or property.

Treasury Shares Shares that a corporation has the authority to issue but that are still unissued.

Trust An arrangement made in a person's lifetime or effective upon death whereby legal title and control of property is placed in the hands of a custodian (*trustee*) for the benefit of another person or group of persons who are known as *beneficiaries* of the trust.

Trustee A person who acts as custodian and administrator of property held in *trust* for someone else.

Undepreciated Capital Cost The cost of depreciable assets minus accumulated *capital cost allowances* previously claimed.

Vesting The process whereby a right to property passes unconditionally to a particular person, such as where an employee becomes entitled to the full benefits from contributions previously made by an employer to a pension program.

Will A legal statement of a person's wishes about what shall be done with his or her property after death.

Whole Life Insurance Life insurance that remains in force until the insured dies, irrespective of when this occurs. Whole life insurance policies usually have cash values, which increase over time and which may be borrowed against, or for which the policy may be surrendered.

Year End The end of the business cycle each year. For tax purposes, a business must file an annual report disclosing its profits. Initially, the year end may be selected to fall on any date. However, no change in the year end may be made subsequently without the permission of the Revenue authorities.

Yield Return on investment, usually computed as the percentage of the anticipated (or realized) annual income relative to the capital invested.